LEGENDARY LOCALS

OF

FITCHBURG

MASSACHUSETTS

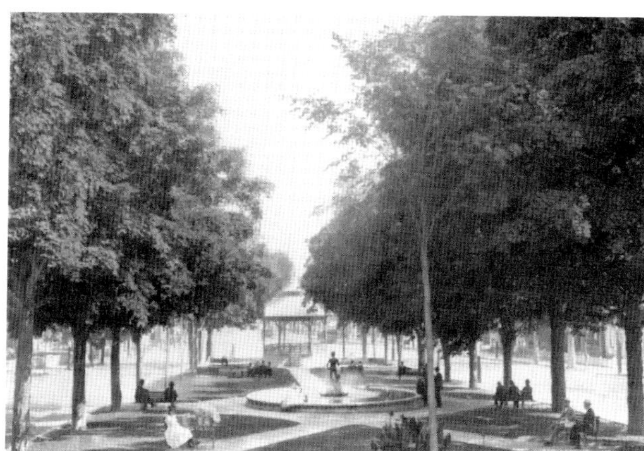

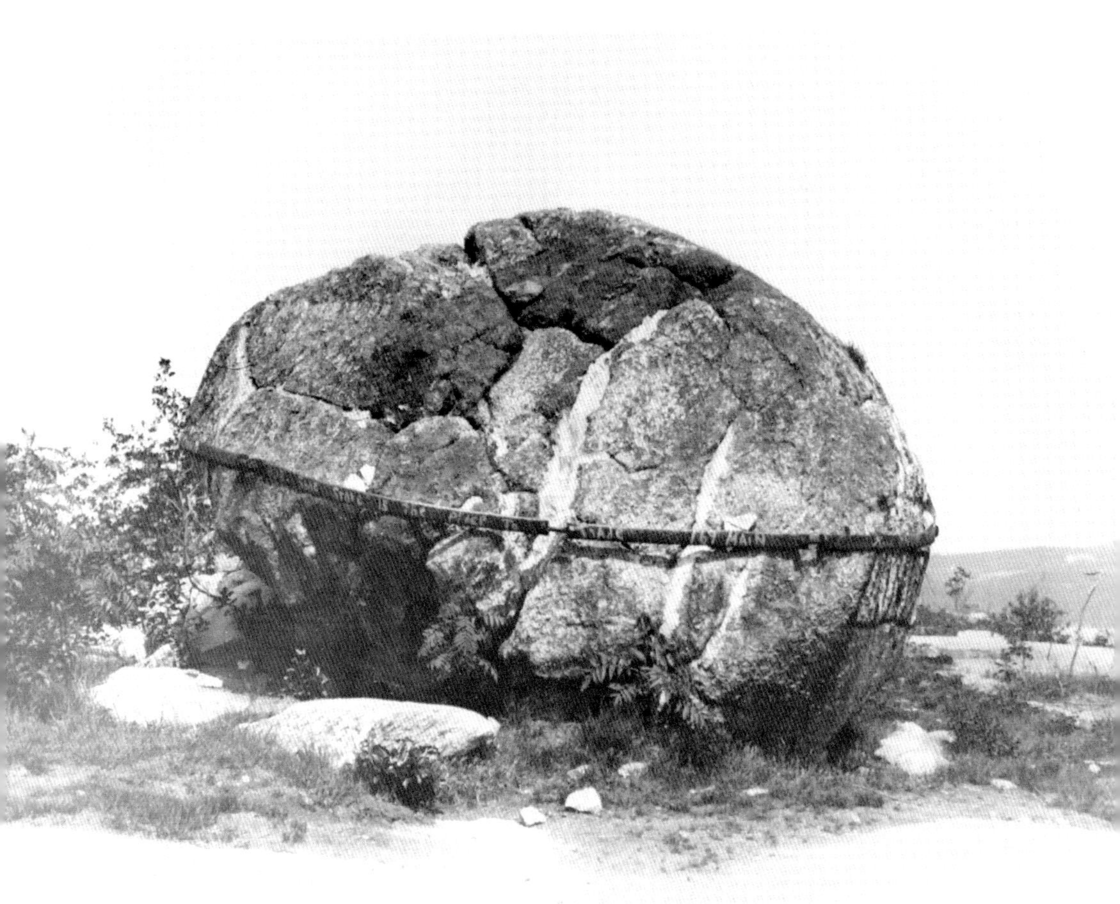

The Granite Boulder

The Granite Boulder, originally at the Rollstone Quarry on Rollstone Hill in Fitchburg, was taken apart in 1929 and moved to the Upper Common, where it was reassembled in 1929–1930. (Courtesy of Fitchburg Historical Society.)

Page 1: *The Fountain of the Boy and the Turtles*

The Fountain of the Boy and the Turtles, a sculpture by Samuel Herbert Adams, welcomes visitors to the Upper Common of Fitchburg. (Courtesy of Fitchburg Historical Society.)

LEGENDARY LOCALS

OF

FITCHBURG

MASSACHUSETTS

FITCHBURG HISTORICAL SOCIETY

LEGENDARY LOCALS

ISBN 978-1-4671-0110-3

Legendary Locals is an imprint of Arcadia Publishing
Charleston, South Carolina

Printed in the United States of America

Library of Congress Control Number: 2013939922

For all general information, please contact Arcadia Publishing:
Telephone 843-853-2070
Fax 843-853-0044
E-mail sales@arcadiapublishing.com
For customer service and orders:
Toll-Free 1-888-313-2665

Visit us on the Internet at www.arcadiapublishing.com

Dedication

This book is dedicated to those who have recorded and preserved the history of Fitchburg over the years.

On the Front Cover: Clockwise from bottom left:
Henry Coggshall, donator of Coggshall Park in Fitchburg (Courtesy of Fitchburg Historical Society, page 30); Ellen Di Geronimo, first woman associate commissioner of Massachusetts Public Works, 1977 (Courtesy of Ellen DiGeronimo, page 38); Carmelita Landry Bernard, North American women's speed-skating champion, 1941 and 1942 (Courtesy of Fitchburg Historical Society, page 95); H.M. Francis and son Frederick, premier Fitchburg architect from 1868 to 1908, (Courtesy of Fitchburg Historical Society, page 11); Alfred Woollacott, mayor of Fitchburg, 1938–1948 (Courtesy of Fitchburg Historical Society, page 34); Amasa Norcross, first mayor of Fitchburg, 1872–1874, (Courtesy of Fitchburg Historical Society, page 10); and Elizabeth "Betsy" Stanton, state representative, 1952–1962, and postmistress of Fitchburg, 1962–1979 (Courtesy of Fitchburg Historical Society, page 37); Lisa Wong, first Asian woman mayor in Massachusetts, current mayor of Fitchburg (Courtesy of Lisa Wong, page 17); Robert and Jeanne Antonucci, president of Fitchburg State University and his wife, an ambassador for the university (Courtesy of Fitchburg State University, page 67).

On the Back Cover: From left to right:
Fitchburg Longsjo Classic (Courtesy of Fitchburg Historical Society, page 96); Fitchburg Historical Society bicentennial float, 1964 (Courtesy of Fitchburg Historical Society, page 15).

CONTENTS

ACKNOWLEDGMENTS

The Fitchburg Historical Society has dedicated volunteers who put together their quarterly newsletters. This group gladly took on the project of identifying, researching, and writing about the *Legendary Locals of Fitchburg*. The core group of writers was Simone Blake, Joy Contois, Kathleen Flynn, Cindy Jones, Helen Obermeyer Simmons, and Shirley Wagner. Simone, Helen, and Shirley have each served as the president of the society. Cindy is currently the clerk, and Joy was formerly the educational coordinator. Kathleen also serves on the annual House Tour Committee. We were fortunate to have two interns working with us during spring of 2013: Katrina Brown, a senior communications media major, and Nathan Burns, a senior English major. They helped with editing, found missing dates, located and scanned photographs, and wrote some of the profiles within this book. Both graduated from Fitchburg State University in May 2013. Pamela Tash, a volunteer who came to the society in spring of 2013, also researched and wrote some profiles. The following people loaned photographs to the society: Joseph Addante, Simone Blake, Fitchburg Access Television (FATV), Fitchburg Public Library, Fitchburg *Sentinel & Enterprise*, Fitchburg State University, Rebecca Rice Flanagan, Kathleen Flynn, Elizabeth Fuller, Eleanor Gilmartin, Andre Gelinas, Patricia Goguen, Rick Jollimore, John Koutonen, Ann Lawler, Jack Mitchell, Robert O'Hara, Teresa Pierce, JR Photo, Special Collections at the University of Massachusetts, Charles Sternaimolo, Alan Thibault, Dolores Munoz Thibault, Peter Timms, Kit Tucker, Washington Speakers Bureau, Mary Whitney, Lisa Wong, and Elliott Zide.

Unless otherwise noted, all images are from the archives of the Fitchburg Historical Society.

INTRODUCTION

Rollstone mountain, thee we hail,
Girded with thy granite mail!
Many a legend, story and song
Round thy steadfast grandeur throng.

—Excerpt from *Rollstone* by Martha D. Tolman

Not much is known about the Nashaways, who migrated through the part of Massachusetts now known as Fitchburg. A few artifacts have been found, but it is not clear whether there was actually a permanent settlement on the Nashaway River, now known as the Nashua. The General Court's land grant of 1719 confirms that Samuel Page and his wife, Martha, were the first family in Lunenburg, in a section called Turkey Hills, later known as Fitchburg. One of the Pages' children was David, Fitchburg's first settler, along with his wife, Priscilla. Legend says that David traded fur pelts with the Indians but often "tipped the scales," making it necessary to move on before being caught. Legend also says that the first child born in today's Fitchburg was the Pages' daughter Priscilla, born in 1735.

Archaeological remains exist from another early settler, Joseph Spofford, whose wife's wedding band records their marriage in 1740. Another early land grant of 1,000 acres in West Fitchburg was given to surveyor Samuel Fullam in 1741. By 1745, Amos and Ephraim Kimball also moved to the area, building the first dam and mill in Fitchburg. In 1748, Samuel Poole, Samuel Hunt, Isaac Gibson, Joseph Spofford, and John Fitch all had garrisoned homes. While attacks were uncommon, the garrison of John and Susannah Fitch was ravaged in July 1748. Two soldiers were killed, and John, Susannah, and their family were captured and forcefully marched to Montreal. Ransomed in the following fall, Susannah died before they reached Fitchburg. Two other settlers were fired upon the next day, but after that time, no other skirmishes were recorded. In 1757 and 1762, Samuel Hunt and others unsuccessfully petitioned Lunenburg to become a separate town. In 1763, John Fitch, Amos Kimball, Samuel Hunt, Ephraim Whitney, and Jonathan Wood took their petition directly to the General Court. In February 1764, the act passed the legislature, and Fitchburg became a separate town.

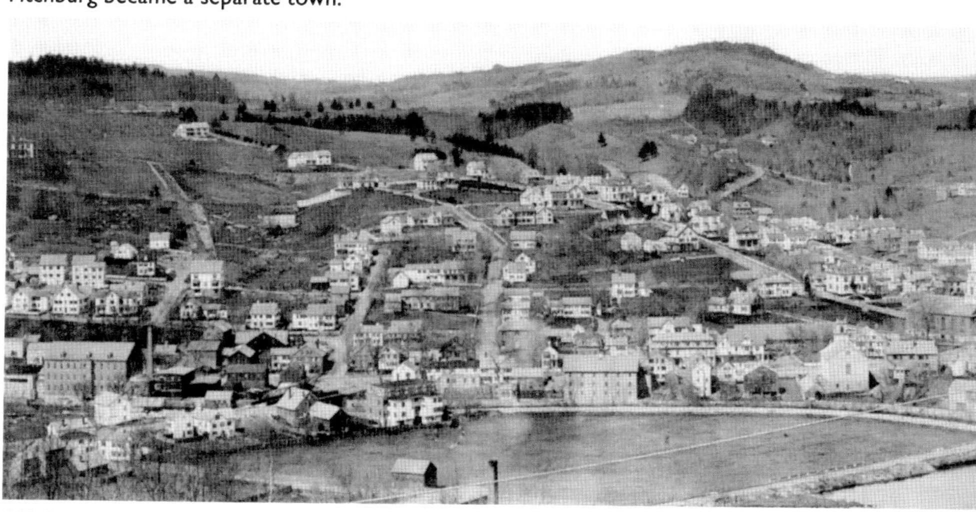

All-America City
Known for being one of the hilliest cities in the United States, Fitchburg, with a population of nearly 40,000, was named an All-America City in 1970.

The incorporation of Fitchburg as a city occurred in 1872, after the town had pooled its resources during the Civil War. The Fitchburg Fusiliers had immediately answered the call to provide Union troops. This was not a surprise since the majority of the citizens were antislavery; in fact, antislavery congregants had formed the Trinitarian Church. The townspeople helped provide for the soldiers as well as their families while they were at war. There are records of clothing, blankets, bandages, and food being sent to the Fitchburg men at war. Dr. Alfred Hitchcock provided inoculations for the men and also traveled to battlefields as a surgeon. The entire community congregated at the town hall to hear news from the battlefronts. Soldiers took time to write letters that were sometimes published in the *Sentinel* or the *Reveille*. Men who died on the battlefield were brought back to Fitchburg by relatives, and community funerals were celebrated in the town hall.

The post–Civil War period brought increased growth to Fitchburg's industries in the 1870s through 1900, defined as the Golden Age of Industry. It was also the time when H.M. Francis, the city's famed architect, was designing many of the buildings that would give Fitchburg its unique look. New businesses moved to Fitchburg. Burbank Hospital, the Burbank School of Nursing, and Fitchburg Normal School were founded. Factories manufacturing machinery, paper, textiles, scythes, and rattan provided jobs for the workers but also dumped waste in the Nashua River, leaving pollution that would need to be addressed in the future.

The generation that grew up in the 1950s and 1960s remembers those years fondly, as a time when Fitchburg exemplified the virtues of a small city. Main Street and neighborhood businesses provided the goods people needed, and Friday nights found the downtown stores filled with shoppers and thriving theaters.

The opportunity to write *Legendary Locals of Fitchburg* came at a perfect time because, in 2014, the City of Fitchburg will be celebrating the 250th anniversary of its incorporation as a separate town. Since 1893, the Fitchburg Historical Society has collected artifacts, papers, and books that document many aspects of Fitchburg history. In 1912, the Fitchburg Historical Society's home at 50 Grove Street was built. Designed by H.M. Francis, the building served the society well for a hundred years. In 2012, the society moved to its new location at 781 Main Street, thanks again to the generosity of the donors who contributed to the Capital Campaign.

In writing *Legendary Locals of Fitchburg*, the authors came across hundreds of stories they wanted to tell. A number of these made it into this book, while others will be told in future newsletters. There are many wonderful stories yet to be told, and hopefully, this project will encourage others to share their knowledge about individuals whom they believe to be "legendary locals."

The chapters in the this volume provide an overview of the ways in which individuals and groups have contributed to the history and culture of the city. Businesses, community leaders, organizations, churches, ethnic groups, athletes, military leaders, and especially the people next door have all made their mark on Fitchburg. These are neighbors and friends, people who were proud of Fitchburg and who make Fitchburg proud on its 250th anniversary!

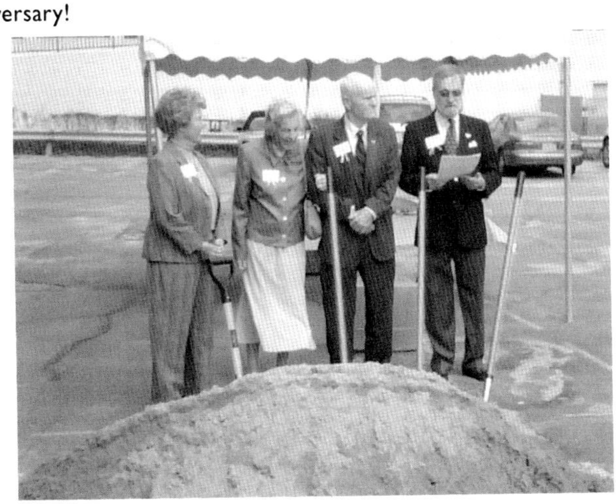

Groundbreaking
Breaking ground for the external elevator at the new home of the Fitchburg Historical Society are, from left to right, Sally Dickinson, chair of the Capital Campaign; Jeanne "Jay" Crocker, cochair of the Capital Campaign; Bigelow Crocker II, cochair of the Capital Campaign; and Dan Mylott, former mayor of Fitchburg and current president of the Fitchburg Historical Society.

CHAPTER ONE

Historic Fitchburg

Nestled among her hills she lies
The city of our love!
Within her pleasant homes arise;
And healthful airs and happy skies
Float peacefully above.

—Excerpt from "Ode to Fitchburg" by Caroline A. Mason

As Caroline Atherton Mason recorded, Fitchburg has always been a beloved city to the many who shaped its history. The organization of the city, from influential mayors to police and fire departments protecting the city, reflect the care and commitment of hundreds. The city itself remains beautiful thanks to visionary philanthropists and architects who saw the city's potential and beauty. Legendary locals who helped record and save Fitchburg's story through newspapers and the historical society make books like this possible. The individuals and groups who have helped preserve Fitchburg history over the years include Nathaniel Wood, Rufus C. Torrey, Henry A. Willis, Atherton P. Mason, James F.D. Garfield, Teresa Garfield, William A. Emerson, Frederick Currier, Barbara Cushing Crocker, Doris Kirkpatrick, the Fitchburg *Sentinel & Enterprise*, Eleanora West, FATV, Philip Jordan, and Barbara Edsall.

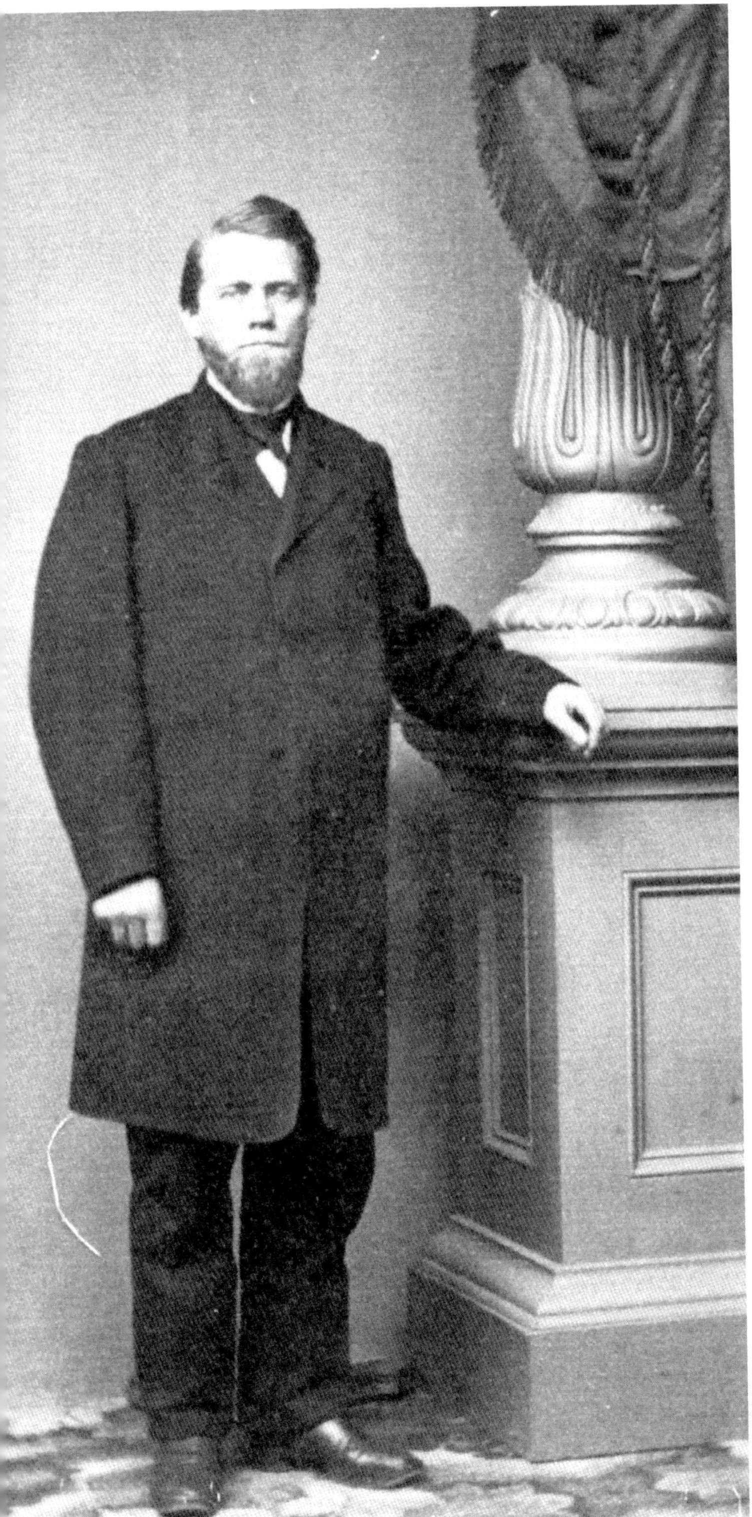

Amasa Norcross (1824–1898)

Born in Rindge, New Hampshire, Norcross moved to Fitchburg to study law at the firm of Torrey & Wood. He passed the bar in 1847 and soon built a strong practice. He became active in the Wide Awakes, a group of young Republicans who supported Abraham Lincoln. A good public speaker, he was often asked to say a few words at public events. When Fitchburg became a city in 1872, Norcross was elected as the first mayor. The city had a significant debt, which some hoped a betterment tax passed by the legislature would lessen. The tax, however, was unpopular in conjunction with the Panic of 1873, which the city survived due to Norcross's leadership. Other immediate concerns were the need for clean water and a sewer system to replace the practice of dumping raw sewage in the Nashua River. An outbreak of typhoid fever made plans for this even more necessary. After his term as mayor ended, Norcross became a representative to the state legislature and senate, later serving from 1877 to 1885 as a US Congressman. His toddler son, Nelson, died in 1863 and his wife, Susan, died in 1869, leaving him and his artist daughter, Eleanor, as a small but devoted family. Eleanor lived in Paris, where her father visited during the winters, and they spent summers in Fitchburg until Amasa Norcross's death in Paris in 1898. He is buried at Laurel Hill Cemetery in Fitchburg.

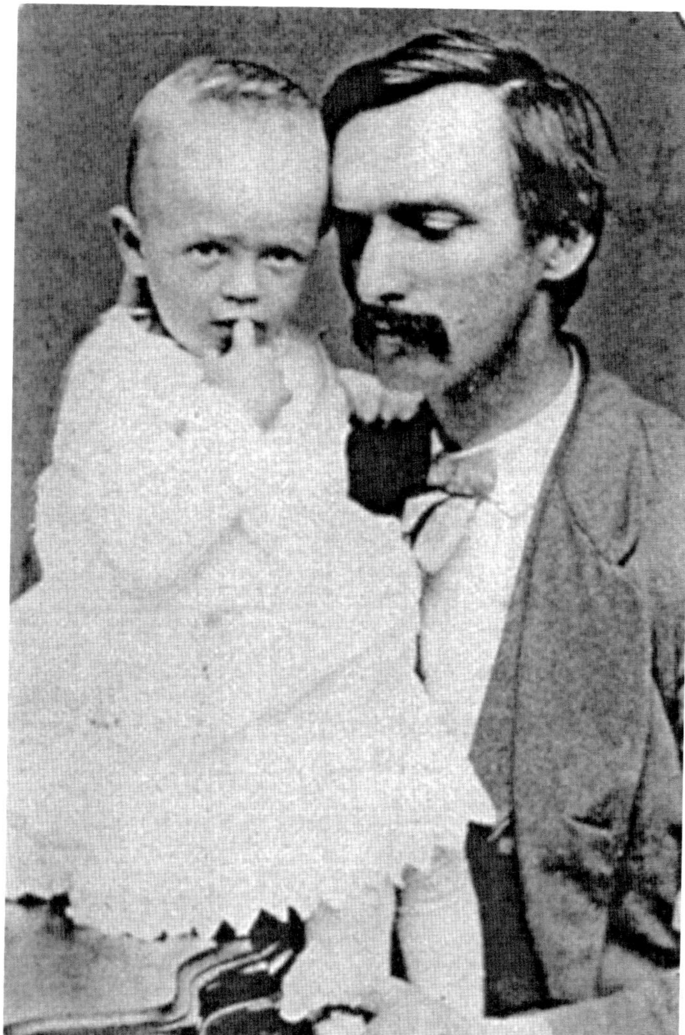

Henry Martyn "H.M." Francis (1836–1908)
Francis was born in Lunenburg, Massachusetts, and educated at Lawrence Academy. Francis first learned the architectural trade as an apprentice in the Framingham firm of New England architect Alexander R. Estey. Between 1864 and May 1868, Francis was employed in the offices of George M. Harding of Portland, Maine, and George Meacham of Boston. In 1868, Francis opened his own architectural firm on Main Street in Fitchburg, where he practiced for more than 40 years. He renamed his company H.M. Francis & Sons in 1902 when his two sons, Frederick L. (pictured) and Albert F., joined the firm. By the time of his death in 1908, Francis left a design legacy in Fitchburg and New England of 30 school buildings, 25 churches, 15 libraries, a large number of public buildings, and several hundred residences. Faith United Parish Church, which is in the National Register of Historic Places, serves as a testament to the architect's skill in the Richardsonian Romanesque style. His sons Frederick and Albert continued to practice architecture in the city until 1943, bringing the H.M. Francis firm's presence on Main Street through three-quarters of a century. In 2008, the Commonwealth of Massachusetts designated a historic district for H.M. Francis Architecture in Fitchburg. The Fitchburg Historical Society owns two H.M. Francis buildings, 50 Grove Street, which was built specifically for the Historical Society in 1912, and 781 Main Street, the new home of the society.

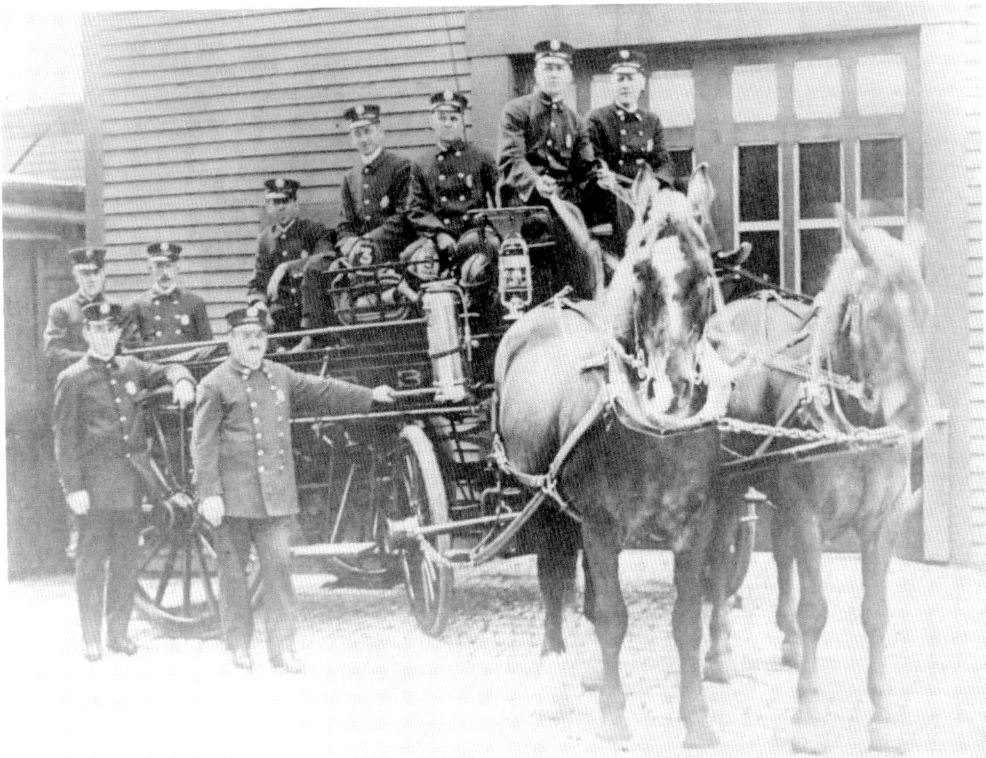

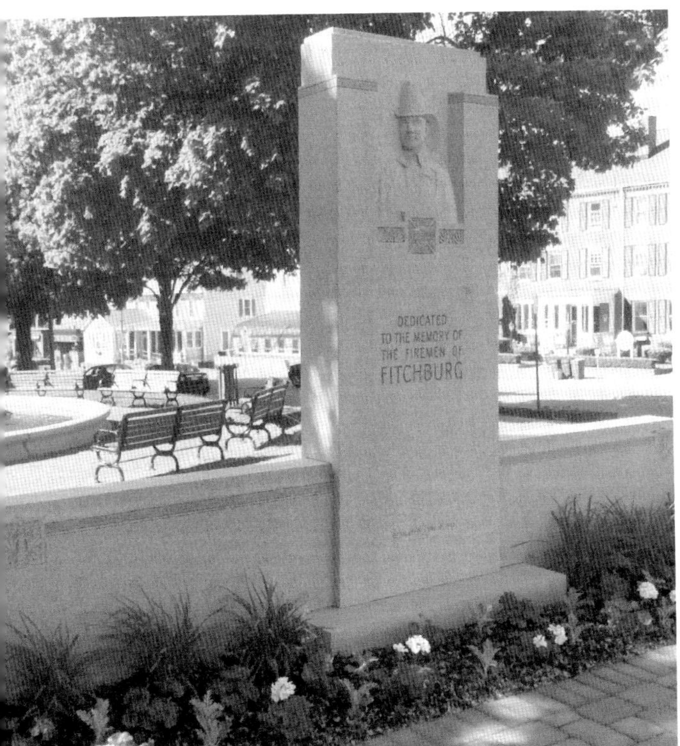

Fitchburg Fire Department (1851–Present)

Retired fireman and historian Philip D. Jordan tells the history of the Fitchburg Fire Department in his book *History of the Fitchburg Fire Department: If These Walls Could Talk* (2012). Fire was always a major threat to Fitchburg businessmen and townspeople, and the entire population turned out to help when the church bell sounded the alarm. Households had leather buckets to carry water and ladders ready for use. In 1851, the formal fire department was created, but firefighters were paid only for the time spent fighting fires. Gradually, full-time firefighters were hired. In 2013, the Fitchburg Fire Department had 76 full-time firefighters and three stations, including its headquarters located on North Street. In 1995, Kevin Roy became chief of the fire department, the youngest man ever to hold that position.

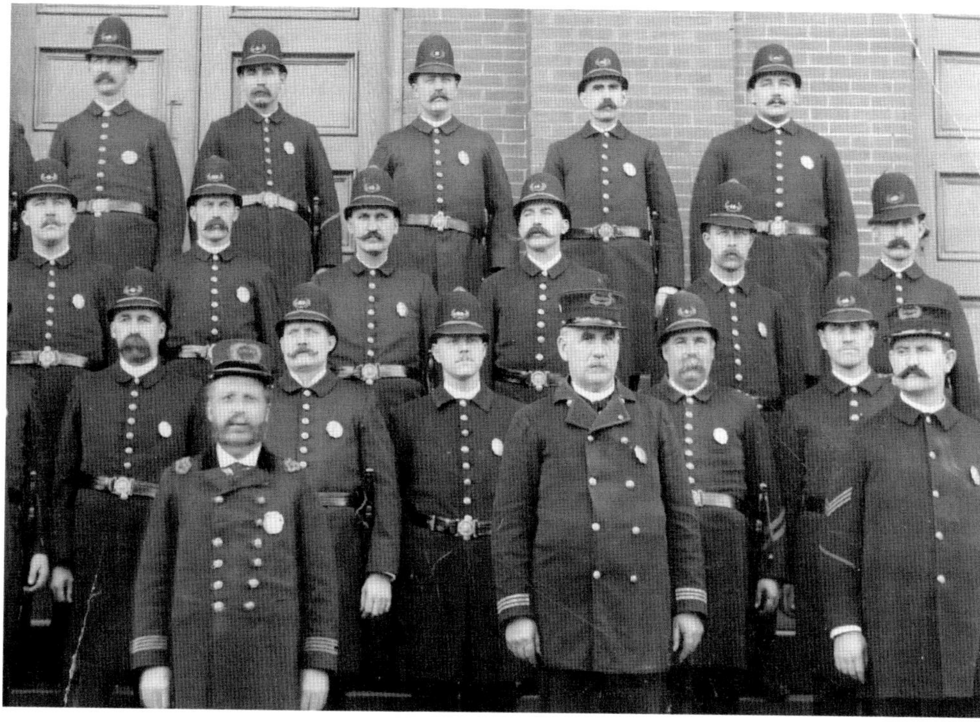

Fitchburg Police Department (1764–Present)
As a town, Fitchburg had a few constables to keep the peace. Throughout the 19th century, there were foot patrolmen, horse-drawn vehicles, and fire police sent to fires to prevent looting and to keep order. By 1872, the City of Fitchburg had a police chief, C.E.F. Hayward, and three patrolmen headquartered in city hall, with holding cells in the basement. In 1894, the station and the district court were located on Elm Street. By 1981, the district court moved to Elm and Grove Streets. In March 1987, the officers moved out of the old building and into the new Elm Street station, which had been built on adjoining land. In 2013, the chief was Robert B. DeMoura. Far from its humble beginnings, Fitchburg now has 56 patrolmen, 10 sergeants, 3 lieutenants, a captain, and a deputy chief protecting the city.

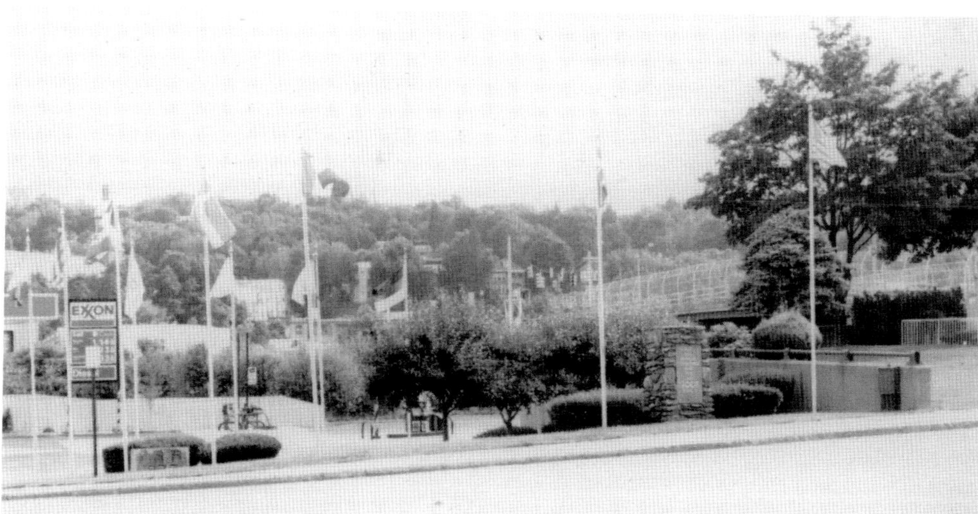

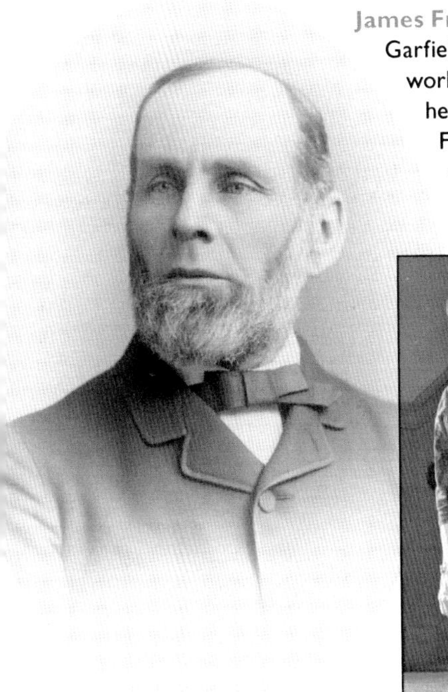

James Freeman Dana Garfield (1828–1911)

Garfield was born in New Hampshire and moved to Fitchburg in 1846 to work for the *Fitchburg Sentinel*, later becoming its editor. A prolific writer, he had always been interested in historical subjects and founded the Fitchburg Historical Society in 1892. He donated land for the society's original building at 50 Grove Street. Construction was completed in 1912, just after his death.

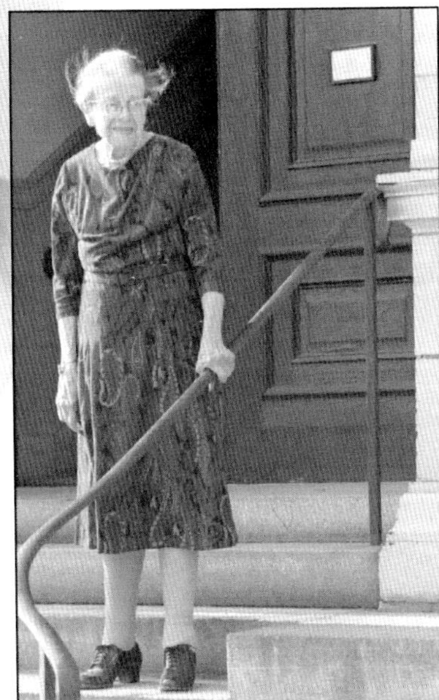

Theresa Newton Garfield (1879–1972)

Garfield was the daughter of James F.D. Garfield and Emily Charlotte (Newton) Garfield. A graduate of Fitchburg High School, class of 1897, and attendee of Rogers Hall in Lowell, Garfield was elected as the librarian of the Fitchburg Historical Society upon the death of her father and was elected as a trustee of the historical society in 1958. Garfield devoted 60 of her 93 years to the Fitchburg Historical Society.

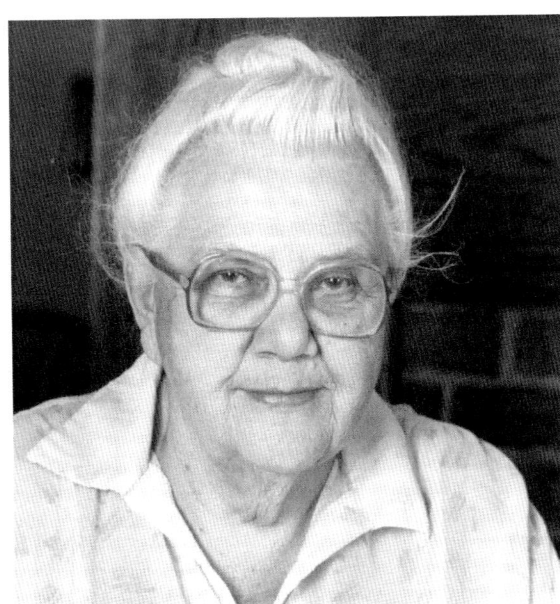

Eleanora Fraser West (1913–2010)

West left her job in Boston in 1965 to help her father, L.O. West, and her brother James in the family businesses in Fitchburg. She was appointed the fourth librarian, or director, of the Fitchburg Historical Society in 1972 and, from that time until her retirement in 1992, was the unofficial ambassador of history in Fitchburg. She spoke in classrooms and at club meetings about "Fabulous Females," "Fine Friends," or "Museum Mysteries." Under her leadership, the society expanded weekly hours, acquired the Vickery House on Prospect Street, and developed a local history course at Fitchburg State University.

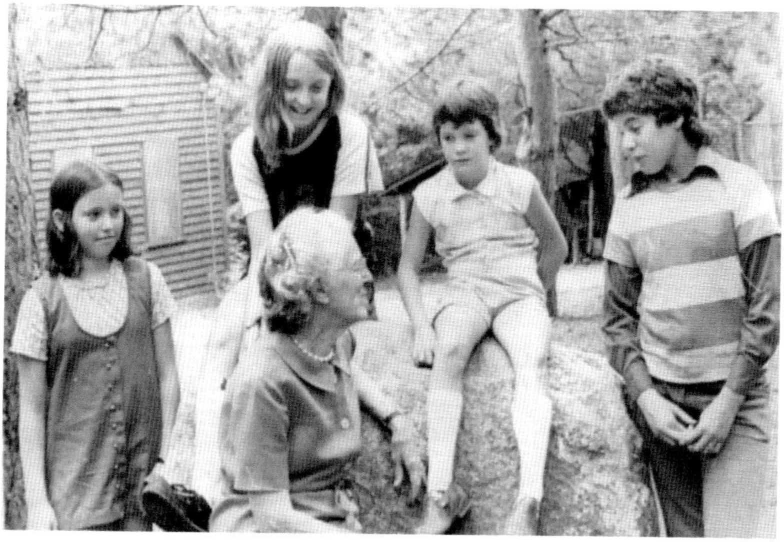

Barbara Cushing Crocker (1897–1981)
Crocker is remembered most for her personal and financial contributions to a variety of causes and projects. During World War II, she opened her home to two English children and assisted three Japanese American families in internment camps. Crocker maintained contact with them, and one of the families visited her in 1968. She was captain of Girl Scout Troop No. 4 and was active in Girl Scouting for many years. She and Helen Vickery, captain of the first Fitchburg Girl Scout troop, were lifelong friends. The Girl Scout Camp Wakitatina near Overlook Reservoir was established on land donated by her. In 1967, she financed the addition of an in-ground swimming pool for the camp. The campers always enjoyed Crocker's visits to the camp. Crocker was a faithful member and benefactor of the Fitchburg Historical Society. She also wrote dramatic vignettes about Fitchburg's history, including *A Bell for Shadrach* with her good friend Doris Kirkpatrick. More controversial was their 1945 study about substandard housing in Fitchburg titled "In Homes Like These." Crocker was chair of Fitchburg's 200th anniversary yearlong celebration in 1964 (pictured below), and in the following years, she provided financial support and encouragement for the writing and publishing of the two-volume history of Fitchburg, *The City and the River* (1971) and *Around the World in Fitchburg* (1975). She was married to Bigelow Crocker, and they had three children—Bigelow Jr., Rosemary, and Carolyn. (Photograph courtesy of Simone Blake.)

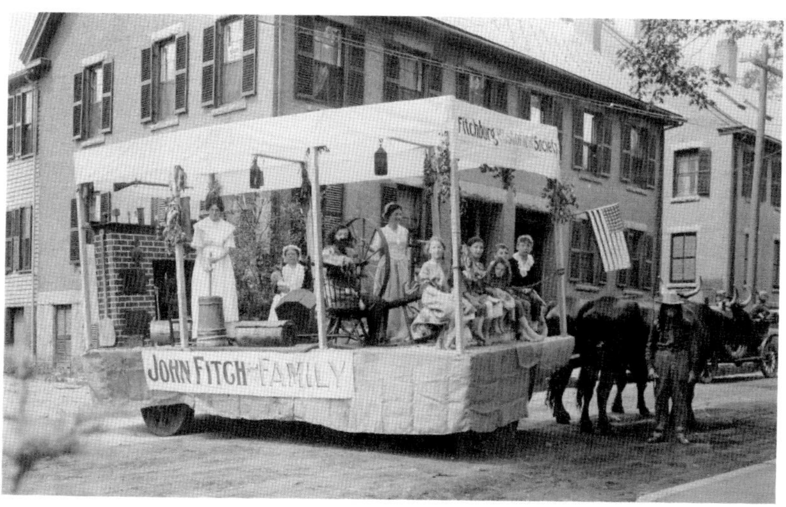

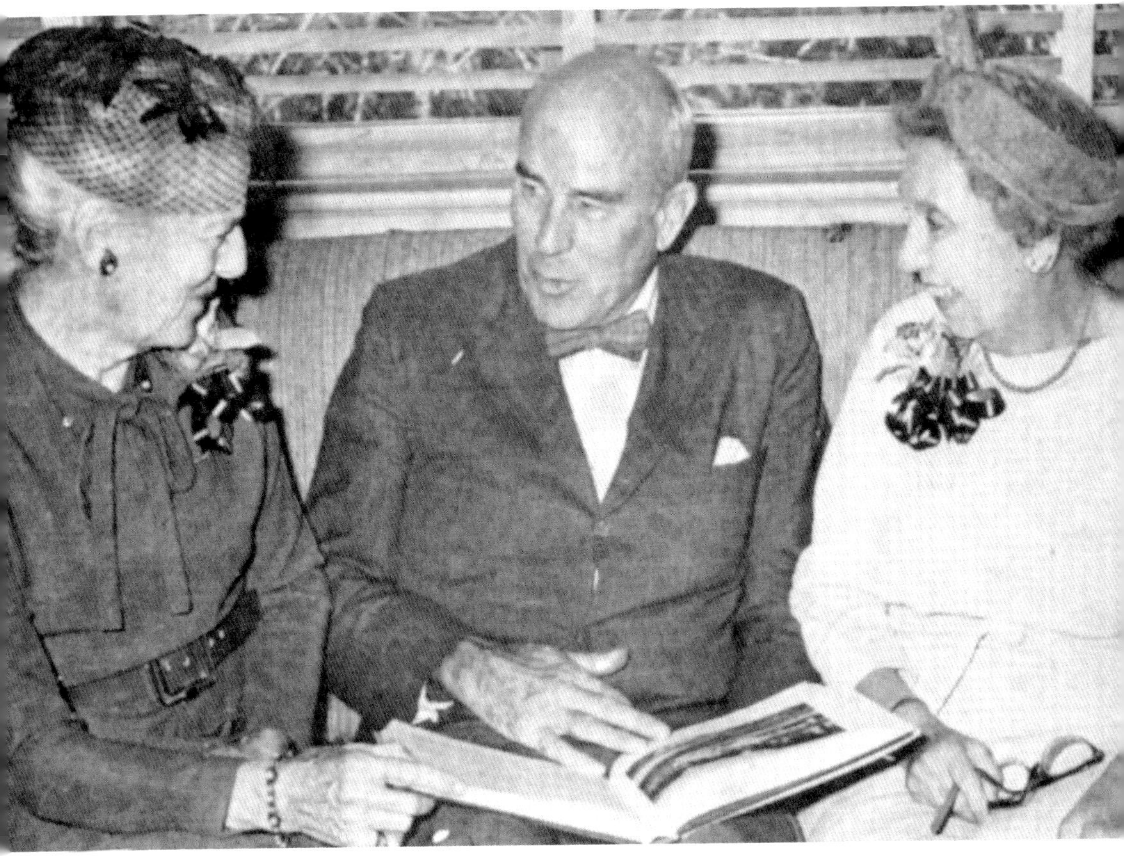

Doris Kirkpatrick (1902–1984)

Kirkpatrick (right) is best known as the author of Fitchburg's history books *The City and the River* (1971) and *Around the World in Fitchburg* (1975). Her writing career spanned more than 50 years, and she wrote in nearly every genre. While the family home was in Whitingham, Vermont, her father, Bradford Upton, left Vermont to take a job as a railroad engineer. Kirkpatrick was born and grew up in Fitchburg. In 1927, she married Clifford Kirkpatrick, son of the late Dr. Edwin A. Kirkpatrick, psychologist on the faculty of Fitchburg State College. They had one daughter, Judy. In 1938, in Germany where her husband was studying, Doris met and interviewed Frau Shultz-Klink, the leader of all German women. She was the first American to do so, and her story was published in the *New York Times*. She was a freelance writer for most of her life but spent 13 years in the Fitchburg office of the *Worcester Telegram*, beginning in 1945. She earned five Associated Press awards, one for an article about the Skyline Engineers' restoration of the Rollstone Congregational Church steeple, which she climbed! Another courageous action involved her and Barbara C. Crocker's research for a controversial study of housing conditions in Fitchburg in 1945. She also wrote the 200th-anniversary pageant *This Land Was Made for You and Me* (1964). Doris, who had retained the family home in Whitingham and loved to relate stories about the difficult winters there, died in Vermont in August 1984.

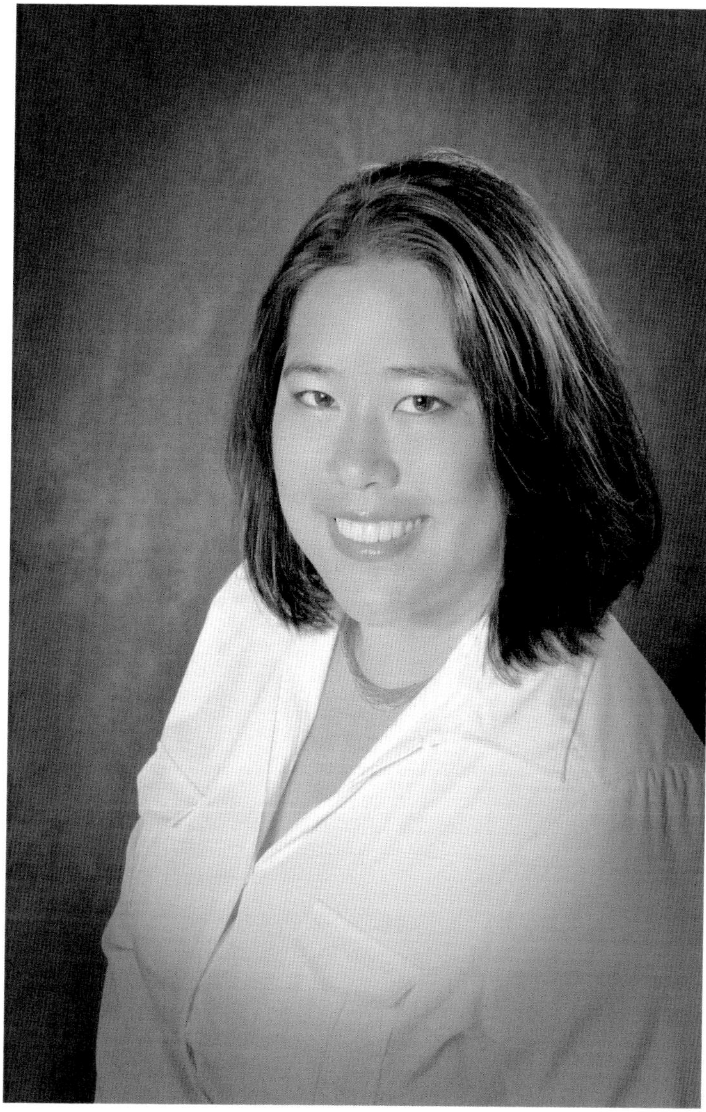

Lisa Wong (1979–present)
Elected in 2007 as the first Asian American mayor in Massachusetts at age 28, Wong continued the tradition of the children of immigrants leading the city. Her parents emigrated from Hong Kong in 1970 and ran two Chinese restaurants in which Wong and her brothers worked during their teenage years. Wong was the valedictorian of her high school class in North Andover and runner-up for "most bashful" senior. She earned undergraduate degrees in international relations and economics at Boston University, as well as her master's degree in economics. These degrees served her well on the Fitchburg Redevelopment Authority, where she became director. In her terms as mayor, Wong supported the creation of more than 300 new small businesses, a lower crime rate, improvements to roofs and boilers in schools, and downtown housing for Fitchburg State University students. Significantly, the city's bond rating was upgraded, while unpopular policies, such as shutting off city streetlights and reducing the city library's hours, created some grumbling among residents. The city streetlights have now been purchased by the city, resulting in savings on annual lighting bills. Currently in her third term, Mayor Wong heads the state's Gateway Cities Initiative. (Courtesy of Lisa Wong.)

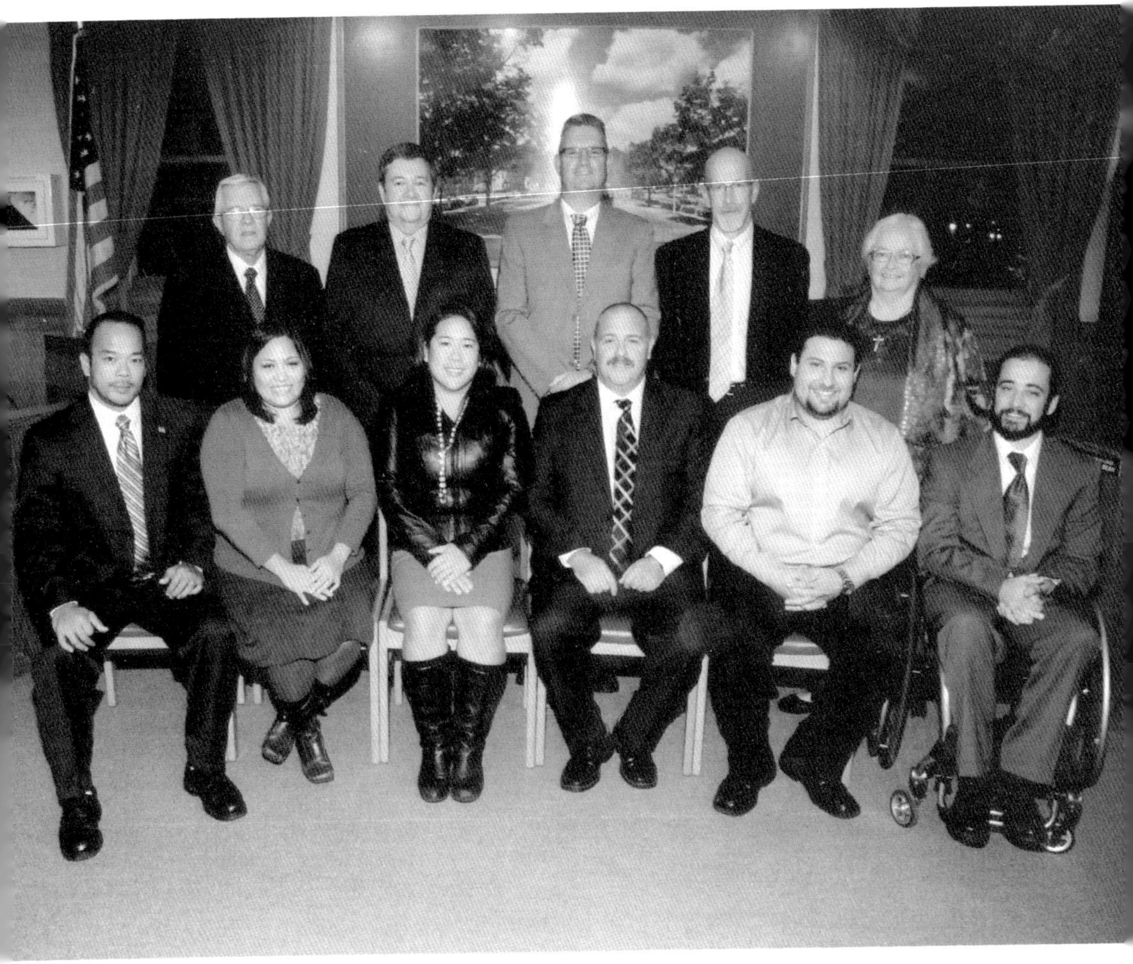

City Council

Working with Mayor Wong in 2013 was a diverse city council of ward councilors and councilors-at-large: from left to right, (first row) Dean A. Tran, councilor-at-large; Dolores Thibault-Munoz, Ward 4 councilor; Mayor Lisa Wong; Jody M. Joseph, Ward 6 councilor; Marcus DiNatale, councilor-at-large; Nicholas Carbone, Ward 5 councilor; (second row) Norman L. Boisvert, Ward 2 councilor; David Clark, Ward 1 councilor; Stephen Hay, councilor-at-large; Jeffrey A. Bean, councilor-at-large; and Rosemary Reynolds, councilor-at-large. (Courtesy of JR Photo and Dolores Munoz-Thibault.)

CHAPTER TWO

Industrialists and Inventors

Her ponderous engineries supply
A thousand waiting needs,
Her wheels revolve, her shuttles fly,
And everywhere the prize hangs high,
Her foot, unfaltering, leads.

—Excerpt from "Ode to Fitchburg" by Caroline A. Mason

Once called "the Machine City" and noted for its paper mills and railroad connections, Fitchburg has been home to many industrialists and inventors, many of whom invented machines to help local, national, and international industries. The Burleigh Drill, the Brown Bag Filling Machine, scythes and knives, clothing patterns, and boilers began in Fitchburg, then were sold around the world. Industries included paper, steam engines, wool and cotton textiles, guns, and bicycles. To support these businesses, the city built several hotels and connected the Fitchburg Railroad to the east and the west. Banking cooperatives were part of the growing industrial city. Credit unions initially formed by immigrants are still serving customers today.

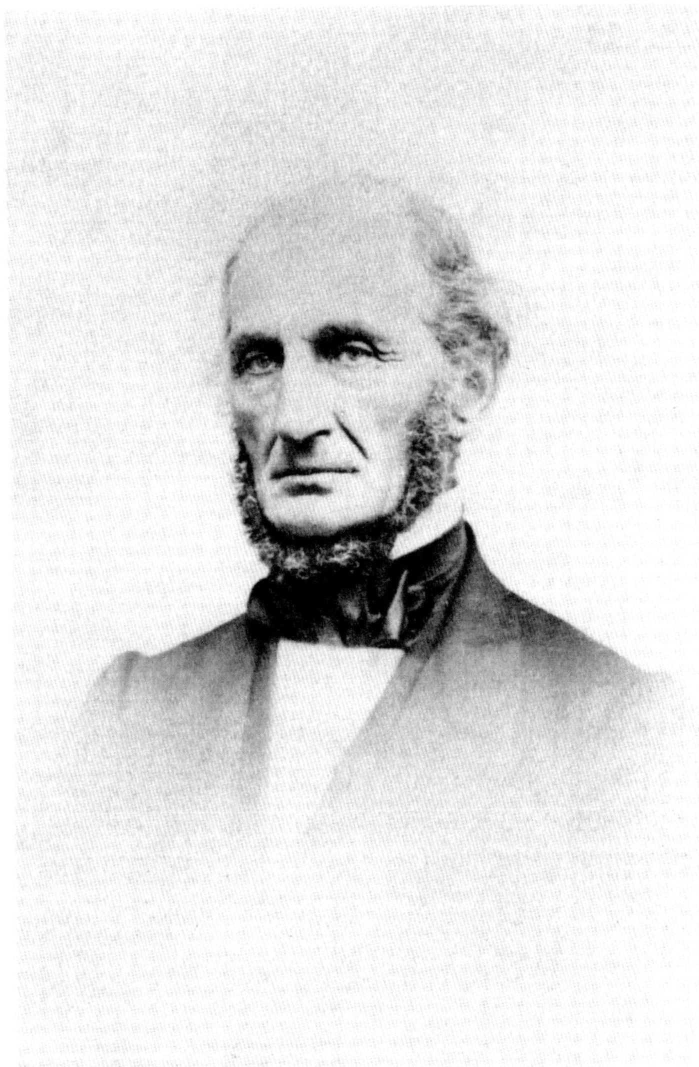

Alvah Crocker (1801–1874)

At the age of eight, Crocker began working at the paper mill where his father was employed in Leominster. He attended a private high school as long as his tuition money lasted and then returned to the paper business until he had saved and borrowed enough to start his first paper mill on the bank of the Nashua River. This first mill was destroyed when the river flooded in 1829, but Crocker rebuilt it. He also purchased the Burbank paper factory, where he had worked as a young man, and borrowed money to purchase more mills. Unfortunately, fate intervened again, and fire struck his most prosperous mill and warehouse. This setback led Alvah to help start the Fitchburg Mutual Fire Insurance Company. After driving his paper to Boston at night to sell, he realized that extending the railroad from Boston to Fitchburg would be beneficial. Later, he realized that a railroad route to the west was also necessary for commerce, so he championed the creation of the Hoosac Tunnel in western Massachusetts to allow the railroad to pass through to the Erie Canal and Hudson River. He also supported the building of Christ Church and served as both state representative and federal congressman. When he died of pneumonia in 1874, congressmen in Washington, DC, wore a badge of mourning for 30 days, and citizens of Fitchburg realized that Alvah Crocker had done more than any other man, living or dead, for the city.

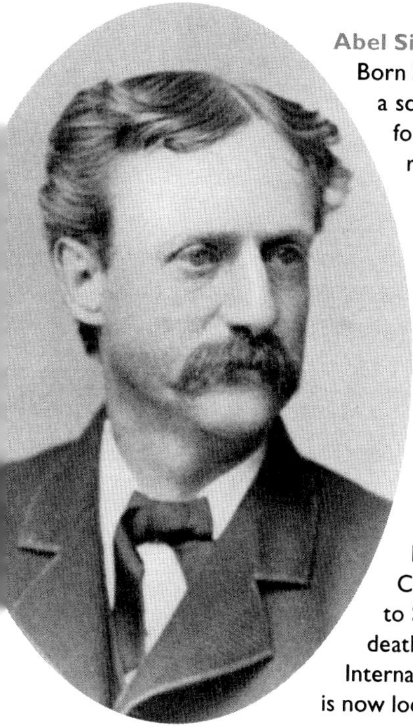

Abel Simonds (1804–1875) and George F. Simonds (1843–1896)

Born in Lunenburg, Abel Simonds served seven years as an apprentice to a scythe maker in Fitchburg. Following his apprenticeship, he worked for two years at Farwell's scythe shop in West Chelmsford. When he returned to Fitchburg, he and Farwell opened a scythe factory on the Nashua River. When McCormick reapers made scythes obsolete, the company switched to the manufacture of saws. Of Abel's 11 children, 8 worked with him in the business. He was known to be generous to his employees, providing medical services, drinking fountains on the factory floors, a recreation club with tennis courts, and an Employees' Aid and Relief Association. After his death, his company opened national and international offices.

George Simonds (pictured), who was the seventh son of Abel Simonds and Jane Todd, worked for his father before and after serving a year in the Civil War. When he took over the business, George used his ingenuity to develop new methods for tempering and straightening circular saws. In his lifetime, George was awarded 100 patents. In 1886, George started the Simonds Rolling Machine Company. George died in a train accident while traveling from Chicago to San Francisco to visit Simonds factories. At the time of George's death in 1896, Simonds employed 200 workers in Fitchburg. Simonds International is still in business today, and the Simonds Factory in Fitchburg is now located on Intervale Street.

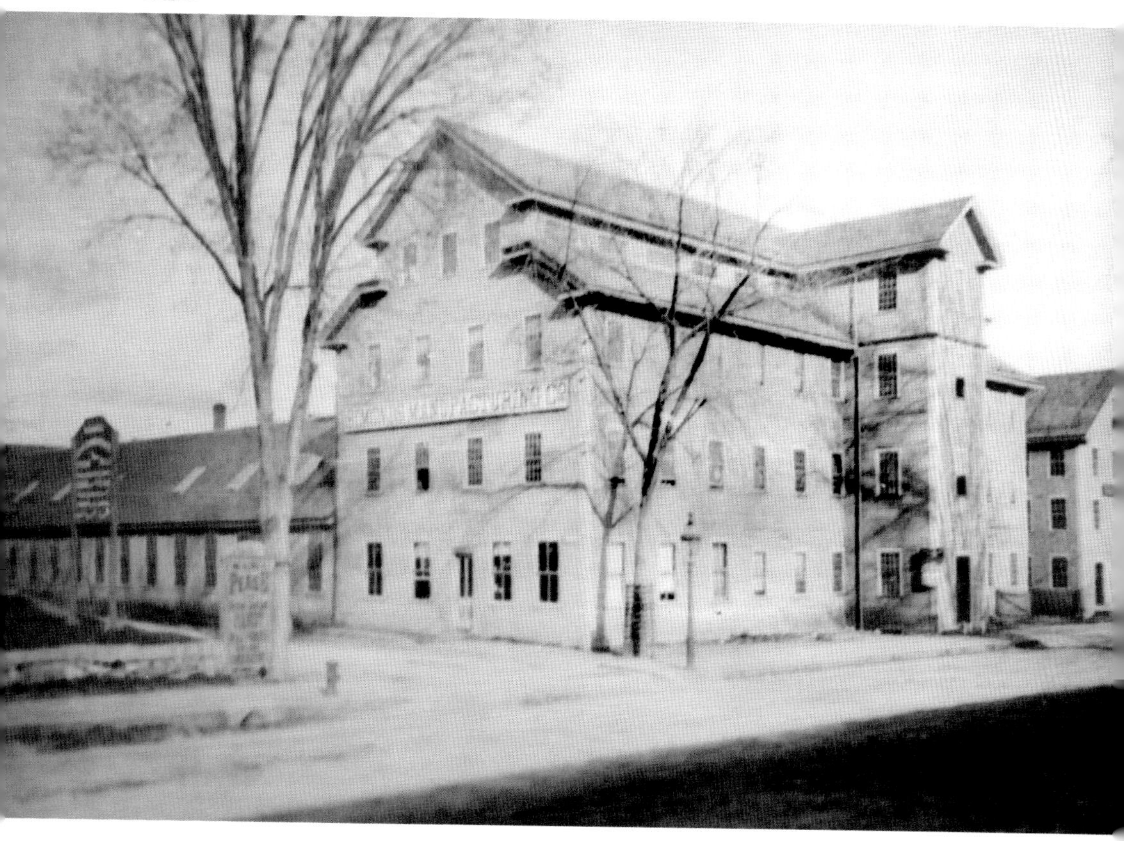

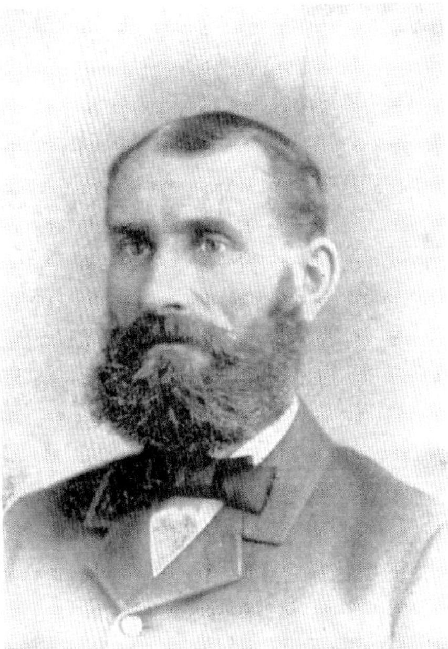

Iver Johnson (1841–1895)
Born in Norway, Johnson began an apprenticeship as a gunsmith at age 16. In 1863, he immigrated to the United States. For eight years, he worked at Allen & Wheelock gun manufacturers in Worcester. He then formed a partnership with another immigrant to make firearms. They had a Worcester-based business that Johnson took over by himself in 1883. In addition to guns, the plant manufactured bicycles, producing high wheelers in 1887 and 1888. In 1890, Johnson became the manufacturer of the safety bicycle, which had front and back wheels of equal size and quickly gained popularity. In 1891, he purchased the Walter Heywood Chair Manufacturing Company factory, built some additions, and moved his production to Fitchburg. When he died in 1895, the family carried on the business. In 1941, the production of bicycles was stopped because of the war, and they were never made again. Johnson's Arms & Cycle Works remained in Fitchburg until 1973.

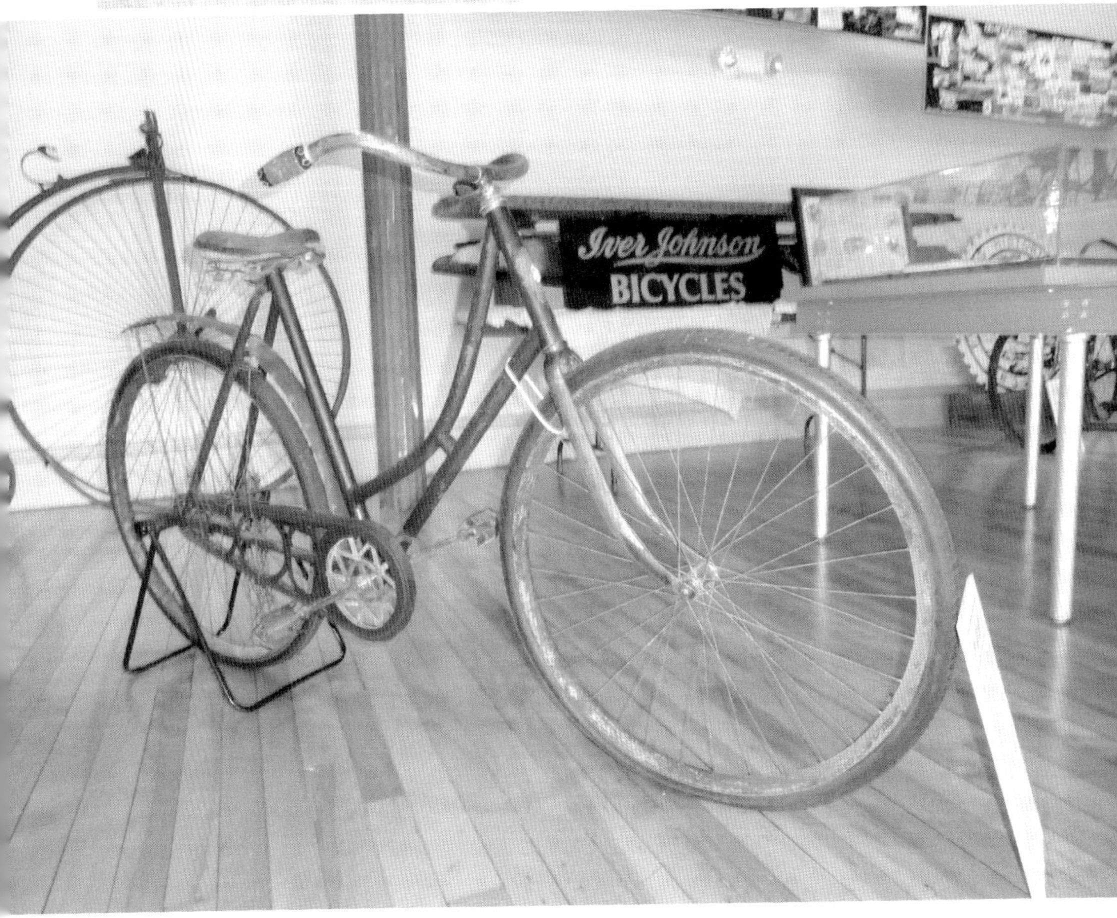

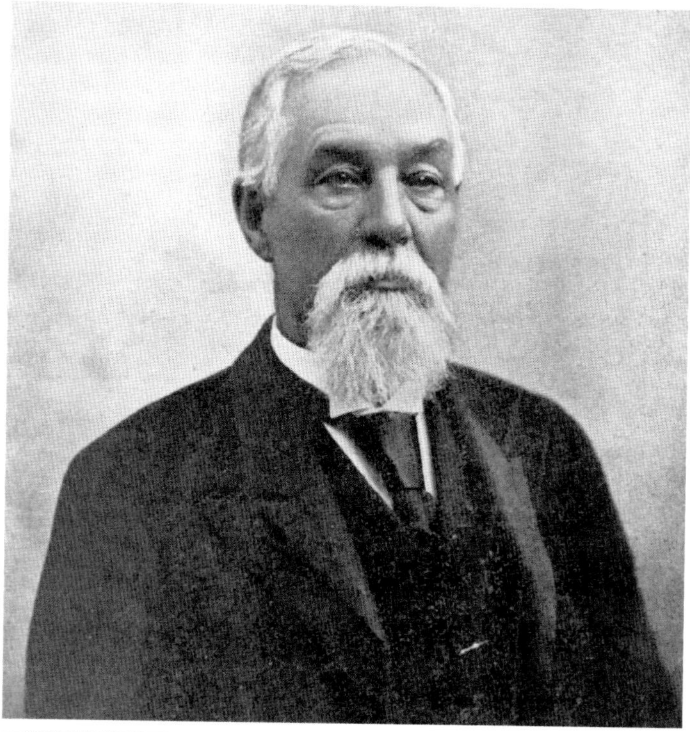

John Parkhill (1823–1906)
Born in Scotland, Parkhill moved to Fitchburg in 1880. He established Parkhill Manufacturing, famous for its dress fabrics, particularly gingham. Over time, the Parkhill Manufacturing Company owned two mills. Parkhill invited Scottish workers to join his new business, which became a major employer in the city with 1,400 people in 1912. Parkhill remained involved in his company until he passed away suddenly in 1906.

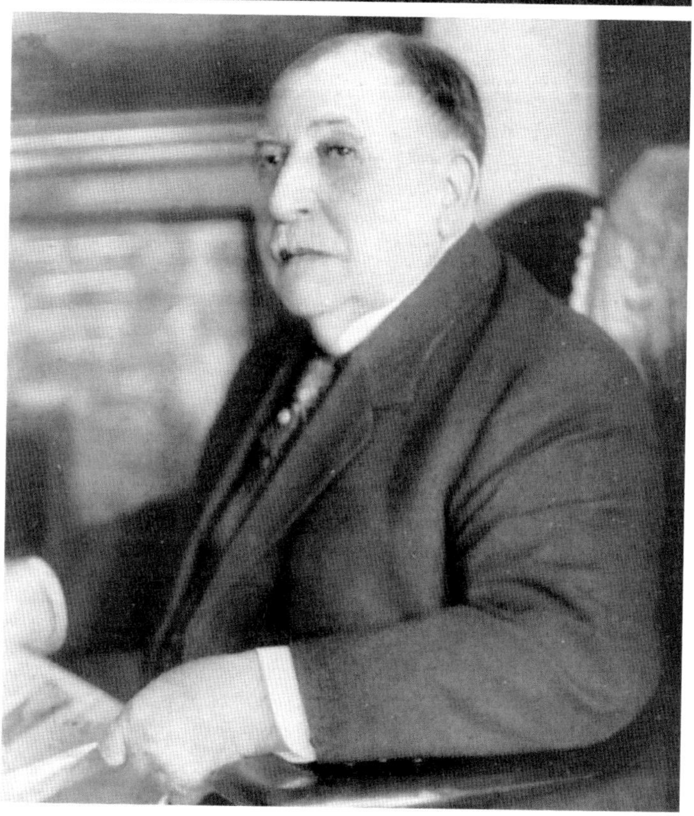

David M. Dillon (1843–1926)
Dillion was born in New Brunswick in 1843 and moved to Fitchburg in 1870. D.M. Dillon Boiler Works made and repaired all sorts of boilers, but his company was most famous for being the first to make boilers out of steel. Dillon boilers, known for their fine workmanship, were sold in every state and many foreign countries.

Charles Burleigh (1824–1883)

Burleigh moved to Fitchburg in 1850 and joined the Putnam Machine Works, where he developed the Putnam Engine, along with Charles H. Brown. After work on the Hoosac Tunnel had slowed drastically, Alvah Crocker asked Burleigh to design a drill to finish the tunnel. The Burleigh Rock Drill was the result. The drill was also used in the building of the Brooklyn Bridge and the Union and Pacific Railroads.

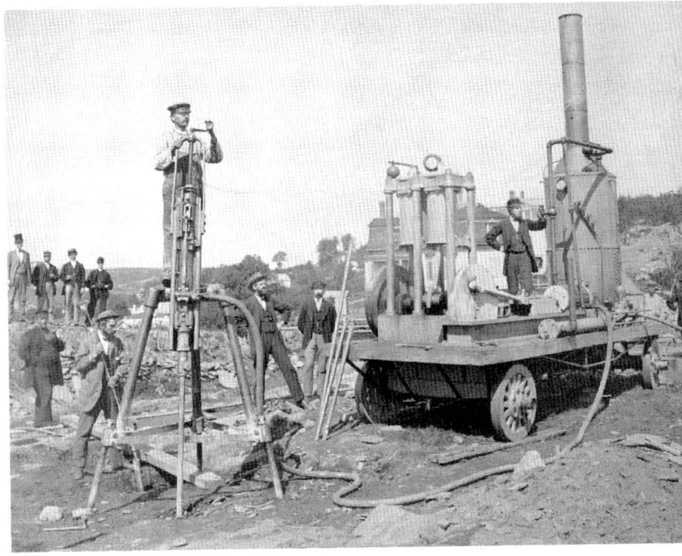

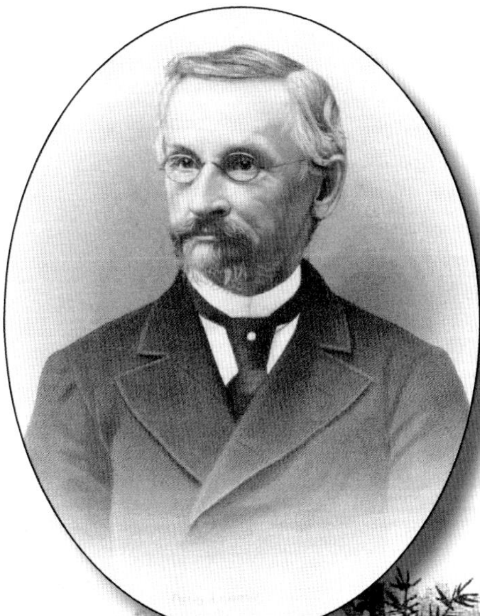

Charles H. Brown (1820–?)

Brown worked for several years in Rhode Island before becoming an apprentice, along with Charles Burleigh, at a Boston steam engine company. He and Charles Burleigh came to Fitchburg to work at the Putnam Machine Company, where they patented the Putnam Engine. In 1863, he founded the C.H. Brown Company. Brown's automatic-cutoff engine won awards at national and international exhibitions and was admired by Thomas Edison.

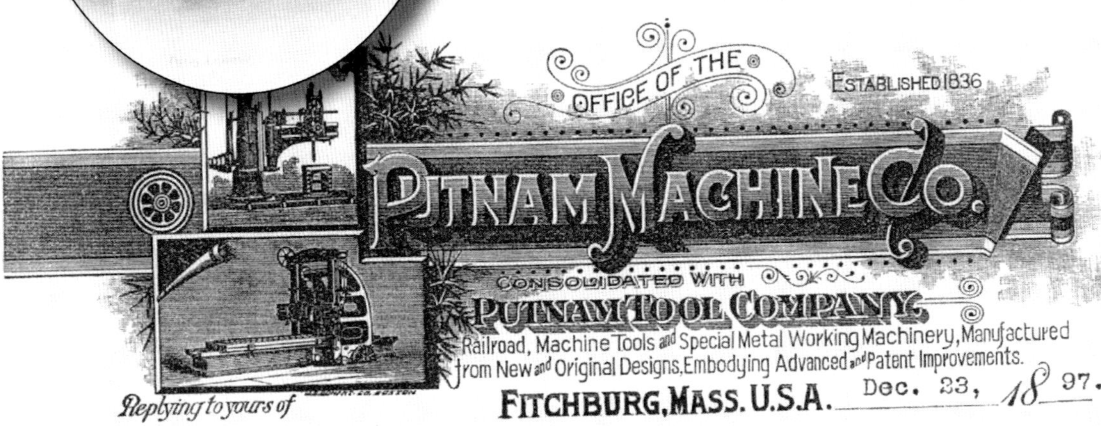

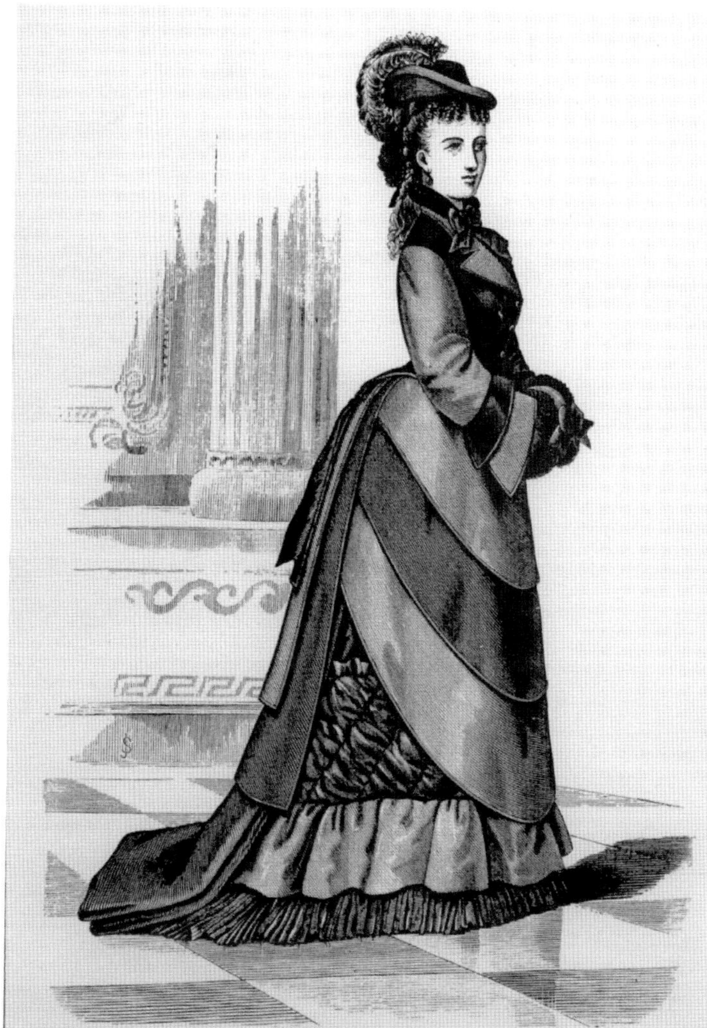

LADIES' WALKING AND CARRIAGE COSTUME.

Ellen (1826–1879) and Ebenezer (1826–1903) Butterick

Ellen and Ebenezer both lived in Sterling. After completing school, Ebenezer clerked at his brother's store and then apprenticed with a tailor in Worcester before opening his own shop. In 1850, he married Ellen Augusta Pollard, who worked in his tailoring business. The story goes that, in 1863, Ellen was drawing a pattern for a baby dress for their son, and as she drew and cut the pattern, Ellen commented to her husband that her work would be much easier if she had a pattern in her son's size. At the time, a pattern would come in one size and the seamstress would make adjustments or draw her own. Taking Ellen's advice, Ebenezer first made patterns for children and men out of cardboard, which was too cumbersome to fold, carry, or mail. Butterick switched to tissue paper, which folded easily and was cheaper to mail or carry. Soon, their Sterling home was too small for their business, and they bought a house in Fitchburg, where women folded the patterns. As business boomed, more space was needed. Ebenezer moved the Butterick Pattern factory to Brooklyn and added ladies' fashions to his lines. By 1871, the Buttericks had already sold six million patterns. Sadly, Ellen died in 1879. In the 1880s, Ebenezer's health began to fail, so when he turned 73, he retired and moved back to Sterling. He died while visiting in Brooklyn and is buried in the Evergreen Cemetery in Leominster, leaving a thriving company that bore his and Ellen's name.

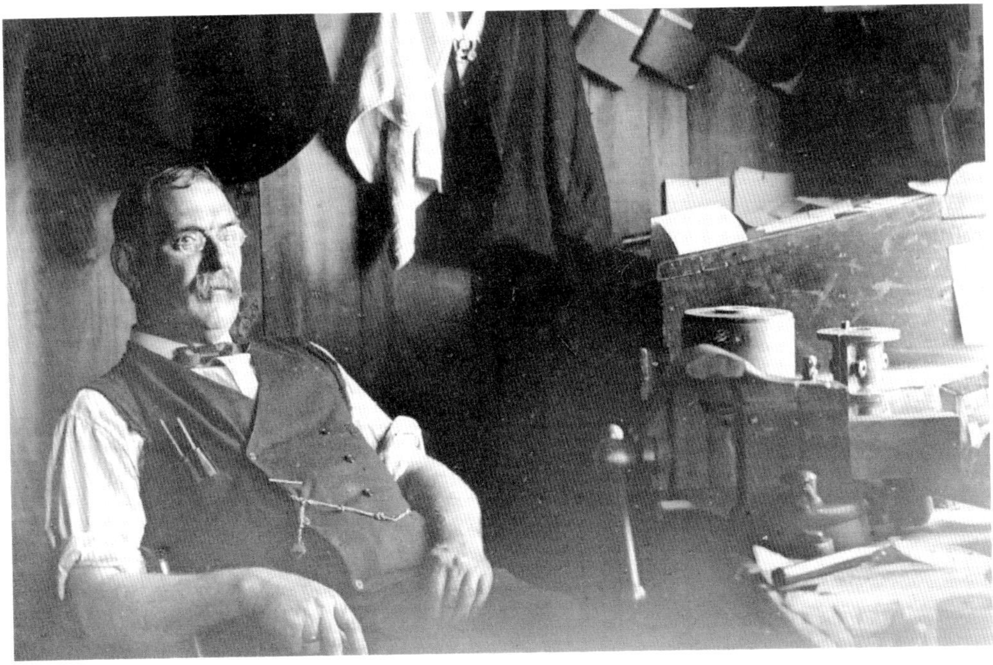

Benjamin Franklin "B.F." Brown (1849–1922)
Brown graduated from Fitchburg High and Amherst College. He taught in Brattleboro, Vermont, and at Fitchburg High and became a principal in Athol and Montpelier, Vermont. His brother Joseph invented the Brown Bag Filling Machine; after Benjamin's retirement, he returned to Fitchburg to help with the manufacture of the Brown Bag Filling Machine. He also served as a school committee member. A new junior high school was named after him in 1924.

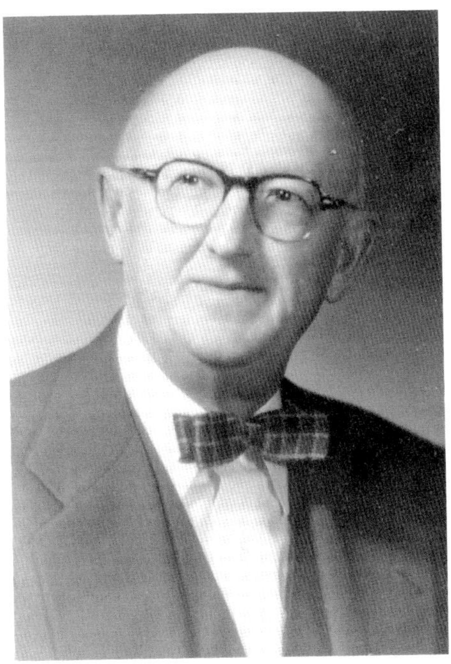

William E. Aubuchon Sr. (1887–1971)
Born in Canada, Aubuchon moved with his widowed mother, Georgiana, to Fitchburg in 1901. There, he worked in a yarn mill, saving his money. In 1908, he opened his first hardware store. The business grew throughout New England and New York. In 1950, his son William Jr. became president, but William Sr. remained very active until his death. Today, there are more than 100 Aubuchon Hardware Stores.

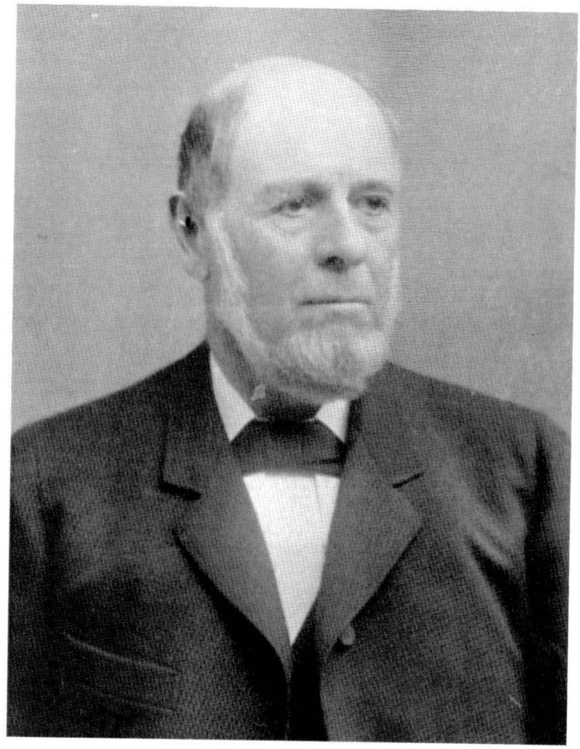

Elijah M. Dickinson (1816–1902)
Dickinson started in business as a cobbler in 1842 and moved his shop to Fitchburg in 1854. In 1877, his son Charles joined the business, and they built a factory to manufacture shoes. Within 10 years, their shoe production numbered 1,500 pairs per day. They erected the Dickinson Block, a prominent architectural feature in Fitchburg.

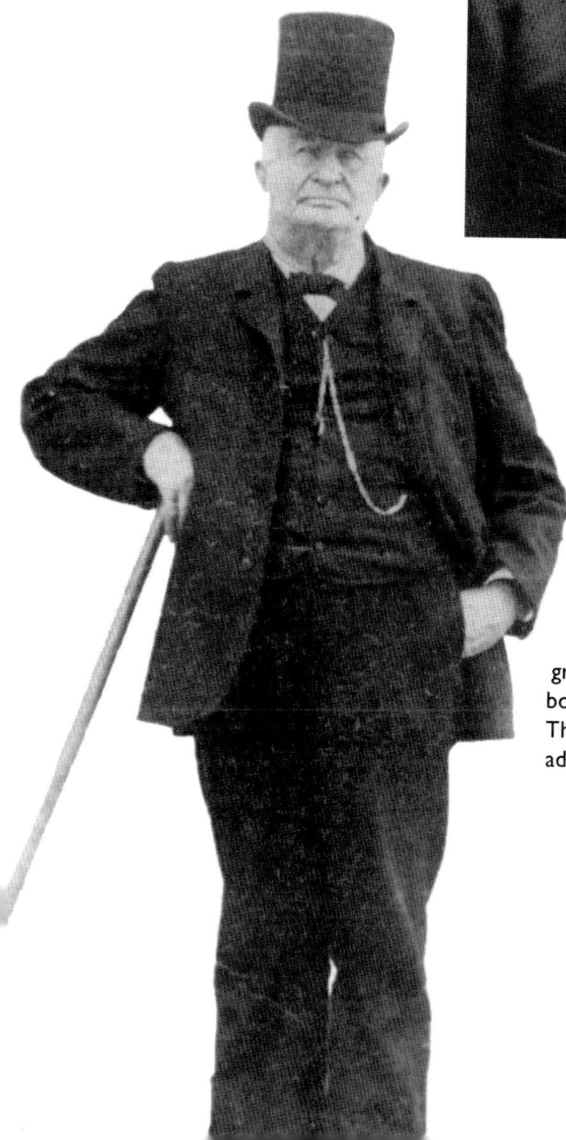

Joseph Cushing (1817–1894)
Cushing was born in Brooklyn, Pennsylvania. His family moved to neighboring Ashburnham when he was 13. Cushing came to Fitchburg in 1844. He owned both a livery business and a lumber business before opening a flour and grain business. In 1868, Cushing and his son Milton bought the Stone Mill and converted it to grain. The grain business was very successful, with 17 additional New England sites.

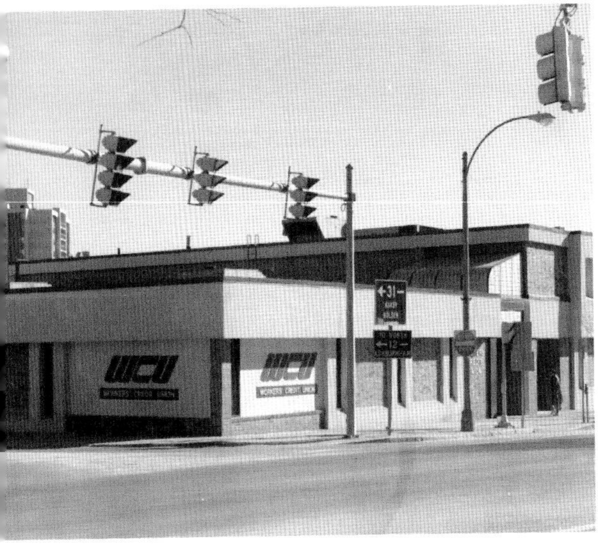

Workers Credit Union (1914–Present)

Finnish immigrants in the publishing office of the *Raivaaja*, the Finnish newspaper, started the Workers Credit Union, with 24 men attending the first meeting. They agreed to submit a charter application to the state and received approval on April 17, 1914. Their purpose was to provide financial assistance to their Finnish members for purchasing property or meeting medical bills. John Suominen, who had initiated the founding meeting, was elected treasurer and served as the credit union supervisor until his death in 1948. His wife, Martha, served as his assistant and bookkeeper. Over the years, Workers Credit Union opened its membership and expanded its growth. Today, it has 15 branches across Massachusetts and assets of $800 million.

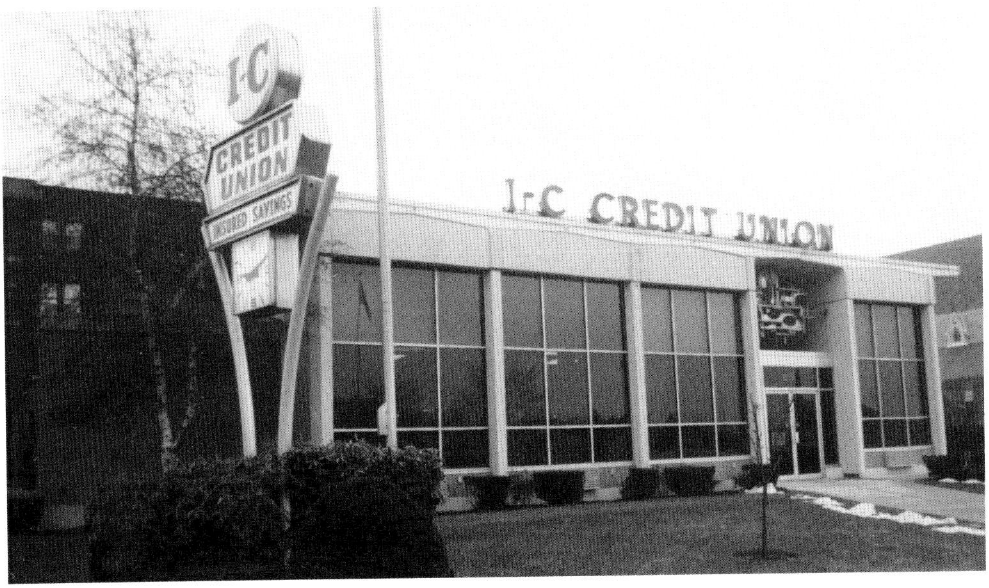

IC Federal Credit Union (1928–Present)

In September 1928, a group of 20 men launched a credit union in the basement of the Immaculate Conception Church, born from a very simple idea: people helping people. From these humble beginnings, the IC Federal Credit Union has grown to one of the largest credit unions in the state of Massachusetts and continues its commitment to its members. Through moves from the church to Main Street, to Blossom Street, and back to Main Street, the credit union continued to grow and serve its members. In 1985, the main office relocated to 300 Bemis Road, with several branches in Fitchburg, Leominster, Westminster, and Ayer. When the charter changed in 1986 from state to federal, IC could include individuals who lived or worked in the Massachusetts counties of Worcester, Middlesex, Franklin, Hampden, Hampshire, and Norfolk. Some of the earliest founders included William E. Aubuchon Jr., Aldei J. Beauchemin, Benjamin Dion, A. Andre Gelinas, and J. Alphonse L'Ecuyer. Today, members recall Norman J. Boudreau, who retired in 2008, as the longest-serving employee in the history of the credit union, having worked there for 45 years. He began as a board member, then treasurer, general manager, and eventually president and chief executive officer.

CHAPTER THREE

Community and Government Leaders

She dons no autocratic airs,
In scorn of humble days.
But shapes her fortune and affairs
To match the civil wreath she wears
And justify her bays.

—Excerpt from "Ode to Fitchburg" by Caroline A. Mason

Many of Fitchburg's mayors are included in this section, including the first female mayor, Mary Whitney. Two leaders—Henry Coggshall and Marcus Coolidge—gave land to the city to build parks still used today. Bill Flynn is remembered for his support in cleaning up the Nashua River and Alfred Woollacott for his support in building the Fitchburg Airport. Fitchburg has sent several men to the US House of Representatives and Senate. A. Andred Gelinas, Worcester district attorney, and his son Andre A. Gelinas, who became an associate justice for the Massachusetts Appeals Court, had the district courthouse renamed in their honor.

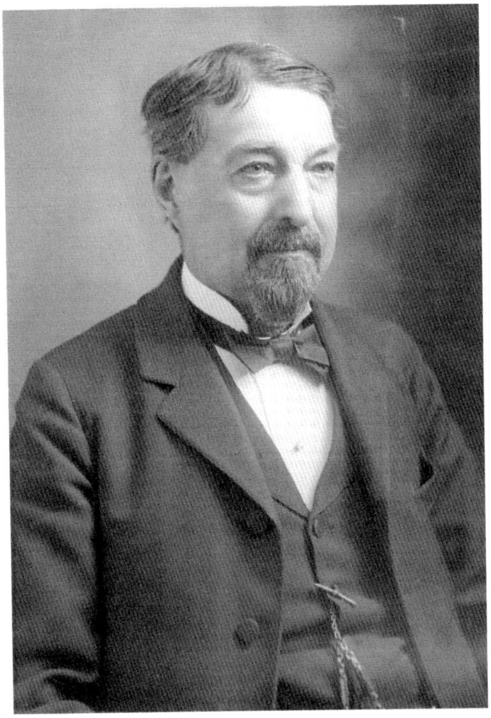

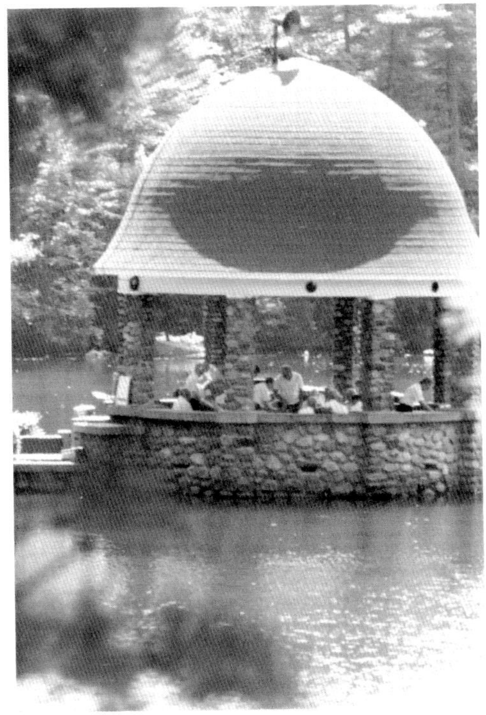

Henry Fayette Coggshall (1823–1912)
Coggshall supervised the construction of Fitchburg Gas and Electric Company and served as general manager from 1853 to 1906. In 1894, he presented the city with 160 acres, the site of his summer home, and, later, 52 more adjoining acres, a dam to create Mirror Lake, and a trust fund for the park's maintenance. The original stone house at Coggshall Park was built as a memorial to the Coggshalls.

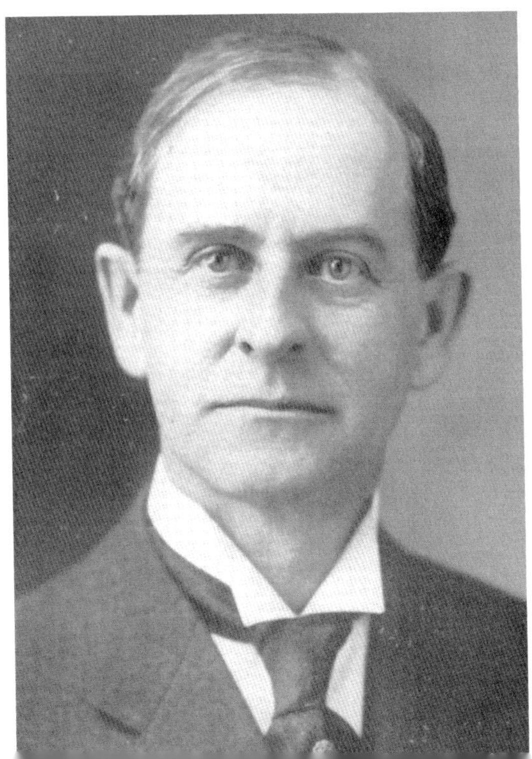

Marcus Coolidge (1865–1947)
Coolidge moved to Fitchburg in 1895 and was elected mayor in 1916. A US senator serving from 1931 to 1937, he was chair of the Committee on Immigration, voted to repeal Prohibition, and helped secure WPA funding for the high school. Pres. Woodrow Wilson sent him to Poland as an envoy in 1919. In 1939, Coolidge donated land to the city for Coolidge Park.

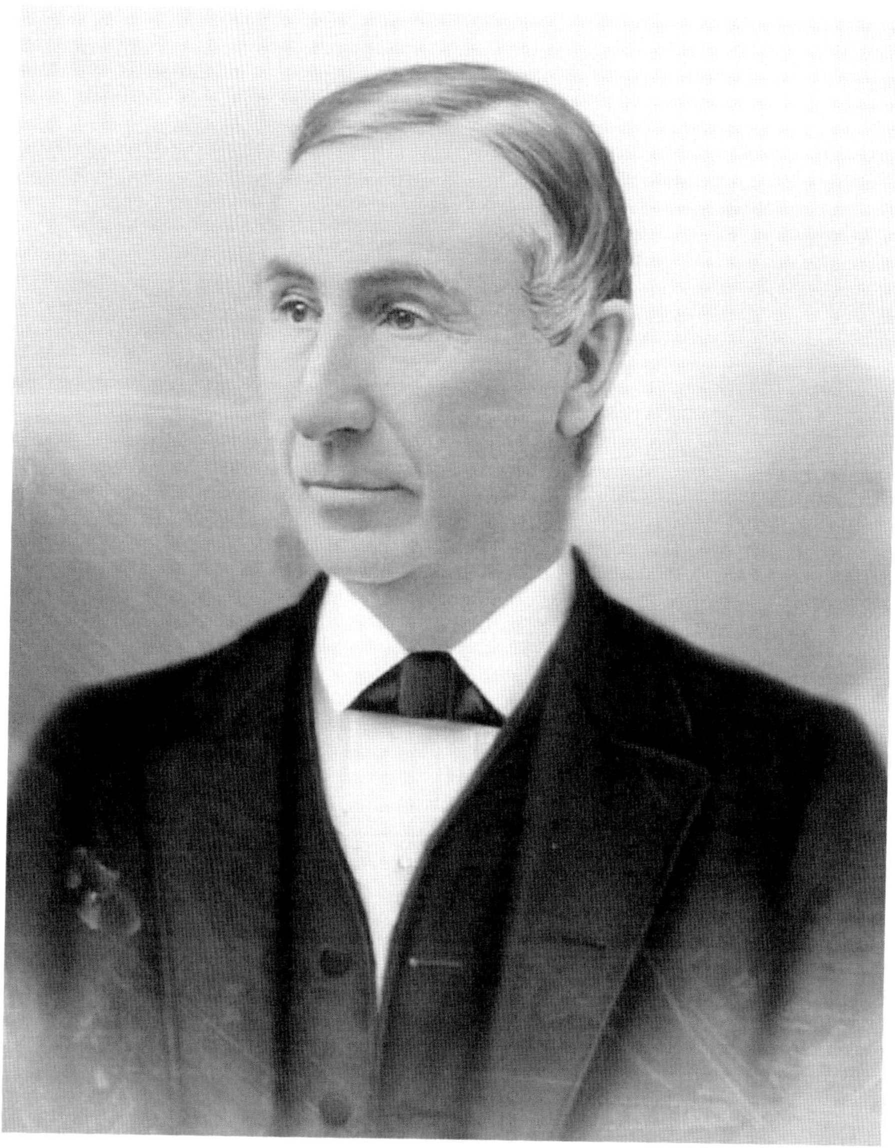

Rodney Wallace (1823–1903)
Born in New Ipswich, New Hampshire, Wallace left home at an early age to work on a farm in Ashburnham. When he was not allowed to complete the entire school term, Wallace strived to continue his education and to create opportunities for others to do so. He moved to Fitchburg in 1853 and opened a bookshop on Main Street. The bookshop also sold stationery and paper stock and dealt in cotton waste. When he and his partner divided the business, Wallace retained the cotton waste part of the business. After the Civil War, Wallace obtained two paper mills in West Fitchburg. To help his mills, he built a stone dam and his own freight station. Embracing the need for education, he promoted the library in town hall and donated the Wallace Library and Arts Building, complete with furnishings, in 1885. Wallace was instrumental in building the railway station in Fitchburg. Still in existence, the Wallace Way staircase to the high school (now Longsjo Middle School) was his gift to inspire students to rise to the stars through education. Wallace served on the board of selectman in 1864, 1865, and 1867 and was a US representative from Massachusetts from 1889 to 1890.

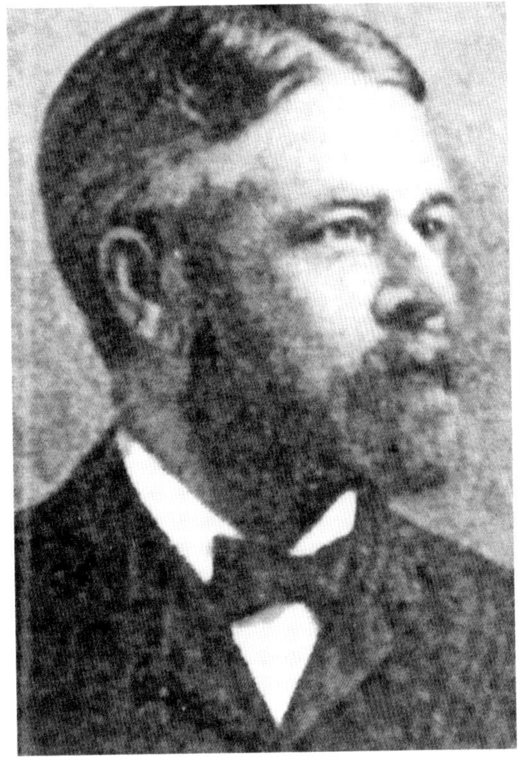

Eli Culley (1840–1890)
Culley emigrated from England in 1855. He served in the Massachusetts 43rd Infantry during the Civil War, mustering out in 1863 after being wounded. He came to Fitchburg in 1867, moving his file works company with him. As the sixth mayor of the city, he was the first to serve six terms. Culley also served as a representative to the Massachusetts legislature.

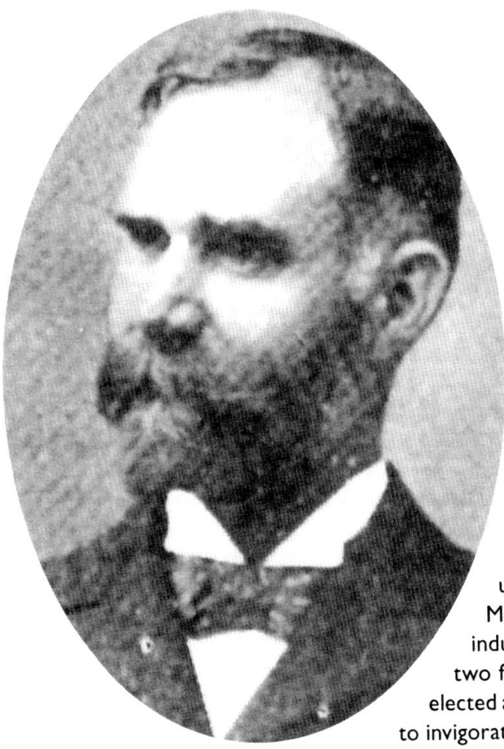

Arthur H. Lowe (1853–1932)
Lowe moved to the city as a toddler. Arthur worked in his father's meat and produce business until he became the agent and manager of the Parkhill Manufacturing Company and expanded the gingham industry. Lowe married Annie Parkhill, thus uniting the two families and their manufacturing concerns. He was elected as the mayor of Fitchburg and was known for helping to invigorate Fitchburg's economy.

David Ignatius Walsh (1872–1947)

Walsh was born in nearby Leominster. He graduated from Clinton High School and College of the Holy Cross, then earned a law degree from Boston University in 1897. He opened an office in Fitchburg, where he began a long career in law and politics. He took on cases where he battled for labor and against corruption in government. Walsh became well known, making friends with people like John "Honey Fitz" Fitzgerald, while crossing swords with the likes of James Michael Curley. Walsh was elected as the first Irish Catholic governor of Massachusetts in 1913. Later, he was elected as a Democrat to the US Senate, serving from 1919 to 1925 and from 1926 to 1946. Walsh fought hard to increase minimum wages and enact child labor laws. In Boston, there is a bronze statue of him as a tribute for all he did for the US Navy while he was in the Senate.

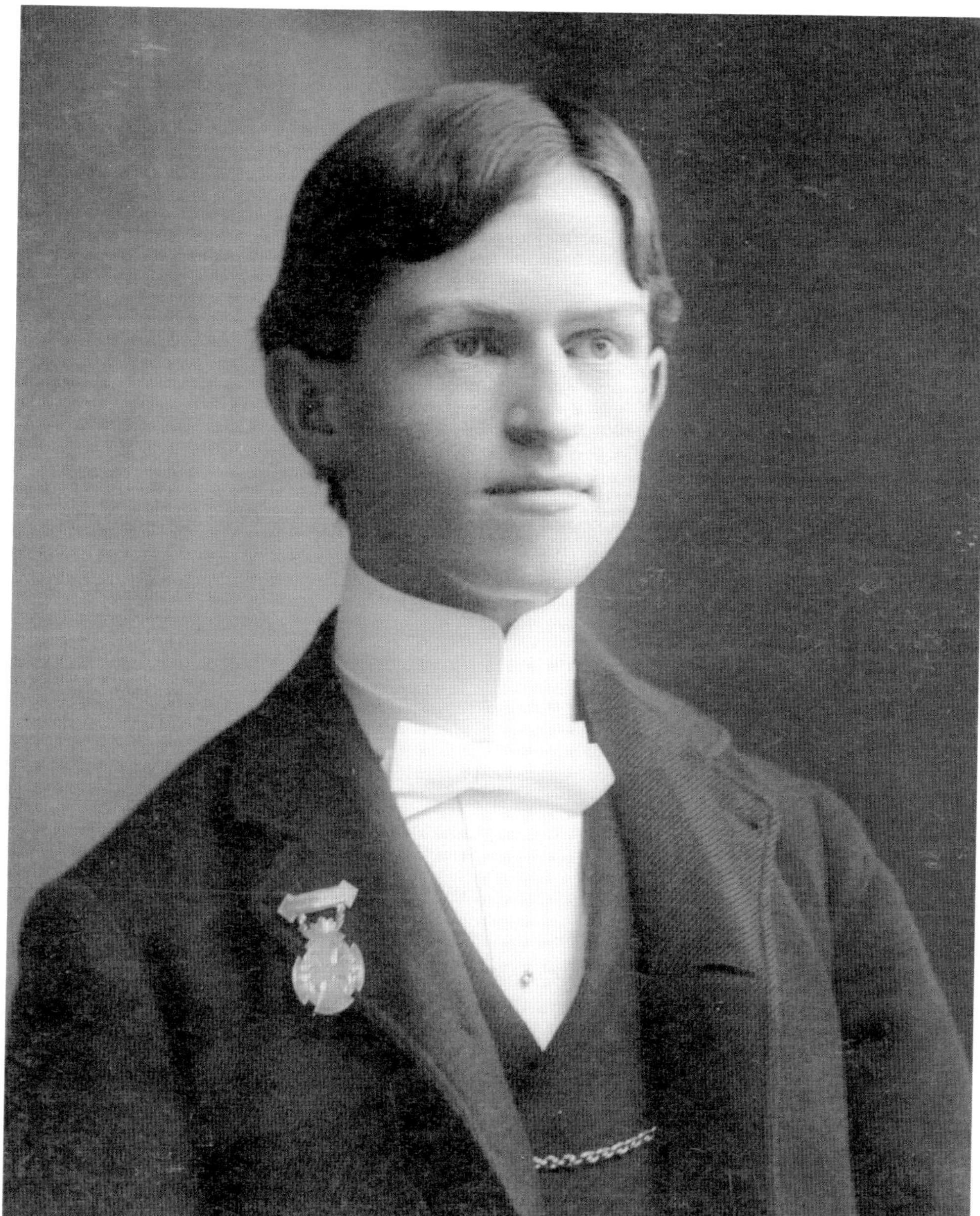

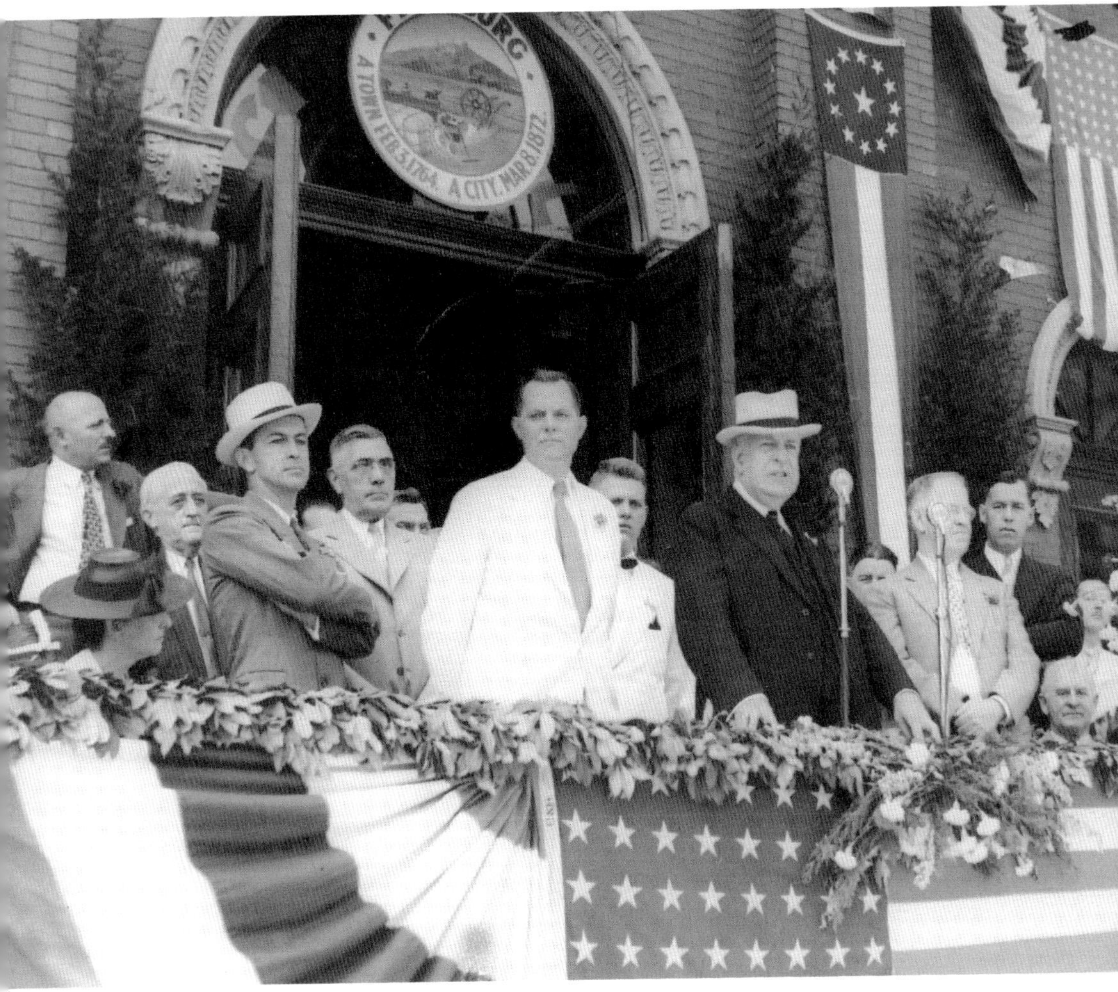

Alfred Woollacott (1892–1986)
Woollacott was one of 11 children of parents who emigrated from England in the late 1800s. He worked in a florist shop after school while a student at Fitchburg High and later owned his own shop, where he worked while mayor of the city from 1938 to 1948. Woollacott served in the Medical Corps in France during World War I and never forgot the carnage he saw there. While mayor, Woollacott had the WPA build an underpass for pedestrians, started the Mayor's Hospital Fund, the Mayor's Milk Fund for children, and summer playground programs and was instrumental in the development of the airport. Also while mayor of the city, he began the much-loved Hospital Street Fair; later, he served as president of the Fitchburg Historical Society. Though Mayor Woollacott upset local Catholics by allowing contraceptives to be sold in city drugstores, he became popular with Finnish voters when he shared a sauna with the visiting first prime minister of Finland, a photograph of which was published in the newspaper. In 1981, the city dedicated a square to Mayor Woollacott at the corner of Main and Prichard Streets.

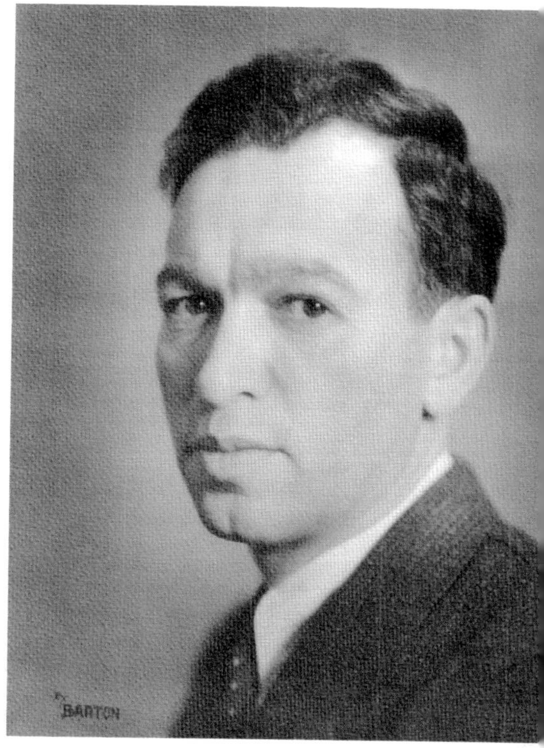

The Honorable A. Andre Gelinas (1894–1978)

Gelinas moved to Athol from Quebec when he was two. He attended school there and in Canada. In 1914, Gelinas entered Assumption College, which he attended for two years before joining the Army during World War I. His service also earned him US citizenship. He returned to Assumption and then entered Harvard Law School, graduating in 1923. In 1924, Gelinas moved to Fitchburg to establish a law practice. He served the large French-Canadian population of the city and represented several industrial companies. Among many community activities, he and eight others founded the IC Federal Credit Union in 1928. He remained a director until the time of his death. He also served as city solicitor and was a special justice of the Fitchburg District Court, hearing cases while maintaining his private practice. From 1952 to 1958, Gelinas served as the district attorney for Worcester County. (Courtesy of Andre A. Gelinas.)

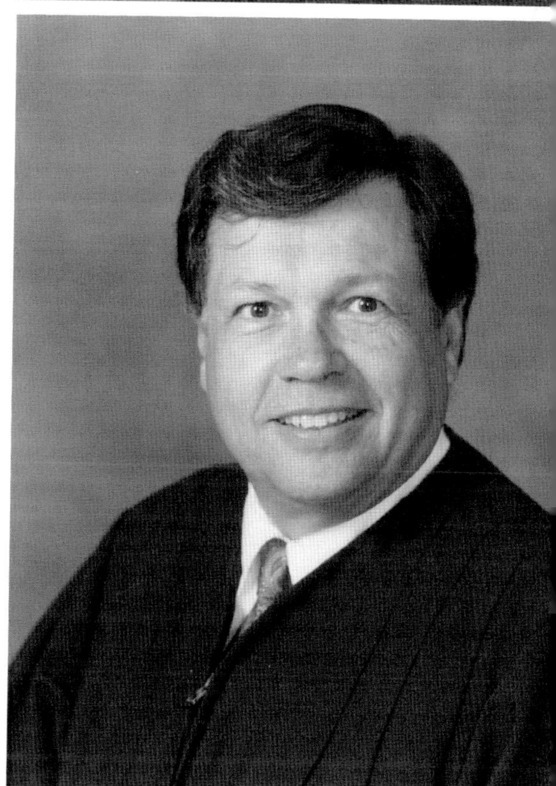

Andre A. Gelinas (1938–Present)

The son of A. Andre Gelinas, Andre A. Gelinas was born in Fitchburg in 1938. He graduated from St. Bernard's High School and Assumption College, then earned his law degree at the University of Michigan. Gelinas returned to the family firm, where he practiced law until 1979, at which time he began his 20-year term as a full-time judge of the district court. He organized a group of citizens to create a mediation program in the district court as an alternative to adversarial conflict resolution and established a one-room schoolhouse, located in the courthouse, for truant children. He served as a director of the Fidelity Cooperative Bank and the Safety Fund National Bank, as trustee and chair of the Burbank Hospital and HealthAlliance Hospital, and as trustee and president of the Fitchburg Art Museum. In 1999, Judge Gelinas was appointed an associate justice of the Massachusetts Appeals Court in Boston, where he served until 2008.

In 2009, the district courthouse in Fitchburg was rededicated as the Gelinas Courthouse to honor both father and son "for their many contributions to the judiciary, the bar, and the city of Fitchburg." (Courtesy of Andre A. Gelinas.)

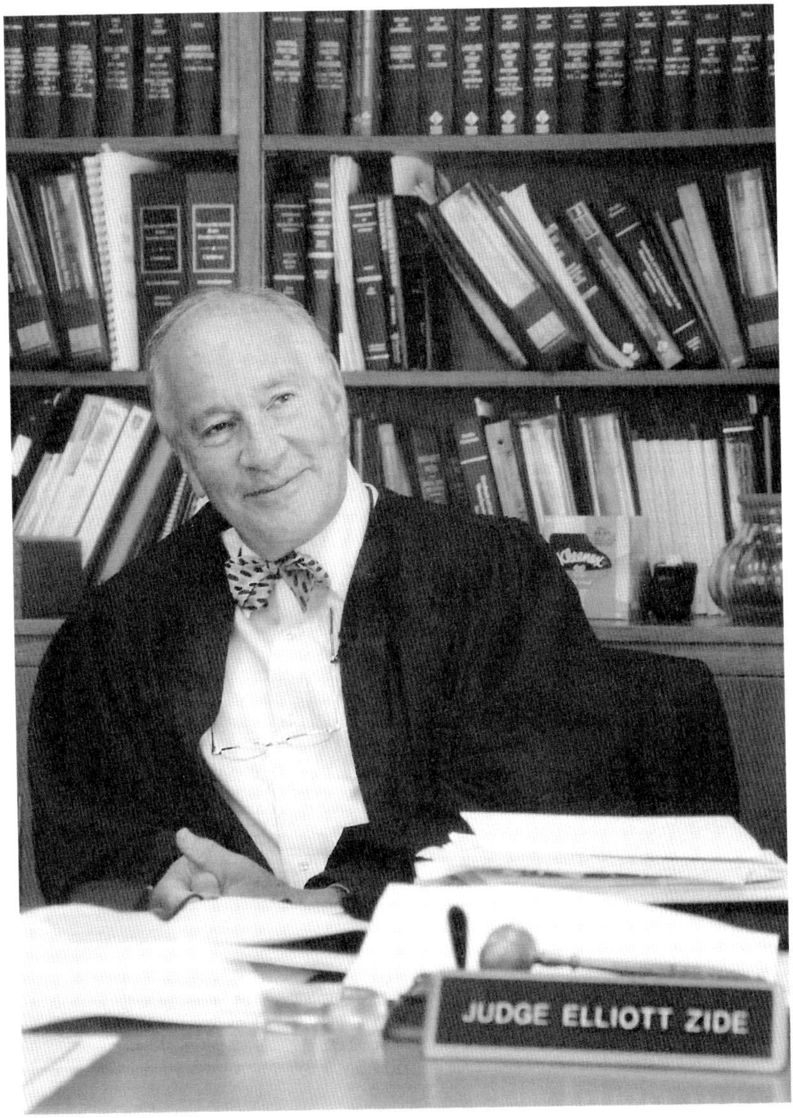

The Honorable Elliott Zide (1942–Present)
Zide was born in Boston but moved to Fitchburg at age six. He traces his familial roots to Russia, from which all of his grandparents emigrated. He attended Goodrich Street Elementary School and the Hebrew School at the Agudas Achim Synagogue, where he met his lifelong friend Allen Rome. Moving on to B.F. Brown Junior High School was an experience he remembers well since it was the first time he encountered the many ethnic groups in the city. He recalls the pleasures of Friday nights in Fitchburg in the fifties when families shopped in bustling Main Street stores. He went to Groton Academy for high school and then completed his undergraduate work at Duke University. Elliott earned his law degree at Boston University Law School and was admitted to the bar in 1968. He first practiced in Boston and then joined a firm in Gardner. In 1971, Zide opened a private law office at 280 Main Street in Fitchburg and was elected as a city councilor-at-large. He explained that he returned to Fitchburg because he always felt it was his home, a place where he felt comfortable and secure. In 1978, he merged his firm with Ward & Gelinas. He was sworn in as an associate justice of the district court in 1986. He retired from the court in 2012. Zide is married to Michele Moran Zide, and they have three daughters. (Courtesy of Elliott Zide.)

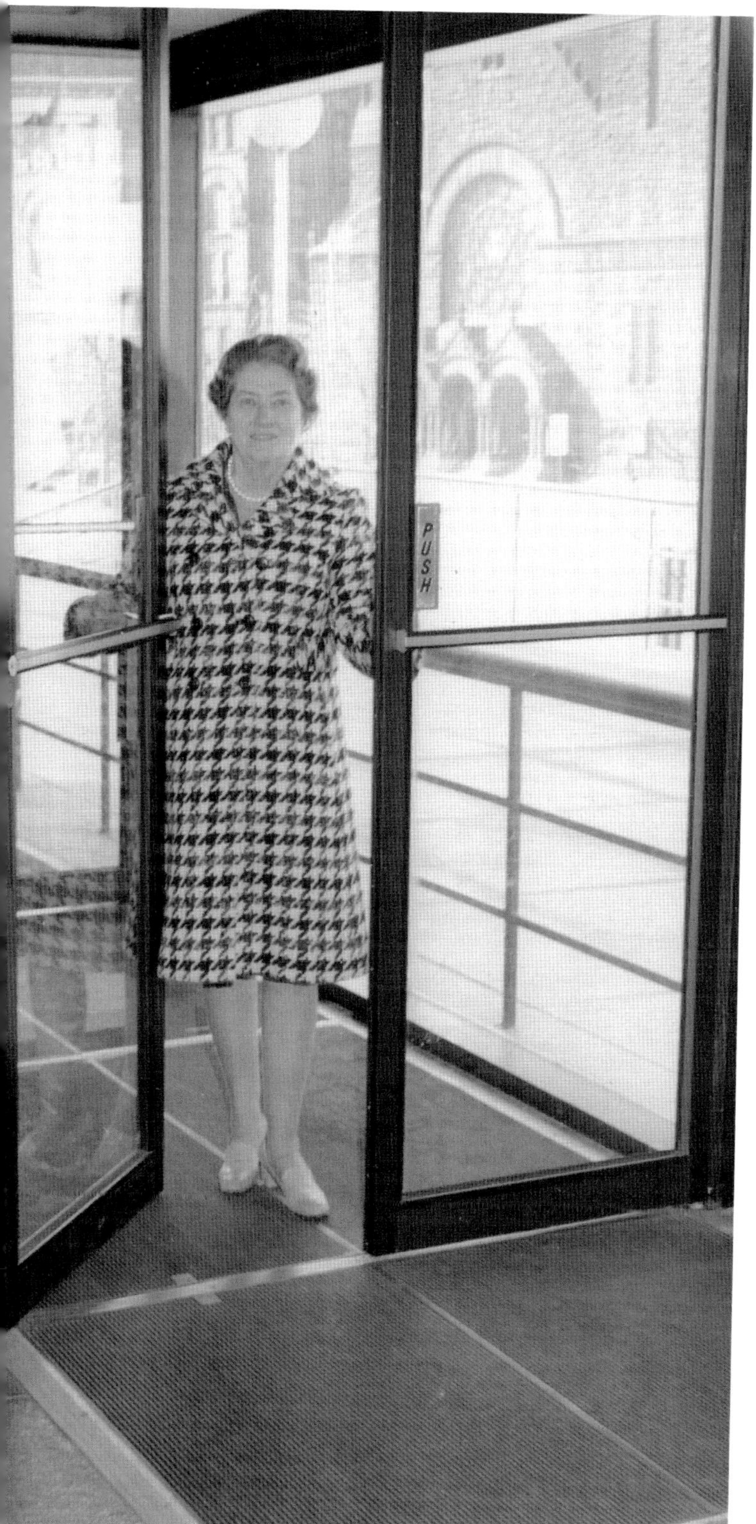

Elizabeth "Betsy" Stanton (1909–1982)
Stanton lived in Fitchburg for her entire life. She was a graduate of Fitchburg High School and earned a bachelor of science degree in education from Fitchburg State College. She was married to George Stanton, who served as mayor of Fitchburg from 1948 to 1950 and as a state senator from 1950 to 1952. When George died, Elizabeth ran for the post he had held. She was elected as state senator and served for 10 years. During her first year in office, she introduced a bill to ensure that women would not be barred from teaching after they married. She was a Democratic National Committee Woman from 1956 to 1962. In 1962, Pres. John F. Kennedy appointed Stanton as postmistress of Fitchburg, and she remained in that position for 17 years, retiring in 1979.

Ellen M. DiGeronimo (1935–Present)

Ever dedicated to service, DiGeronimo was the second woman elected to the city council, serving Ward 1, where she grew up, for three terms beginning in 1971. Her most significant contribution was her participation in the vote to clean the Nashua River. In 1977, Gov. Michael S. Dukakis appointed Ellen the first woman associate commissioner of the Massachusetts Public Works Department. She worked on the Highway I-190 project and assisted cities and towns with upgrading and replacing their infrastructure. This eventually led to her appointment as executive director of the Salem Chamber of Commerce in 1991; she participated in that city's revitalization until 2001. She and her husband, Ralph, returned to Fitchburg, where she continues to share her experience and passion, working with businesses and organizations to identify historic and cultural assets on Main Street. (Courtesy of Charles Sternaimolo.)

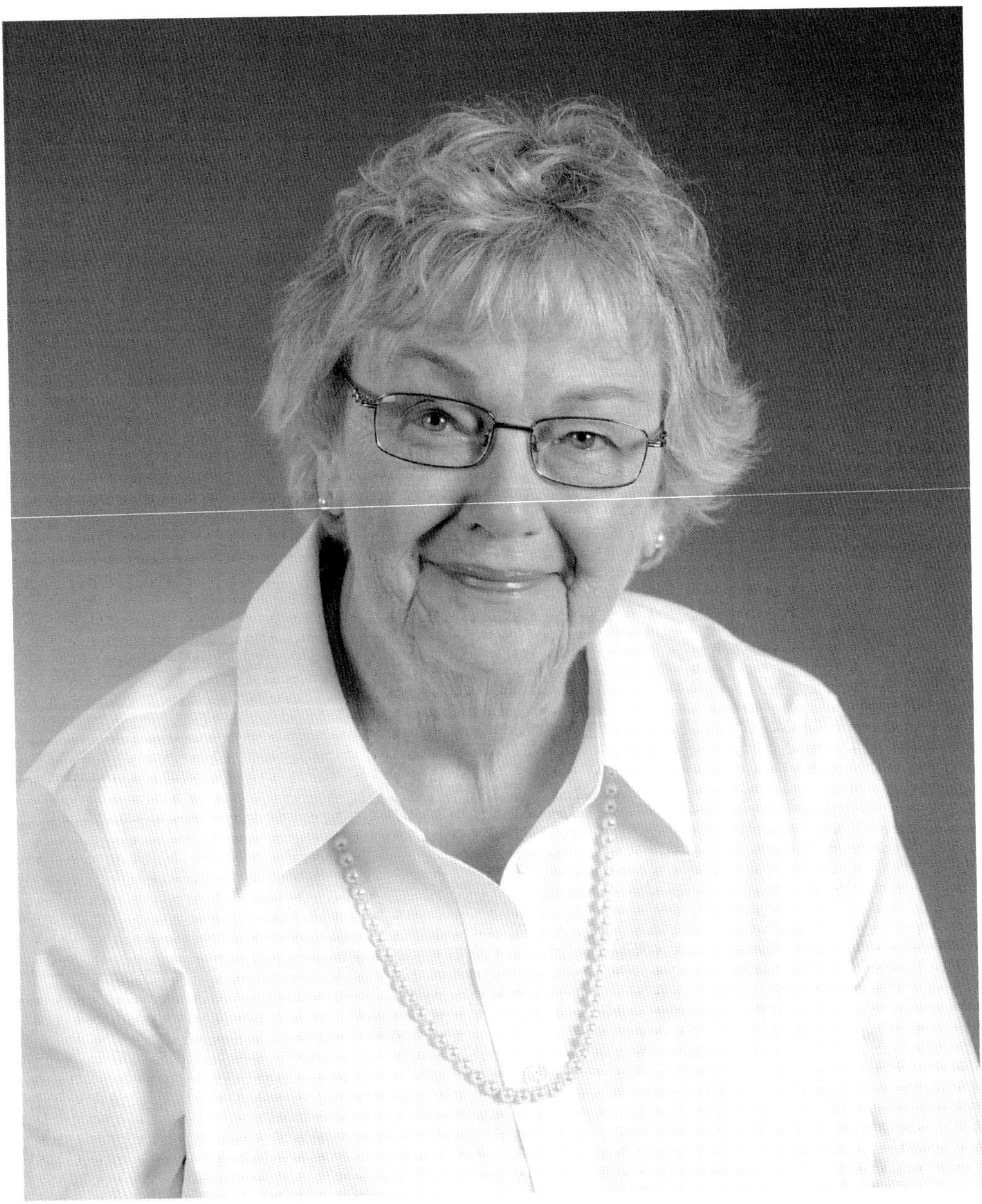

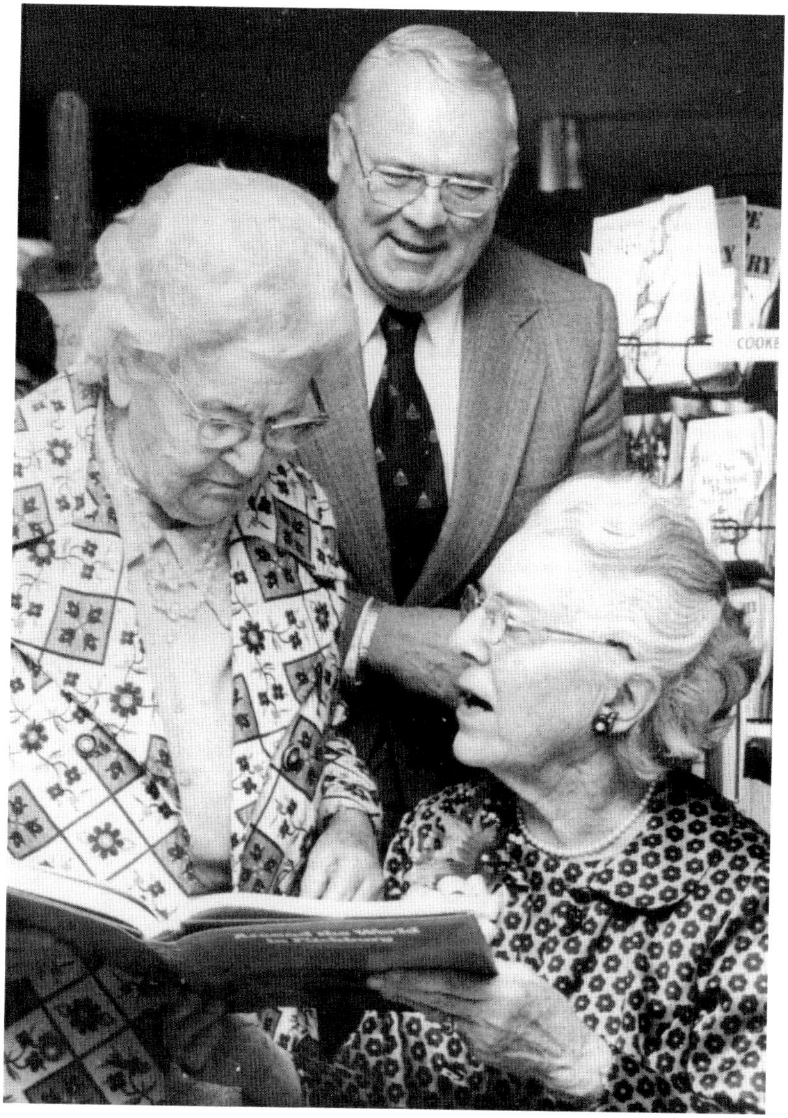

George J. Bourque (1913–2011)

Bourque was born in Joggins Mines, Nova Scotia. His family moved to Fitchburg soon thereafter, and eventually, the family comprised 13 children. At age 16, George left school to become a paperboy to help support the family. Through his first job, he learned to interact with customers and to handle money. Later, he started an industrial catering company for Simonds Saw and then had his own catering company for 26 years. He was very athletic and coached various sports teams through the years and served on the city council and the parks commission. Bourque served four terms as mayor of Fitchburg, from 1960 to 1967. While he was mayor of Fitchburg, Reingold, Memorial, and Crocker Schools were built. Under his administration, the Fitchburg Longsjo Classic began, as did Civic Days. He was also elected president of the Massachusetts Mayors' Association. When his term ended, Bourque served 20 years in the House of Representatives for the Third Worcester District, until 1992. Mayor Bourque is especially remembered for his long service to the IC Federal Credit Union, begun at his church, which often extended loans to those who could not acquire them at other banks. In January 2013, the gymnasium of the McKay School at Fitchburg State University was named in his honor.

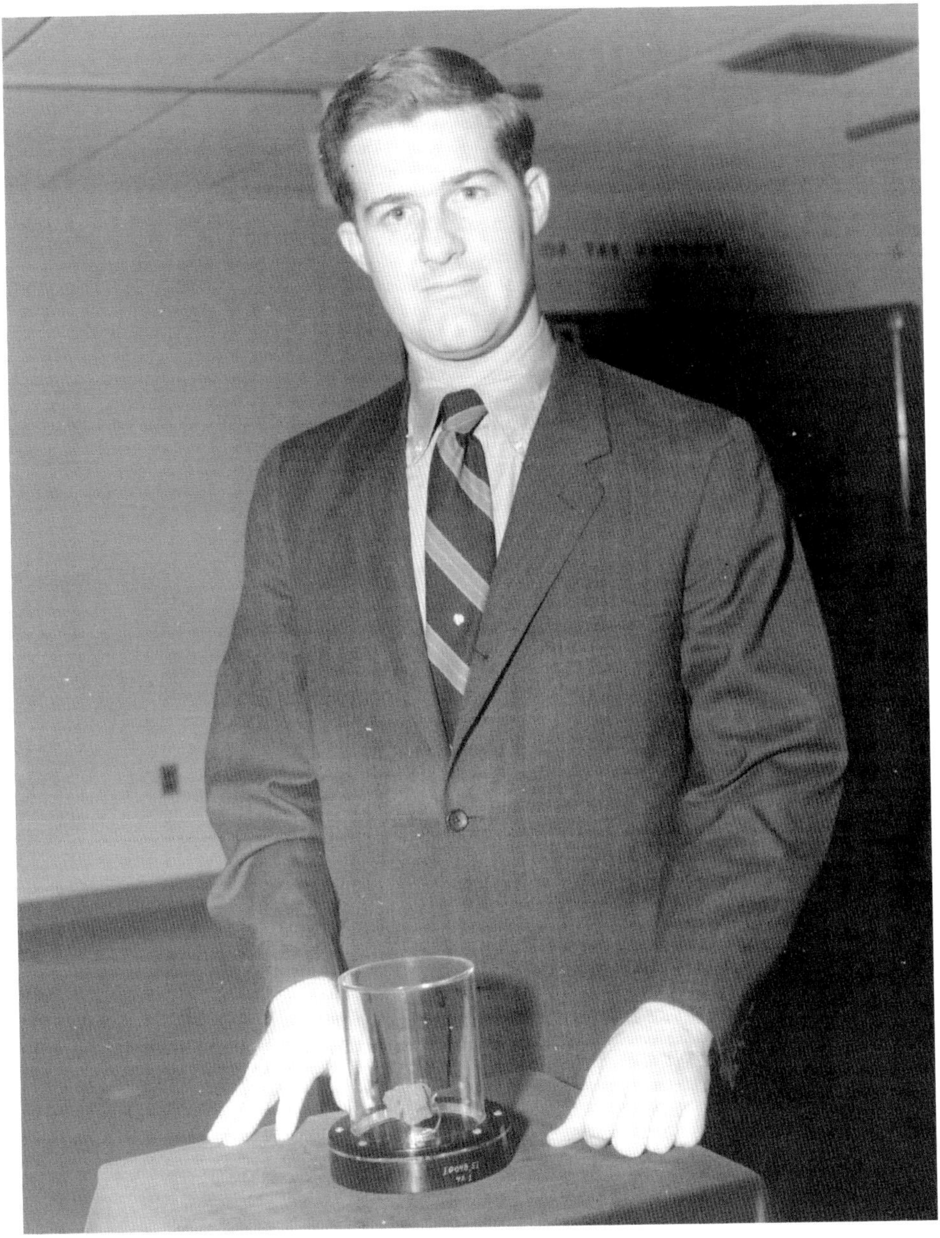

William "Bill" Flynn (1942–present)

The youngest person elected mayor, Flynn was referred to as "the lad" during his campaign. Flynn was serving on the city council and attending the University of Massachusetts as a graduate student when he ran for mayor. He launched his campaign with only $35 and went on to defeat incumbent George Bourque. Elected mayor in 1967 and again in 1969, Flynn made the job full-time. He advocated for regionalism, championed founding the Montachusett Regional Planning Agency, and created a landfill with the Town of Westminster. During his administration, a new elementary school and a reservoir were built. In 1970, his initiatives earned Fitchburg national recognition as an All-America City. Perhaps he is most remembered for his efforts to clean the polluted Nashua River by canoeing the river to call attention to its condition.

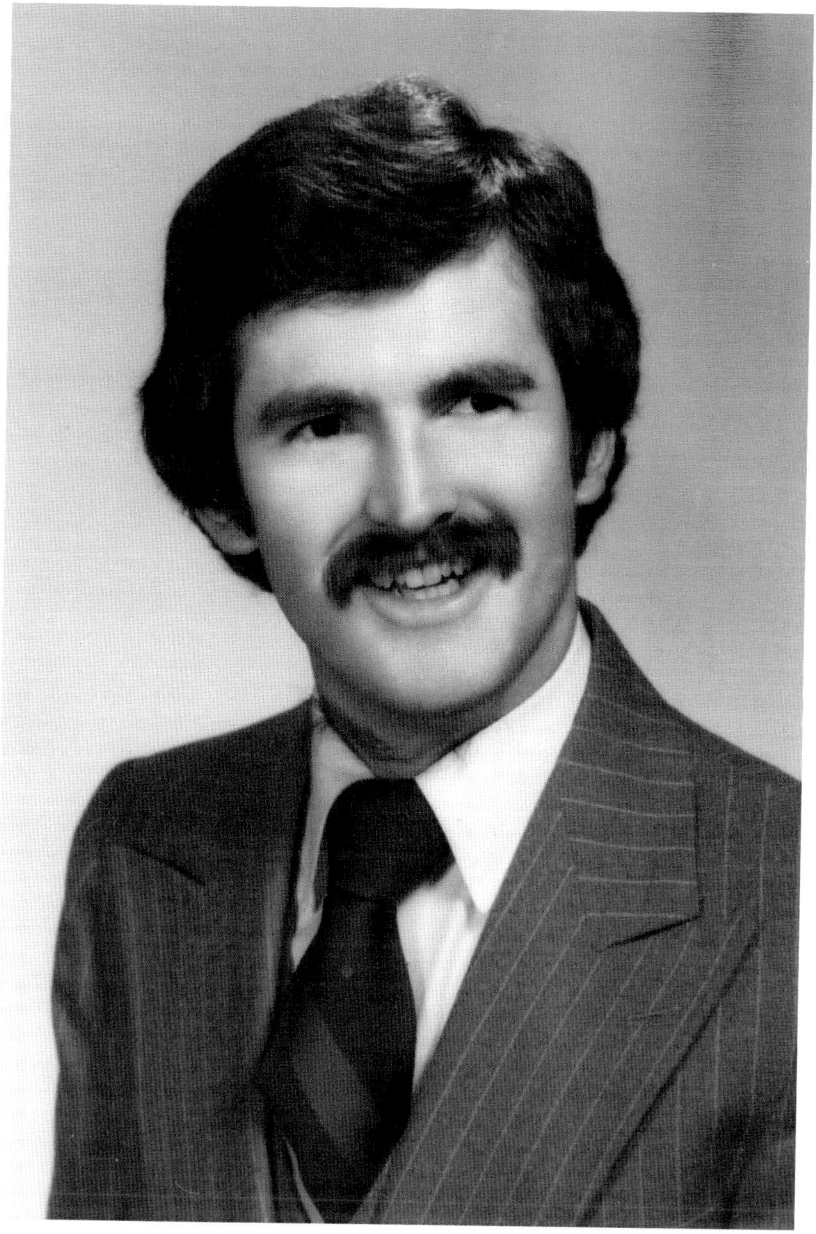

David Gilmartin (1952–Present)
Son of David W. and Eleanor C. Gilmartin, David Gilmartin began his public service career as a Fitchburg firefighter in 1973. He was elected as Fitchburg's mayor in 1978 and served three terms. During that time, he established a regional transit authority, which restored commuter rail service between Fitchburg and Boston. He also created the Fitchburg Senior Center in the old state armory on Wallace Avenue and began the process of replacing Fitchburg's ancient water mains. After leaving office, David continued in public service, eventually becoming director of security for the Massachusetts Water Resources Authority. Gilmartin is a US Navy veteran with 22 years of service and graduate degrees from both Harvard and the Naval War College. He served in Europe, Korea, and both the Bosnian and Iraqi operations and retired as a commander. (Courtesy of Eleanor Gilmartin.)

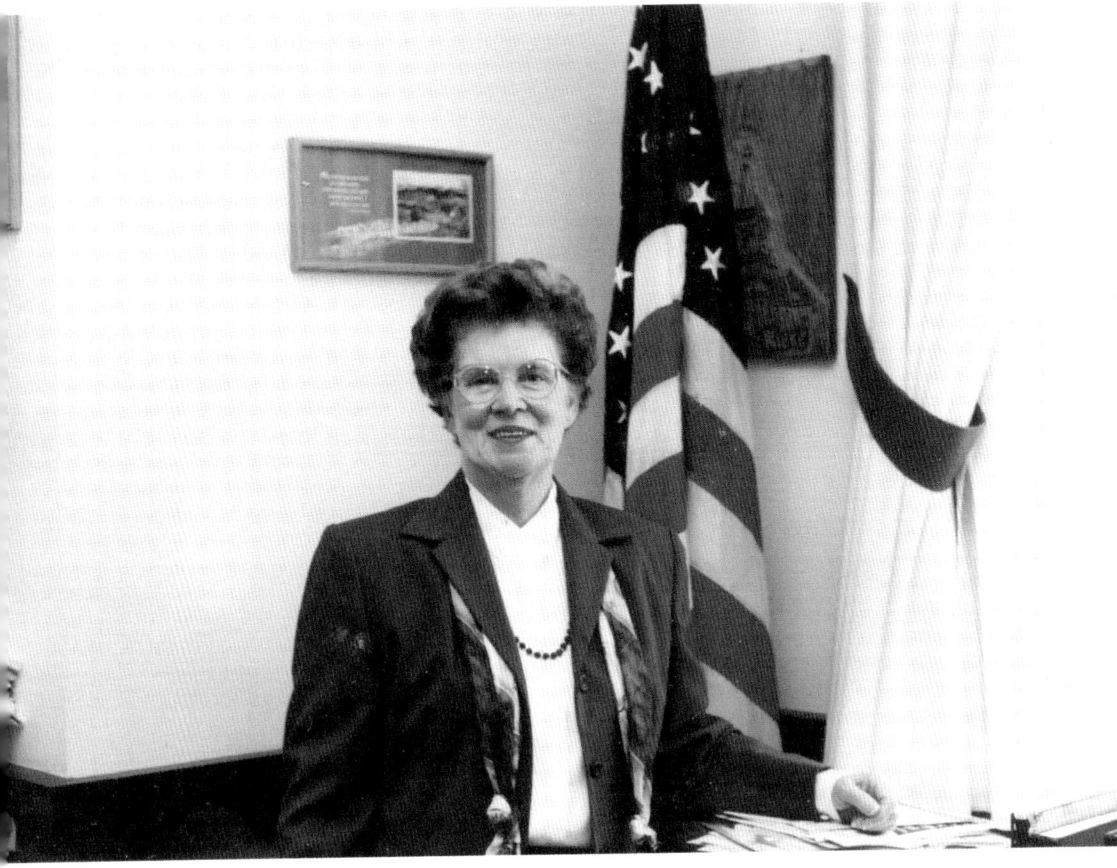

Mary H. Nally Whitney (1935–present)

On June 4, 1998, when Whitney took the oath of office as mayor, she was the first woman to hold that office in Fitchburg as well as the only female mayor in central Massachusetts. She began her more than 40-year political career in 1972 as a member of the school committee. During those 10 years, she was elected president of the Massachusetts Association of School Committees. She went on to serve on the city council for 14 years, becoming the chairperson of every committee, respectively. While mayor, she negotiated the purchase of the closed General Electric plant. Now known as Putnam Place, this is the current site of the city offices. She initiated the block parties held during July Civic Days and was instrumental in bringing the Cancer Center to the Burbank Campus of Health Alliance, where she still serves on the board of directors. Whitney continues a longtime membership in the Rotary Club and presides over the club's municipal employees annual awards night. She is a member of the Friends of Coggshall Park and a commissioner of the Parks Board. She oversaw the rebuilding of the Coggshall stone house after it was destroyed by fire in 2009. She and her husband, Robert, have four children and 10 grandchildren. (Courtesy of Mary Whitney.)

CHAPTER FOUR

Religious Organizations and Leaders

Alert in war, she emulates
The arts of peace as well,
Religion, order, guard her gates;
Wealth, culture, thrift, like happy Fates,
Her destinies foretell.

—Excerpt from "Ode to Fitchburg" by Caroline A. Mason

Fitchburg has been home to a variety of faiths, including Baptist, Congregational, Episcopalian, Greek Orthodox, Jewish, Lutheran, Methodist, Roman Catholic, Unitarian, and more recently, Buddhist and Muslim. Church spires dot the cityscape according to where ethnic groups settled in the city. These centers of worship also provided for education and assisted the poor and newly arriving immigrants. Through the years, many of the churches have closed. The Jewish synagogue is still a house of worship, but not for those of the Jewish faith. The stories here remind us that it is people who make the difference in any religious community regardless of where they worship. They are individuals who provided and continue to provide leadership in parishes, as missionaries, and in the community.

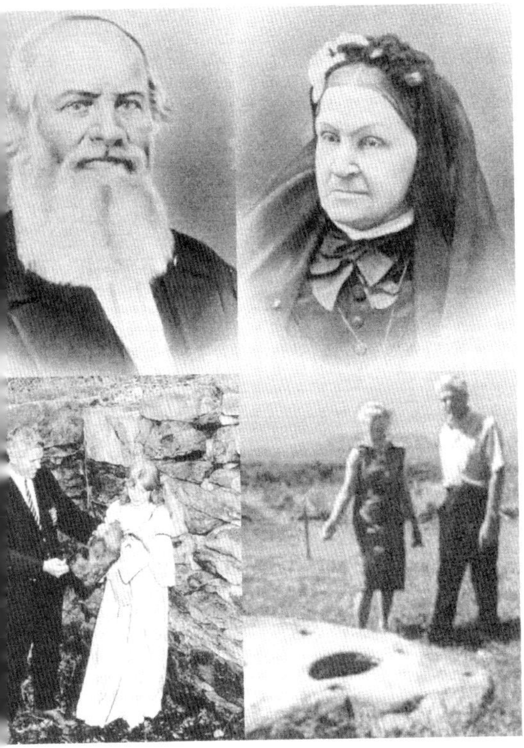

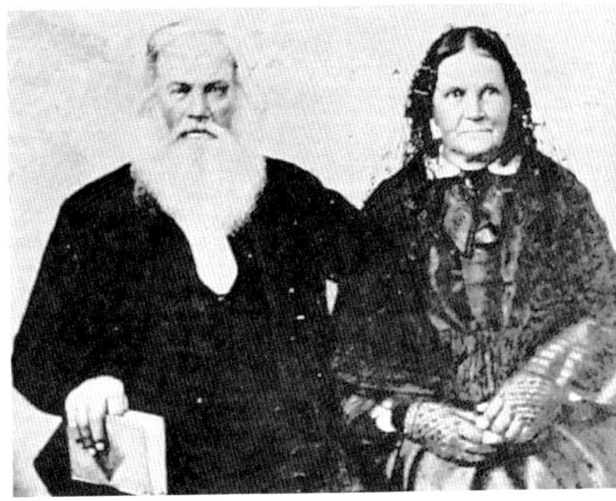

Asa Thurston (1787–1868)
Thurston contracted typhoid fever at 19. He survived, but his mother and two siblings died. This led to his decision to serve God. He completed studies at Yale and Andover Theological Seminary before joining the American Missionary Board. With his wife, Lucy, he was sent to the Sandwich Islands, where they built a home, church, school, and orphanage. Thurston also developed an alphabet for the native language.

Sister Agnes Catherine Fitzgibbon (1899–1993)
Fitzgibbon graduated from Fitchburg High School and Smith College. She taught English at Fitchburg High School before entering the sisterhood and missionary service. In 1933, she left for China to teach at the Morning Star School. After suffering under Japanese occupation, she saw the rise of communism and was declared incompetent for refusing to teach its ideas. Forced to return home, she trained women missionaries until her death. (Courtesy of Eleanor Gilmartin.)

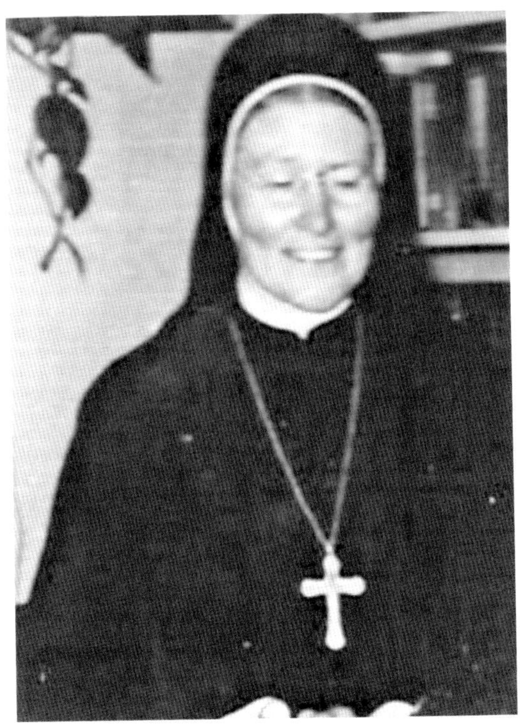

St. Bernard's

St. Bernard's was the first Roman Catholic Church in Fitchburg. It was erected not once but three times. Alvah Crocker recruited workers from the docks in Boston to help build the Fitchburg railroad, completed in 1845. These "railroaders," predominantly Irish Catholic immigrants, lived near Water Street in shanties built by contractor John T. Cahill. Priests came to Fitchburg to celebrate mass in open land or shops near Water Street. Rev. Matthew Gibson of Worcester, who became the first pastor, encouraged the building of a church in 1847. Cahill donated the lumber for what was called the "shanty cathedral." By 1848, a larger church was needed, and First Street was selected as the site. The church was to be granite, but due to costs, another wood structure was completed in 1851. Father Gibson, who acquired land for a graveyard on the other side of the river, was succeeded by Rev. Edward Turpin in 1856 and Rev. Cornelius M. Foley in 1866. That year, land was purchased on Water Street, and the cornerstone for the third and final church was laid in 1869; the first mass was celebrated on Christmas Day. Rev. Philip Garrigan succeeded Father Foley in 1875. In 1886, he built a convent and brought the Sisters of the Presentation to teach the more than 350 children of the parish. A school was built on the foundation of the old church on First Street. Father Garrigan assumed the duties of vice rector of the newly established Catholic University in 1888. The high school was built in 1927, and a new elementary school was built on Summer Street in 1966. Many more pastors led the parish until the church was closed as a place of worship in 2010 and the parish merged with St. Camillus De Lellis, founded in 1953. The last mass in the third Shanty Cathedral was on June 27, 2010.

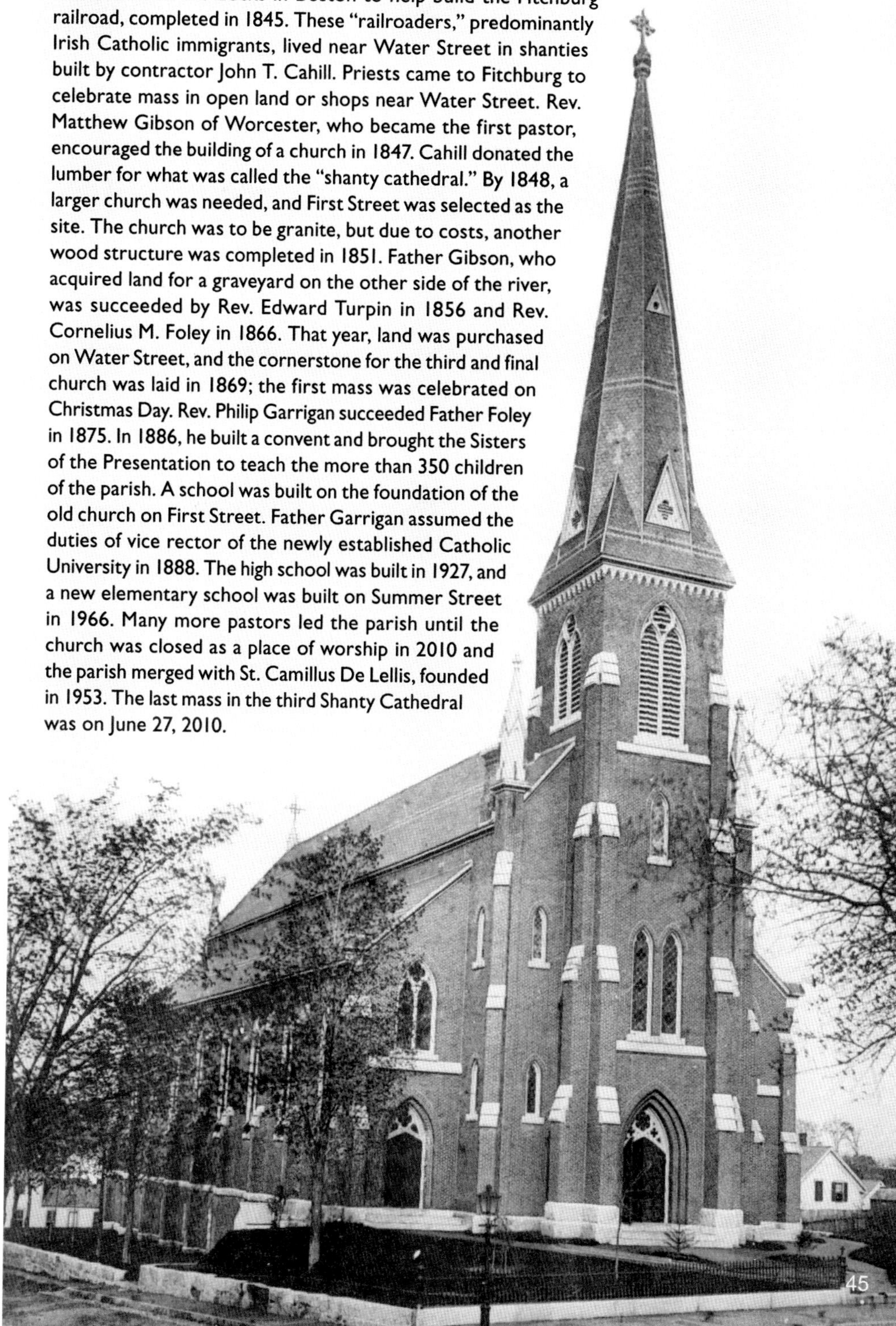

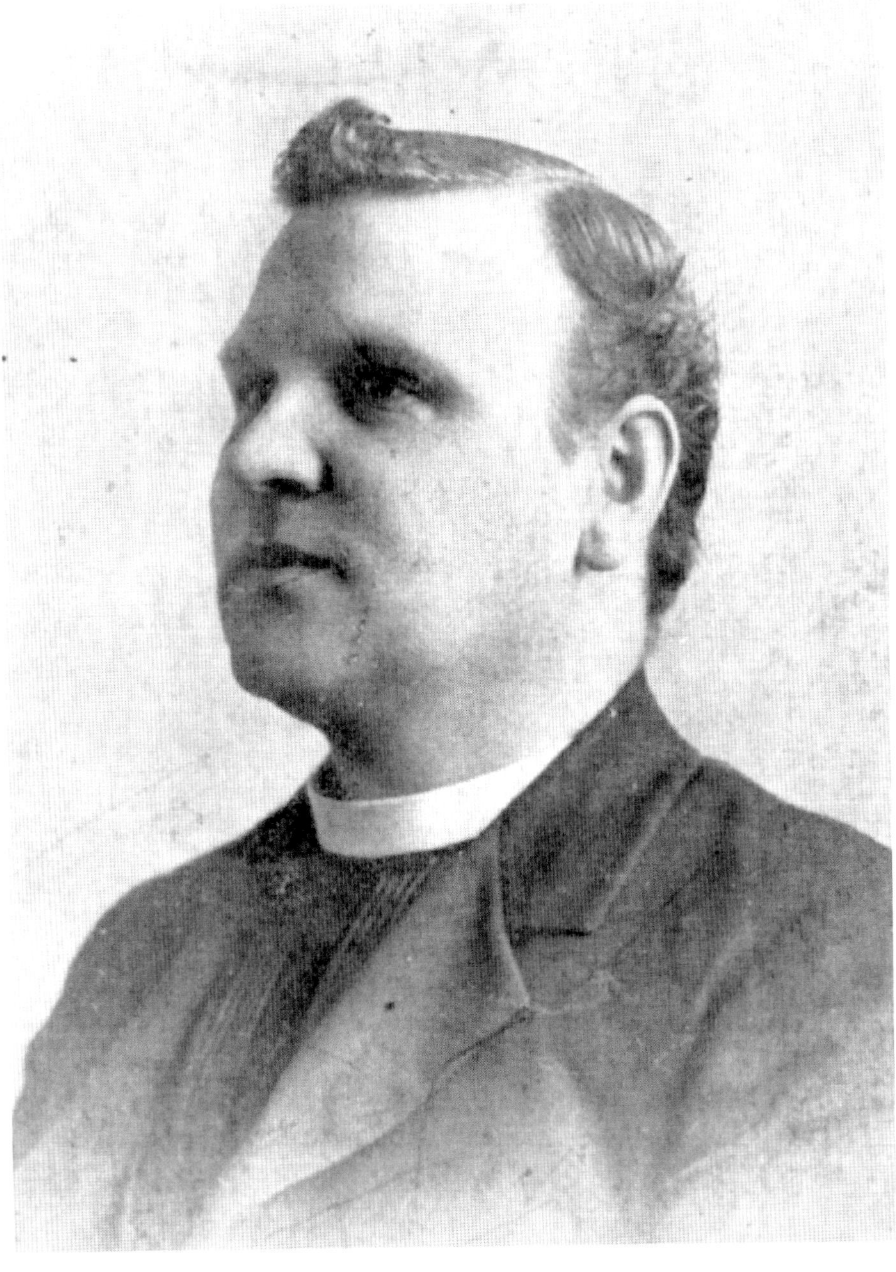

The Reverend Thomas S. Hanrahan (1860–1933)
Hanrahan began more than three decades as pastor of West Fitchburg's Sacred Heart Parish in 1897. The love for him was evident at his funeral on a rainy April day when, with pomp and circumstance in the presence of more than 100 religious representatives from the Springfield Diocese, hundreds of parishioners from Sacred Heart and other city parishes celebrated the life of this humble man in the small, beautiful church on the hill. After the mass, he was laid to rest in the heart-shaped lot in front of the edifice. The Fitchburg *Sentinel & Enterprise* covered his death and funeral and noted that, despite the downpour, "the crowd lingered until the casket was lowered from sight." Sacred Heart, dedicated in 1879, was closed in 2010 but is used for youth programs, a legacy of Father Hanrahan. (Courtesy of Teresa Pierce.)

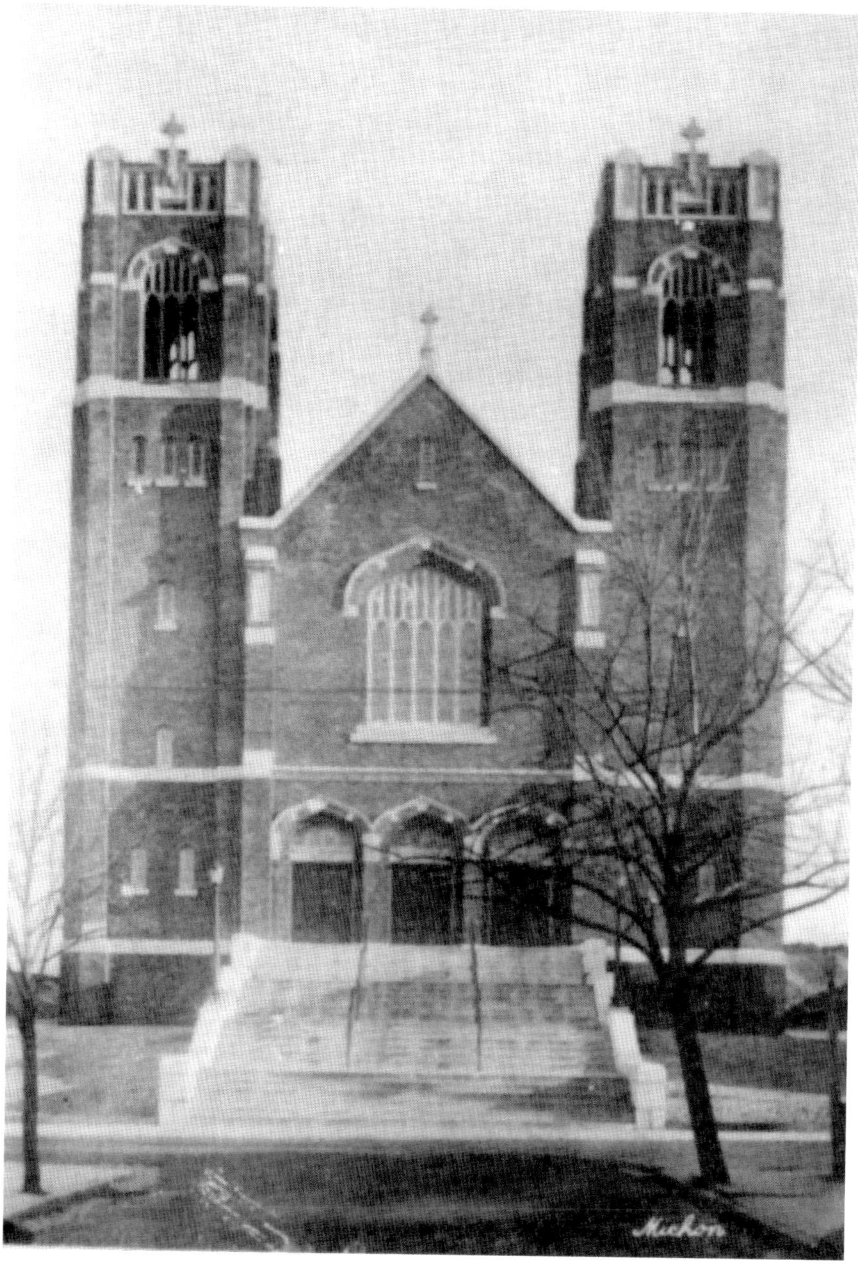

St. Francis of Assisi (1903–Present)

The plan to build a school for Immaculate Conception parishioners in South Fitchburg developed into a new parish, St. Francis of Assisi. Beginning with 200 families, primarily of Franco-American descent, the parish had approximately 635 families by 1978. Rev. Emerito Ortiz, pastor since 2007, is currently guiding about 700 families, a blend of ethnic groups of American and Hispanic backgrounds. Many, like Father Ortiz, have emigrated from Puerto Rico, Mexico, Ecuador, Uruguay, Argentina, and the Dominican Republic. He stresses that St. Francis is first and foremost a Catholic community, preferring not to differentiate among the several ethnic groups. Services are celebrated in English and Spanish, and the Hispanic community has found a home at St. Francis.

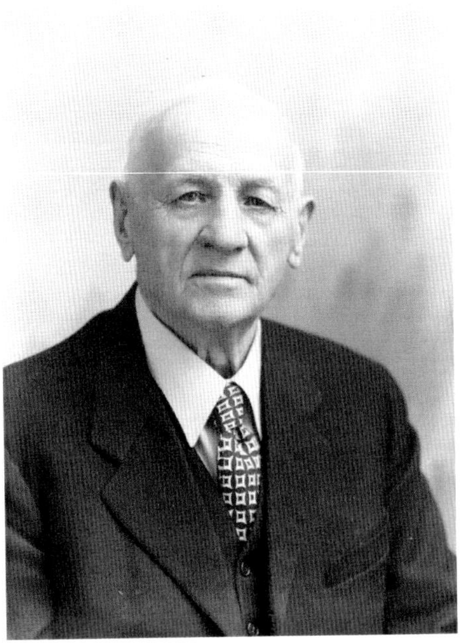

Andrew Groop (1862–1950)

Groop was born in Finland and grew up in Sweden, immigrating to the United States in 1882. He spent 58 years in active ministry, founding 15 Finnish churches. Groop considered Fitchburg his home. He and his wife purchased land for the local congregation of the Finnish Evangelical Mission Church, now the Elm Street Congregational Church. He founded Pilgrim Covenant Church and was a volunteer chaplain for Burbank Hospital.

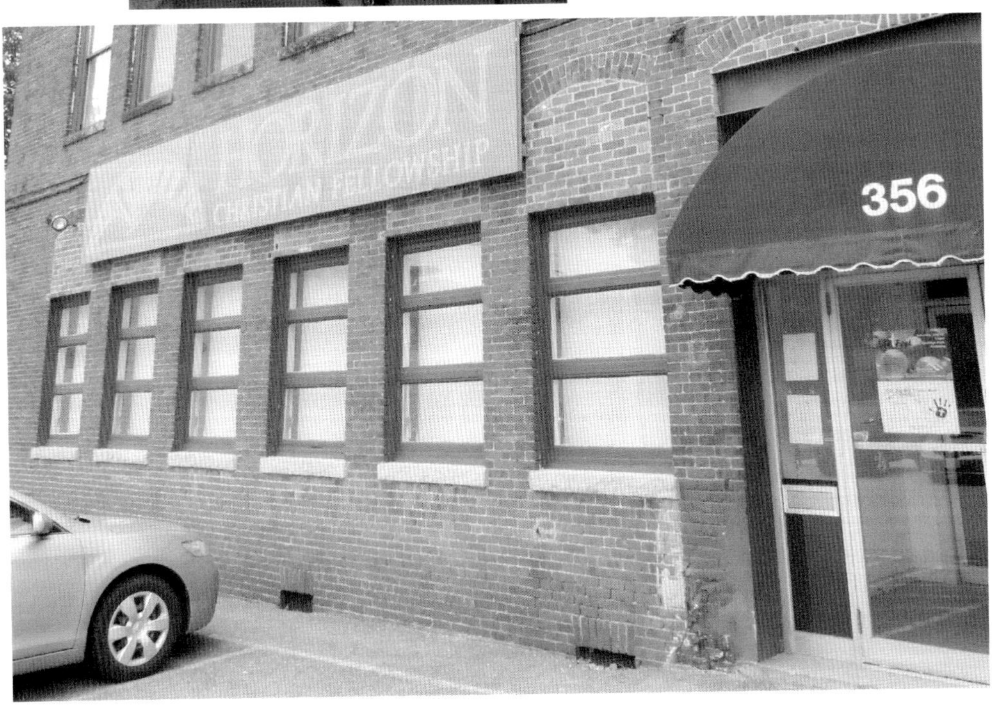

Horizon Christian Fellowship

Nondenominational, interdenominational, and storefront churches have been growing in Fitchburg. Pastor George Small, his wife Paula, and three children came to Fitchburg in February 1995 to "plant" a nondenominational church, Horizon Fellowship, and begin a Christian radio ministry. Horizon Fellowship meets in an old mill building where Pastor George leads two Sunday services, each with approximately 400 congregants. The radio ministry spreads his message even farther.

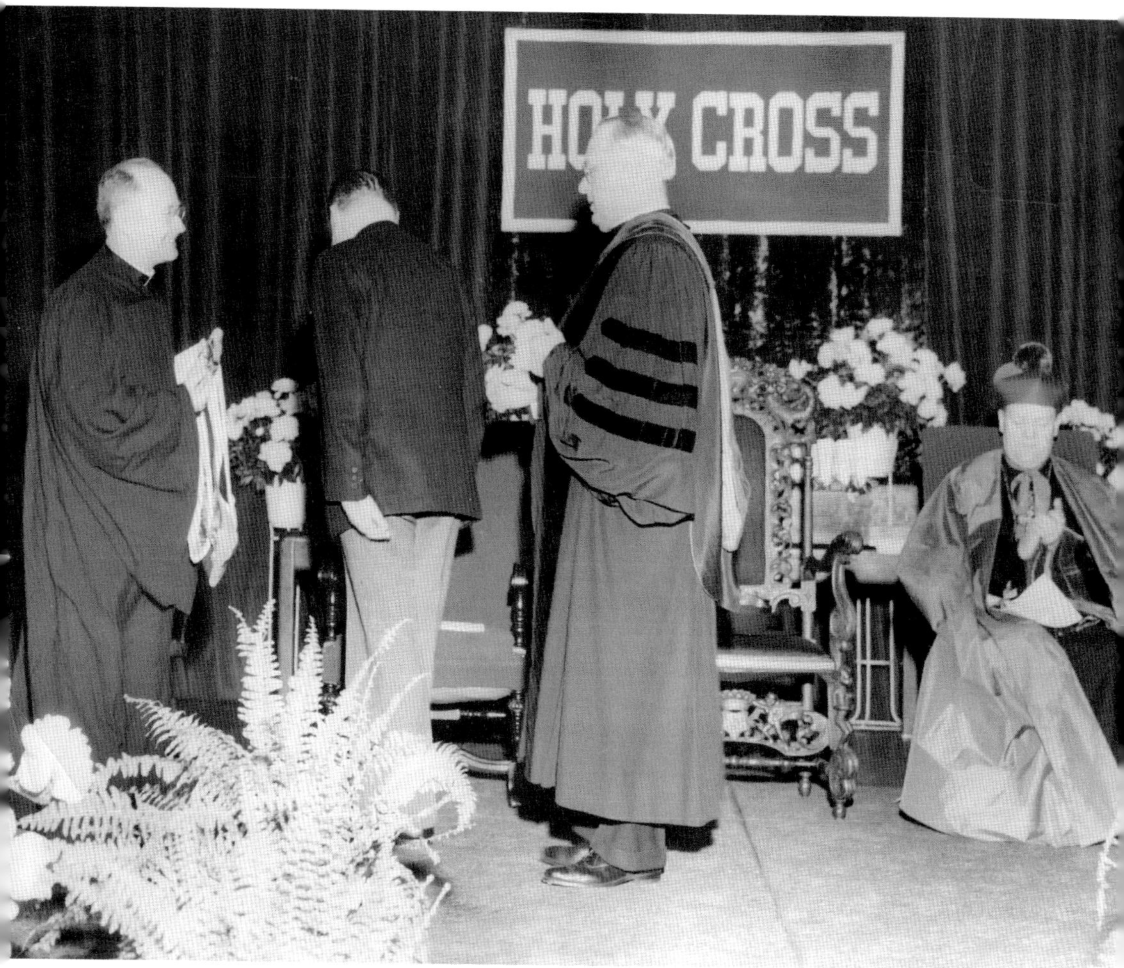

The Reverend Everett Francis Briggs (1908–2006)
Briggs was born and buried in Fitchburg, but he made his mark in Monongah, West Virginia, as an activist for the miners there. Son of Thomas Edward and Mary Lillian Hughes Briggs, he attended Fitchburg parochial schools and graduated from the College of the Holy Cross in Worcester and the Maryknoll Seminary in New York. He was ordained a Catholic priest in 1933 and assigned to missionary work in Otsu, Japan. In 1941, during World War II, he was arrested as a spy. When released, he returned to the United States and, since he was fluent in Japanese, spent several years with Japanese citizens in the internment camps here in the United States. In December 1956, he traveled to Monongah, where he became interested in the Monongah Mine disaster of 1907, considered the worst in American history with the death of at least 360 miners. He wrote articles and books on the topic. He also authored books in Japanese. In 1961, he built St. Barbara's Memorial Nursing Home as a monument to the miners and widows. Another monument he initiated was completed and dedicated after his death. In attendance were dignitaries from Italy, the homeland from which most of the miners had come. There is also a bridge across the West Fork River in West Virginia that bears his name. Father Briggs died in the nursing home he had built in Monongah and is buried in St. Bernard's Cemetery in Fitchburg.

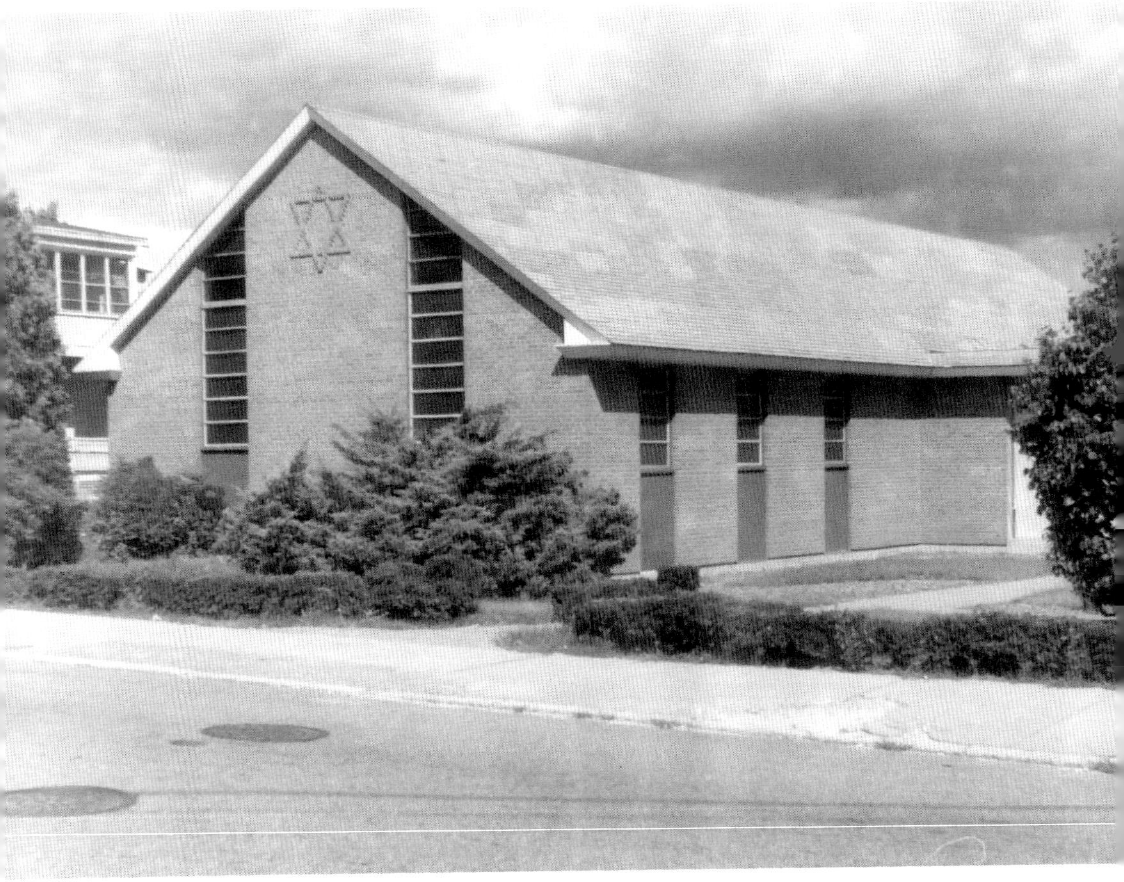

Agudas Achim Congregation (1900–2002) and Faith Christian Ministries (2003–present)
The Agudas Achim congregation was first started in Fitchburg in 1900, when there were 15 Jewish families in the city. In 2000, the congregation celebrated its 100th anniversary, and a short time later, it faced the sad task of closing the synagogue because there were no longer sufficient families to keep it going. The congregation was large enough over the years that it consecrated a cemetery where the Jewish families of Fitchburg could be buried. The original synagogue was a small building on Main Street. The synagogue on Boutelle Street was built of wood in 1905, then later replaced by a brick structure in 1960. Many Jewish families originally lived in the neighborhood around Boutelle and followed customary traditions of walking to the synagogue on the Sabbath and keeping kosher households. In 2003, the building that housed the synagogue was sold to the Faith Christian Church, which identifies itself as a Christian church with Jewish roots and a Jewish heart.

In March 2003, Pastor Don Long purchased the Jewish synagogue on Boutelle Street and moved the Faith Christian Ministries into its new building. Pastor Long chose the synagogue above all other properties because the roots of Bible-believing churches are imbedded in Jewish scriptures. The congregation kept the Jewish symbolism—pews with the Star of David, mezuzahs for the doorways, and the menorah on the outside of the building—intact. Several large paintings created by internationally famed Israeli artist Udi Meriotz still remind the congregation of its Jewish roots. The only two original Meriotz paintings in the United States of Jewish soldiers worshipping at the Western Wall are in this Fitchburg building and the US Air Force Academy in Colorado. The most unusual trait of these paintings is that ground-to-dust Jerusalem stone has been added to the oil paints, following the scripture from Luke 19:40: "even the stones will cry out." Pastor Don Long, received his master of divinity degree from Gordon-Conwell Theological Seminary, and his messages consistently refer to biblical standards and Christian living from Jewish roots.

CHAPTER FIVE

Immigrant Leaders

And coming northward to his native hills
From distant prairies and from tropic isles,
May he whose fame through every zone extends
Find warmest welcome here among his friends.

—Excerpt from an untitled poem by Henry A. Goodrich,
delivered to the Fitchburg Merchants Association, 1899

The potato famine in Ireland, the Russian Revolution, and letters from America were some of the reasons why immigrants flocked to Fitchburg before and after the turn of the century. They all shared the hope of finding a better life than the one they had experienced in their native land. By 1877, approximately 90 passenger trains arrived at Union Station each day, bringing immigrants directly to Fitchburg, where they started businesses, found jobs in their trade, or labored in the paper, textile, and machine mills. These immigrants created ethnic neighborhoods and churches to keep their cultures strong. They believed in hard work and raised their children with strong family values, encouraging them to acquire education and opportunities they never had. There were immigrants like Xenophon Gamvas, an artist from Greece who worked in a gun factory carving gunstocks while pursuing his skill as a painter of religious icons for Greek Orthodox churches. Rocco Pandiscio came from Italy at age six with the dream of singing in all the great opera houses in the United States and Europe—and he did. Today, Fitchburg remains a culturally diverse city with more than 60 ethnic groups represented. More recently, South Americans, Dominicans, and Southeast Asians have left their native lands and immigrated to Fitchburg, where they are beginning a new life like so many have before.

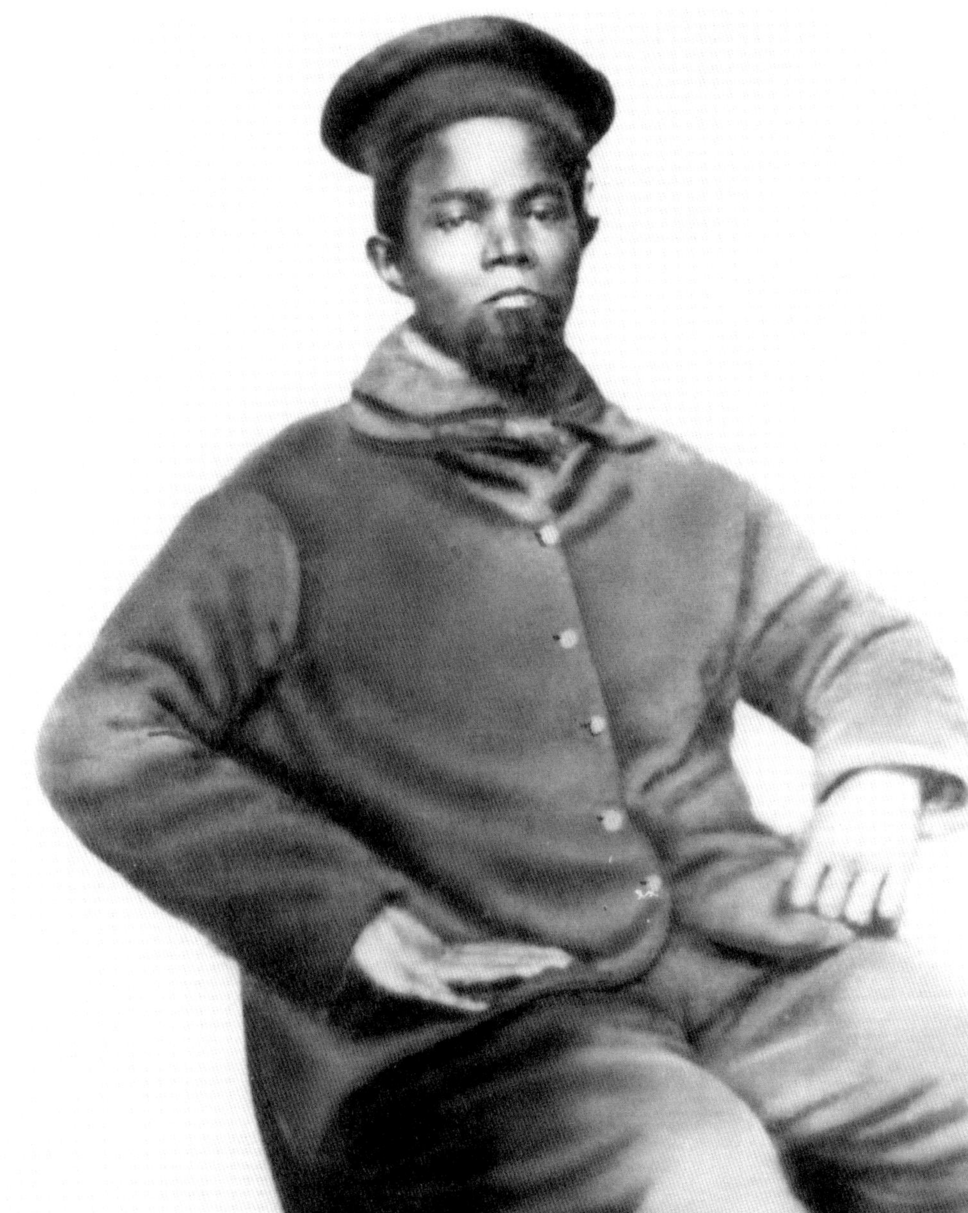

Martin F. Becker (1820–1880)

Fitchburg's first black abolitionist, Becker was also a sailor, soldier, printer, and barber. Born in South Guiana (now Surinam), he immigrated to the United States after college in Europe. Several years later, he and his wife, Caroline, settled in Fitchburg, where he became a barber, printer, and local leader. The Beckers bought a home from Benjamin Snow, an early abolitionist and businessman in Fitchburg. Becker enlisted in a white Union Navy regiment during the Civil War and was stationed on the *Cumberland* until it sank. He then enlisted as a private in Company B of the 55th Massachusetts Regiment. Wounded in battle, he was promoted to quartermaster sergeant. After the war, Becker settled in Charleston, South Carolina, where he was a prominent politician during the Reconstruction era. He died there, but he and his wife are buried in Fitchburg.

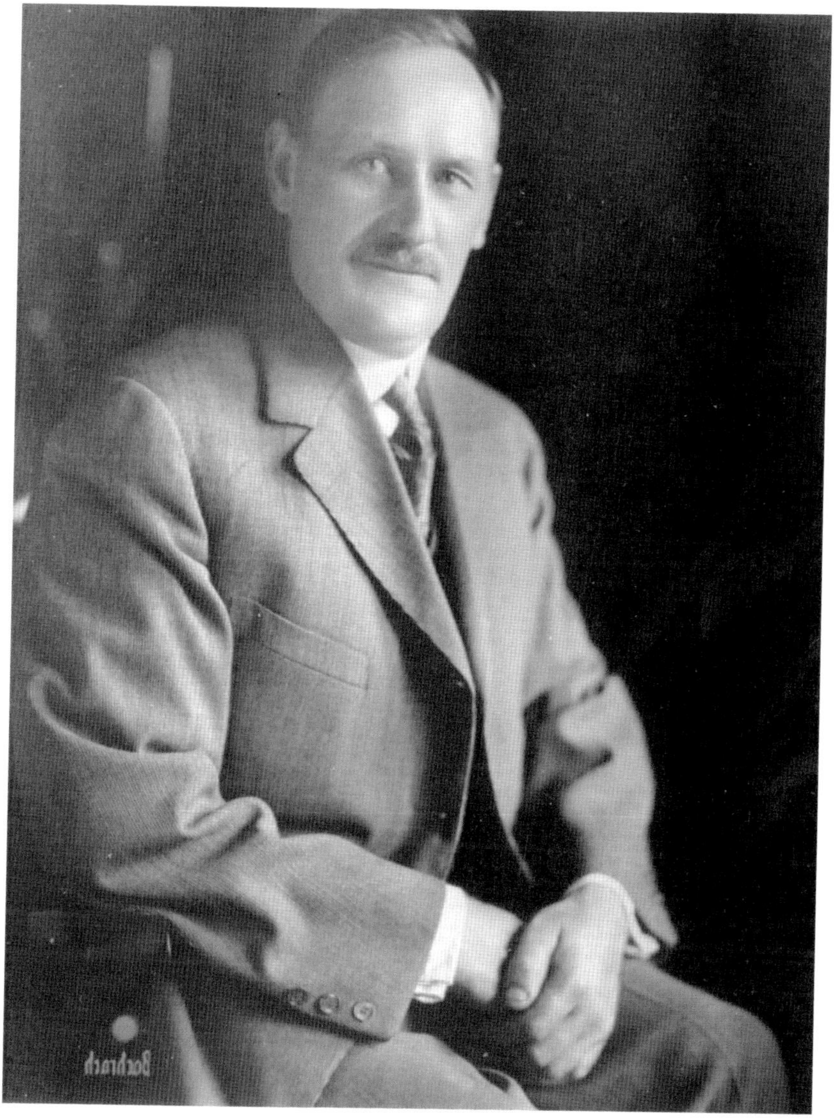

Charles O. Swanson (1871–1930)
Swanson was born in Sweden. At age 16, he came to New York City to work as a carpenter and a builder before contracting malaria. In 1892, while recovering, Swanson decided to visit family in Fitchburg. He found Fitchburg to his liking and soon moved to the city, where he bought the Horton Bakery with his brother-in-law, Sven Nelson. They called it the Nelson & Swanson Bakery Co. Nelson did the baking and Swanson was in charge of deliveries. Their business prospered for 10 years, until Nelson became ill and moved to California. Swanson continued on without Nelson. He bought a bakery in Worcester and called it Town Talk Bakery. In 1913, he was forced to merge with other bakeries to form the Massachusetts Bakery Co., of which he was president. Later, he merged again with Wonder Bread. Swanson, finding the expansions and reorganizations frustrating, decided to retire and take a long vacation to Sweden with his wife, Lily. Two years later, having had enough of retirement, he purchased the Grant Mill on River Street, where he began to expand his Town Talk Company with a new state-of-the-art bakery. Charles Swanson died in September 1930. His son Carl and his grandson Charles O. Jr. continued to run the company until 1945, producing 25 million pounds of bread each year.

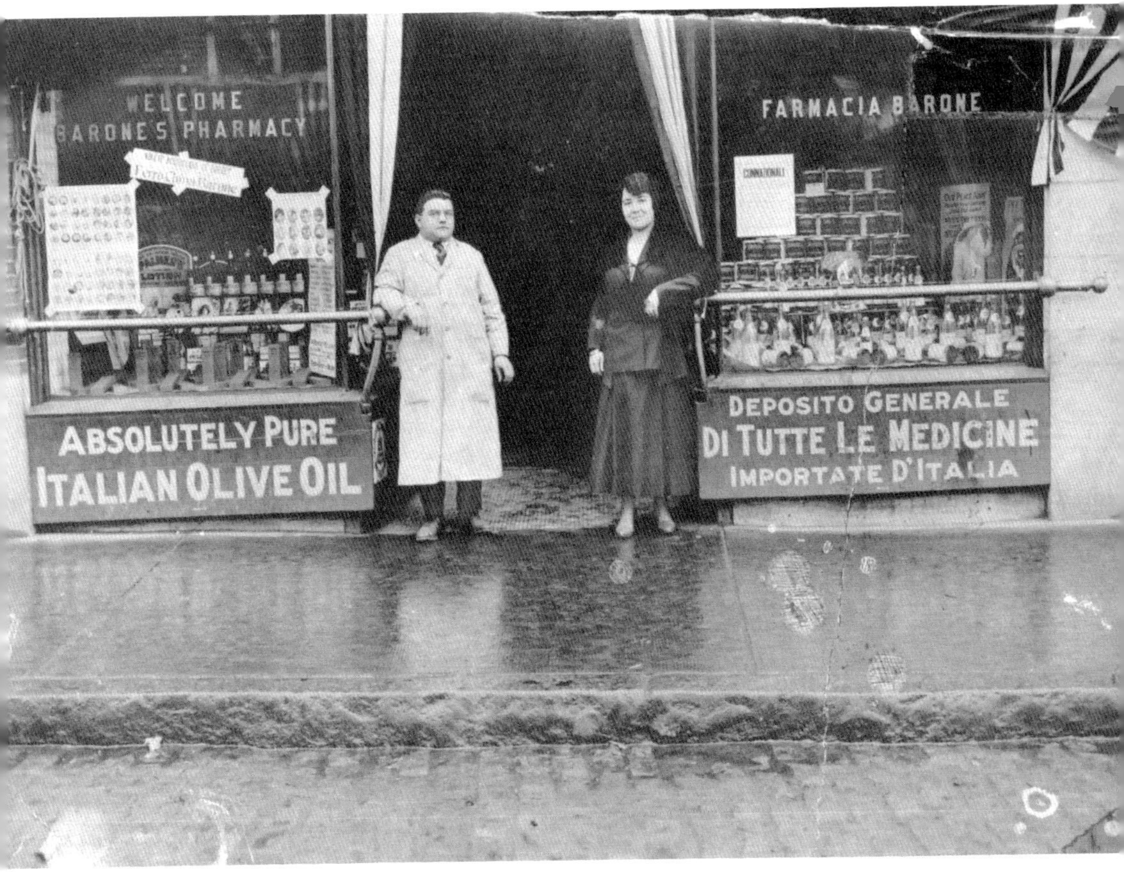

Ciro Barone (1891–1950)
Barone was born in Italy. At seven, his family immigrated to Boston. His father died, leaving his mother to raise eight children. Barone graduated from the Massachusetts College of Pharmacy and worked in the North End. His childhood friend Rev. Angelo Carpinella was assigned to St. Anthony's Church in Fitchburg in 1915, and Barone went to visit him. He liked Fitchburg, and soon after, he moved his family and opened a drugstore on Water Street. Business prospered, and Barone was able to open a larger store on Harvard Street. He and his wife had three sons and a daughter. His three sons became pharmacists, each with his own store. For many years, Barone's was the largest chain of drugstores in Fitchburg and North Leominster, until CVS Pharmacy bought them out.

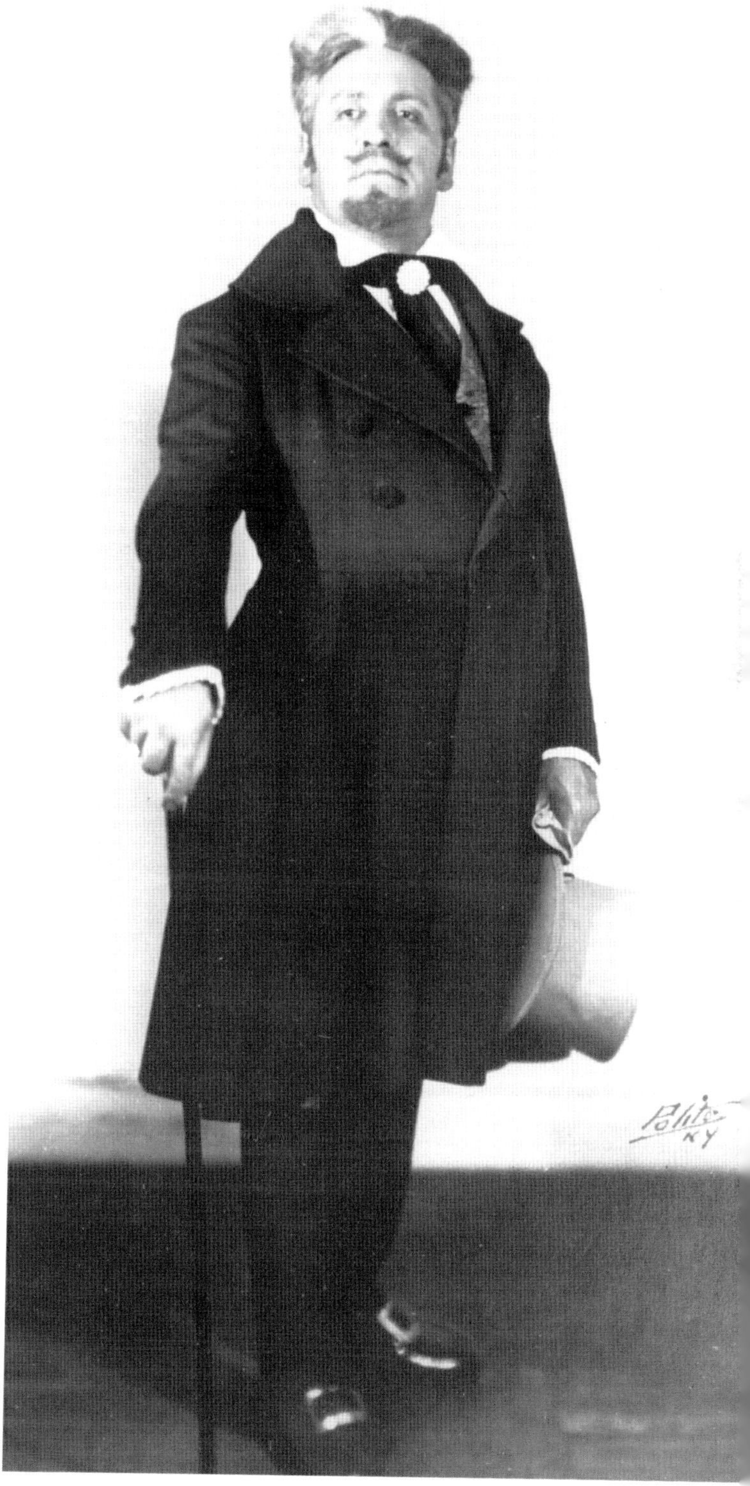

Rocco Pandiscio (1898–1978)
Born in Italy, Pandiscio came to Fitchburg when he was just six years old. Pandiscio's first love became music. At 14, he earned money to pay for lessons. In 1918, he joined the 331st Ariel Squadron to fight overseas, and he entertained his fellow troops by singing opera. After the war, Luisa Tetrazzini, the Italian soprano, heard him sing and encouraged him to train professionally in Italy. In 1920, Pandiscio began studying in Naples and Milan, where Enrico Caruso continued to encourage him and Arturo Toscanini gave him free lessons. Pandiscio went on to a brilliant career and was hailed by critics as the greatest baritone voice of the day, as well as an accomplished actor. His most famous role was that of Germont, the father in *La Traviata*.

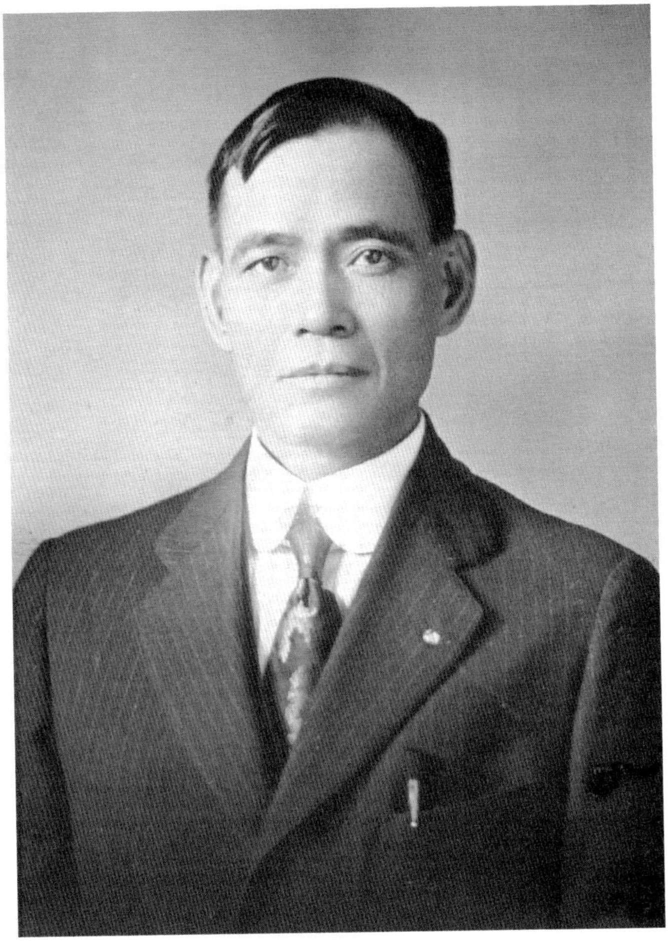

John Fong Ying (?–1940)
Ying was born in Canton, China, in the late 1800s. At a young age, he was orphaned and needed to move to a Catholic mission school. There, he learned to speak English and became very interested in the Catholic religion. At his baptism, he took the Christian name "John," placing it in front of his given name. Ying somehow managed to enter the United States at a time when very few Chinese were allowed into the country. Ying arrived in Boston, and he immediately sought out a church. At the Boston mission, he met Rev. James Donnelly, pastor of St. Bernard's Church in Fitchburg. Soon after, Ying moved to Fitchburg, joined St. Bernard's, and got a job working at one of the six Chinese laundries in the city. At six foot four, Ying was unusually tall, and he possessed a very likable personality that drew people to him. One such person was David I. Walsh, a prominent lawyer who encouraged Ying to open a Chinese restaurant. Ying opened his first restaurant, called the Canton Restaurant, in 1918 with the financial support of some Chinese friends in Boston. The restaurant was a huge success; however, Ying had left a wife and daughter in China. Before he could afford to bring them here, his wife died and his daughter, Fong Wai Oi, remained in China. Ying sent money for her care and education, hoping someday she could join him. In 1920, Fong Wai Oi married Wong Hong Dock. Three years later, Ying asked his son-in-law to join him in the restaurant, and he accepted. Wong and his wife had four children. The Ying family was the first Chinese family to settle in Fitchburg. Years later, with money in his pocket and his son-in-law to help, Ying went back to China to finance the building of a church and to buy land to build a Maryknoll School. John never returned to Fitchburg. He died in China of pneumonia in 1946 while trying to hide from the communists who had come to destroy his church.

Xenophon Gamvas (1884–1971)

Born in Greece, Gamvas studied the sacred art of iconography—the painting of religious images for the worship of the Greek Orthodox Church. Educated at the University of Constantinople, he immigrated to Fitchburg in 1906 and found work at Iver Johnson's Arms & Cycle Works carving gunstocks. In 1913, while visiting his family, he married his wife, Eudoxia, and brought her back to Fitchburg, where they raised six sons and two daughters. In 1919, Gamvas was commissioned to paint the icons for the Holy Trinity Orthodox Church being built in Fitchburg. Iver Johnson respected Gamvas's work such that he granted him extended leaves of absence to complete his paintings. Xenophon Gamvas painted icons for more than 50 Greek churches in the United States.

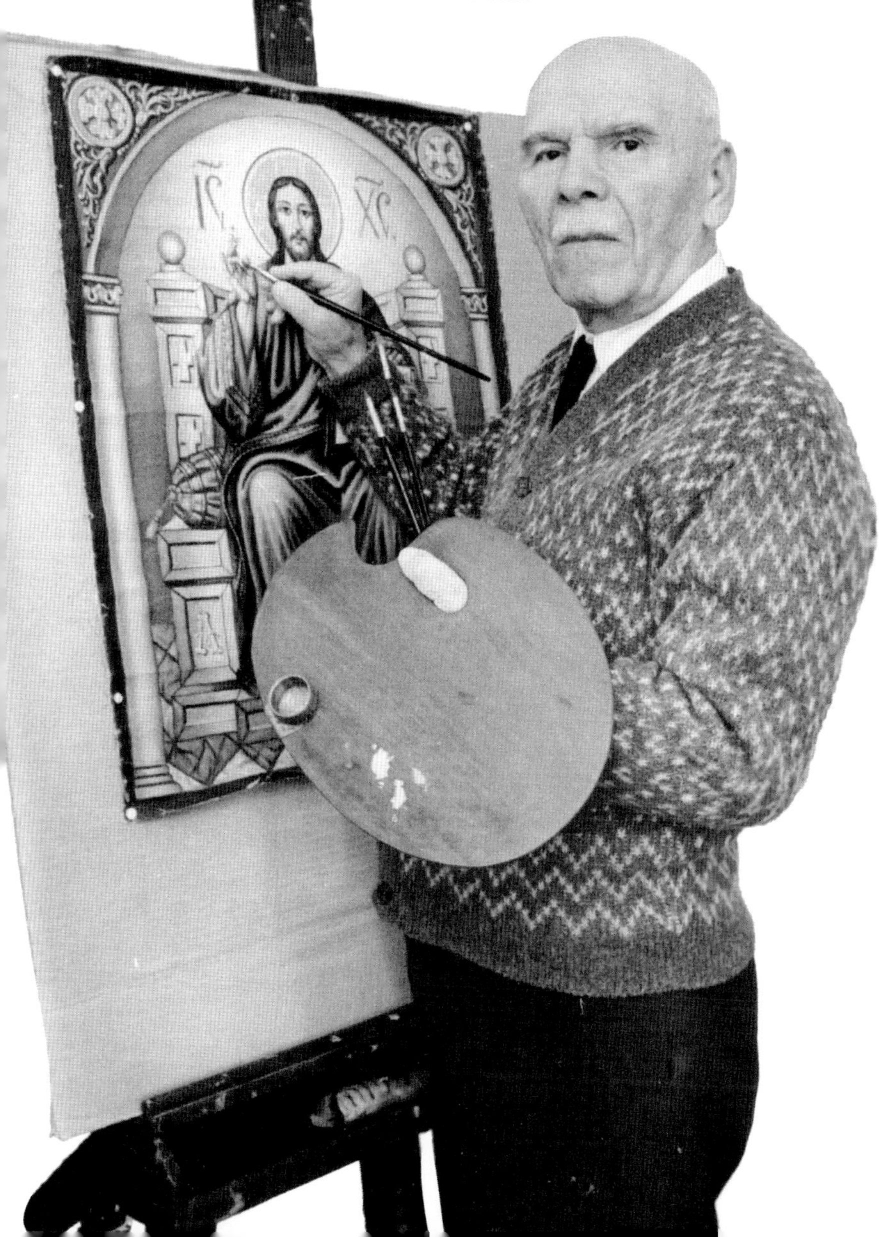

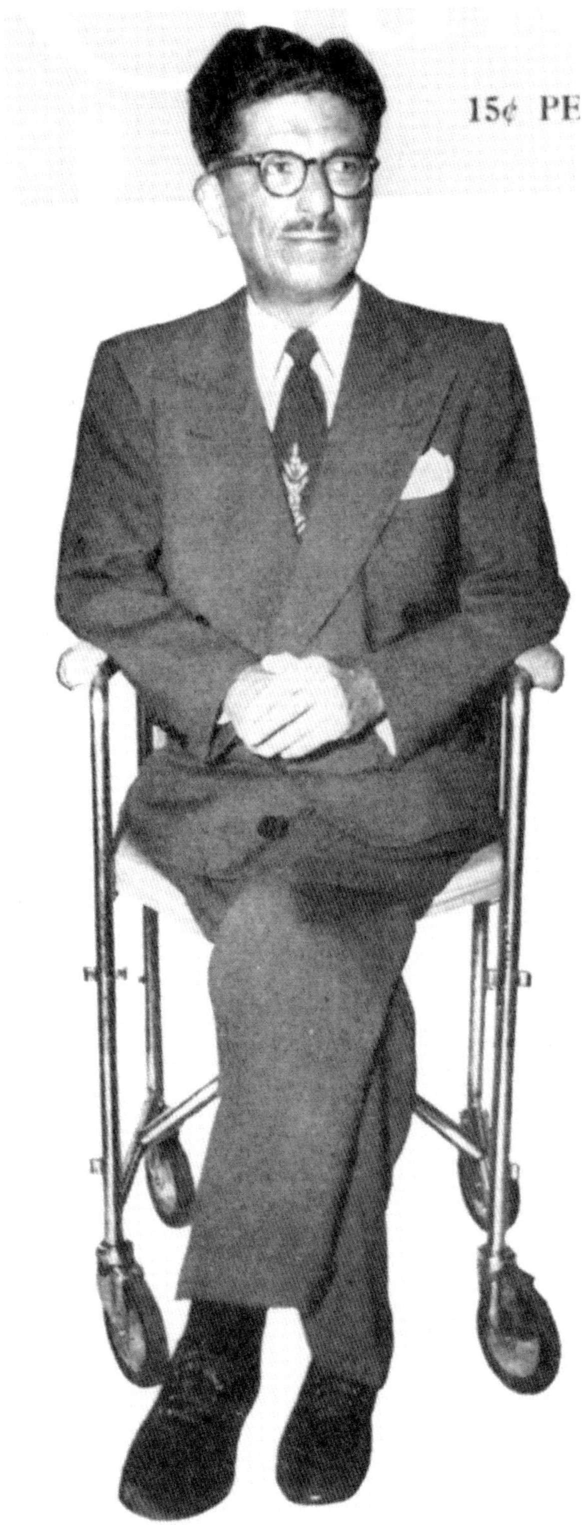

Harry Doehla (1900–1977)
Doehla was born to German immigrants in Fitchburg in 1900. When he was 17, Doehla was diagnosed with rheumatic fever, causing him to remain in a wheelchair for the rest of his life. To help his family, Doehla began to create Christmas cards at home to sell. Doehla Greeting Card grew from the family kitchen to four factories with 630 employees. It posted sales of more than four million cards a year and eventually expanded and moved to Nashua, New Hampshire. Doehla was kindhearted and caring. He hired the handicapped and provided good working conditions for his employees. Doehla also encouraged young artists to send him designs that he would buy, and he set up many educational scholarships in the community. Doehla passed away in New York in 1977 at age 77.

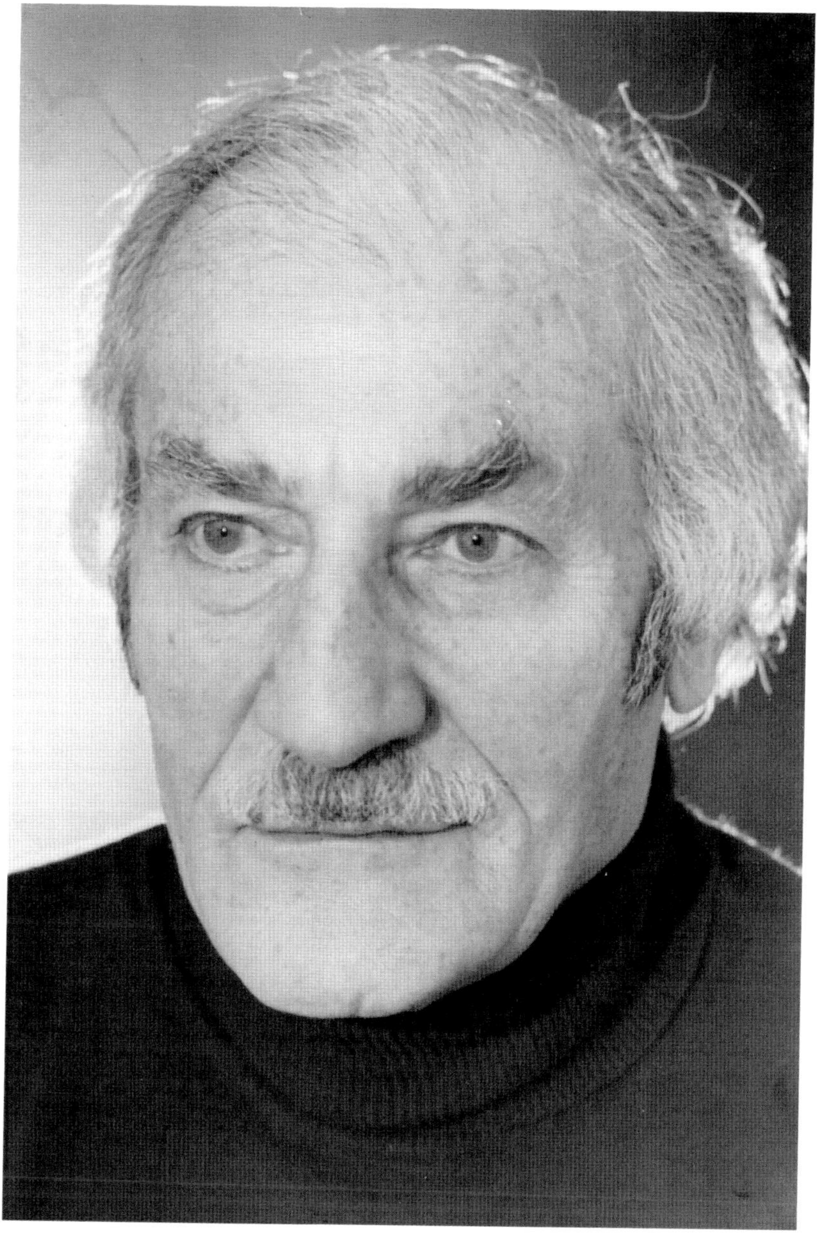

Dr. Maxwell Zide (1907–1992)
Dr. Zide moved his family to Fitchburg in 1949 after having established his podiatry practice there. He continued his practice for more than 50 years, living in both Fitchburg and Leominster. Dr. Zide held leadership roles in his professional life, the Fitchburg community, and B'nai B'rith organizations. He served as president of the Massachusetts Podiatry Society and a director of the New England Society of Foot Surgeons. He was elected as a member of the Royal Society of Health in England in 1965. He was an active member of the Agudas Achim Synagogue and founder of the Fitchburg Community Forum, which was held on Sunday evenings. Dr. Zide was also president of the Achduf B'nai Lodge of B'nai B'rith and a member of the B'nai B'rith Central New England Council. Dr. Zide is buried in Achudas Achim Cemetery in Fitchburg. (Courtesy of Elliott Zide.)

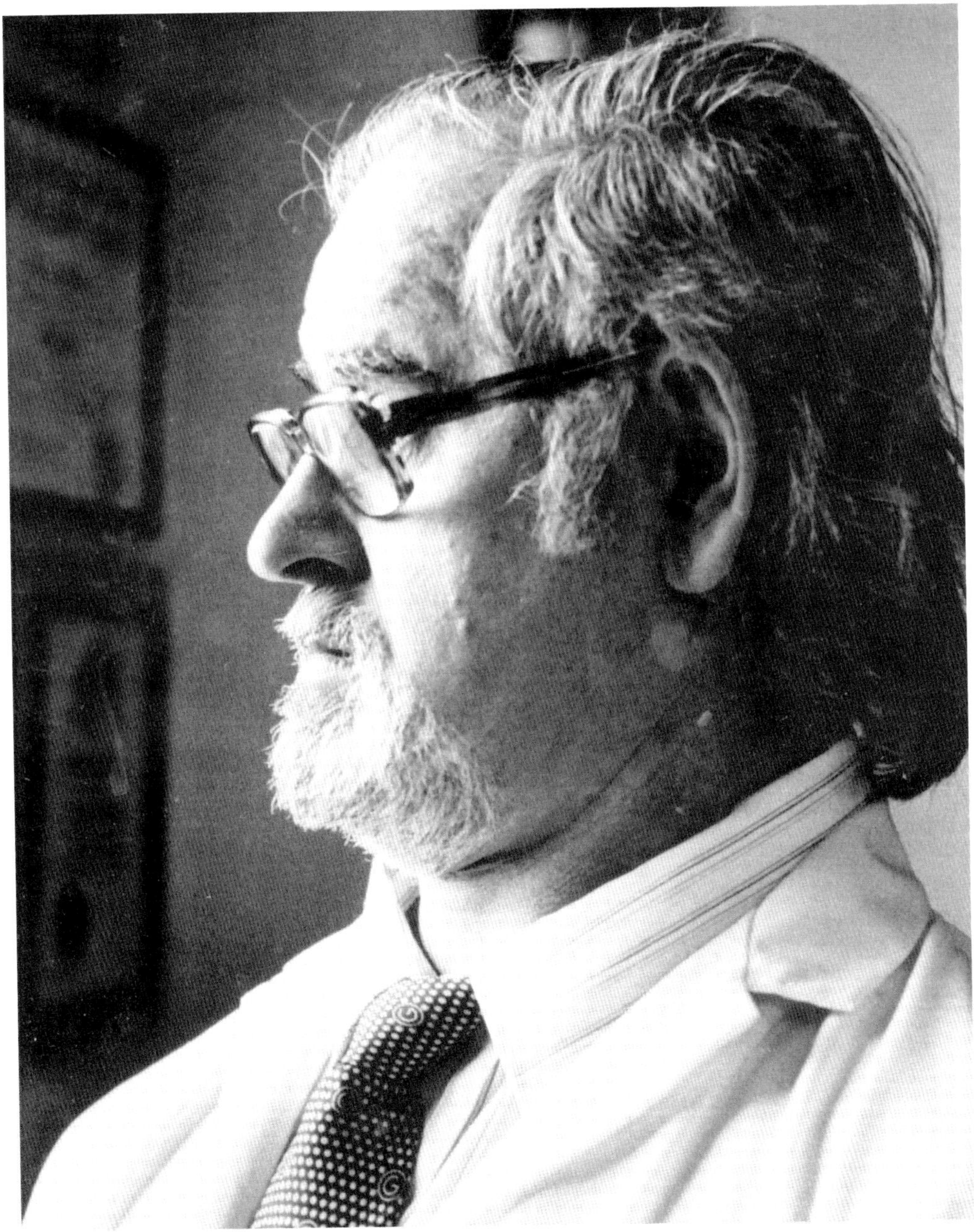

Dr. Warren Litsky (1924–1993)
Dr. Litsky was born in Fitchburg. He was a brilliant student who especially liked science. After graduating from Fitchburg High School in 1941, he went to Clark University in Worcester, Massachusetts, where he majored in biology, graduating in 1945. After obtaining his doctorate, he took a teaching position at the University of Massachusetts (UMASS) as professor of environmental microbiology. Dr. Litsky was renowned in the fields of industrial and agricultural bacteriology. At UMASS, he met his wife, Dr. Bertha Yanis, a fellow microbiologist. Upon his death, his family established the Warren Litsky Endowed Chair in Biology at Clark University, where he is still honored today. (Courtesy of Special Collections at University of Massachusetts Amherst.)

Dr. Joseph B. Addante Sr. (1926–Present)

A world traveler and leader in his profession, Dr. Addante grew up in a bilingual household in Fitchburg. In 1944, he served in China as an airplane mechanic for the Air Force, little realizing that his experience stitching leather in his father's cobbler shop would eventually lead to a medical career. He stitched parachutes and, later, was recruited to assist with stitching wounds. After discharge, Dr. Addante attended Temple University, specialized in podiatry, and opened an office in 1954. Soon after his retirement in 1997, he and his wife, Alice, mourned the tragic loss of their two sons—Jay and Bart—and he accepted an invitation to lecture at the University of Sapienza in Rome, beginning an 18-year association with this university. He is most proud of having met two popes—John Paul II and Benedict. (Courtesy of Dr. Joseph B. Addante.)

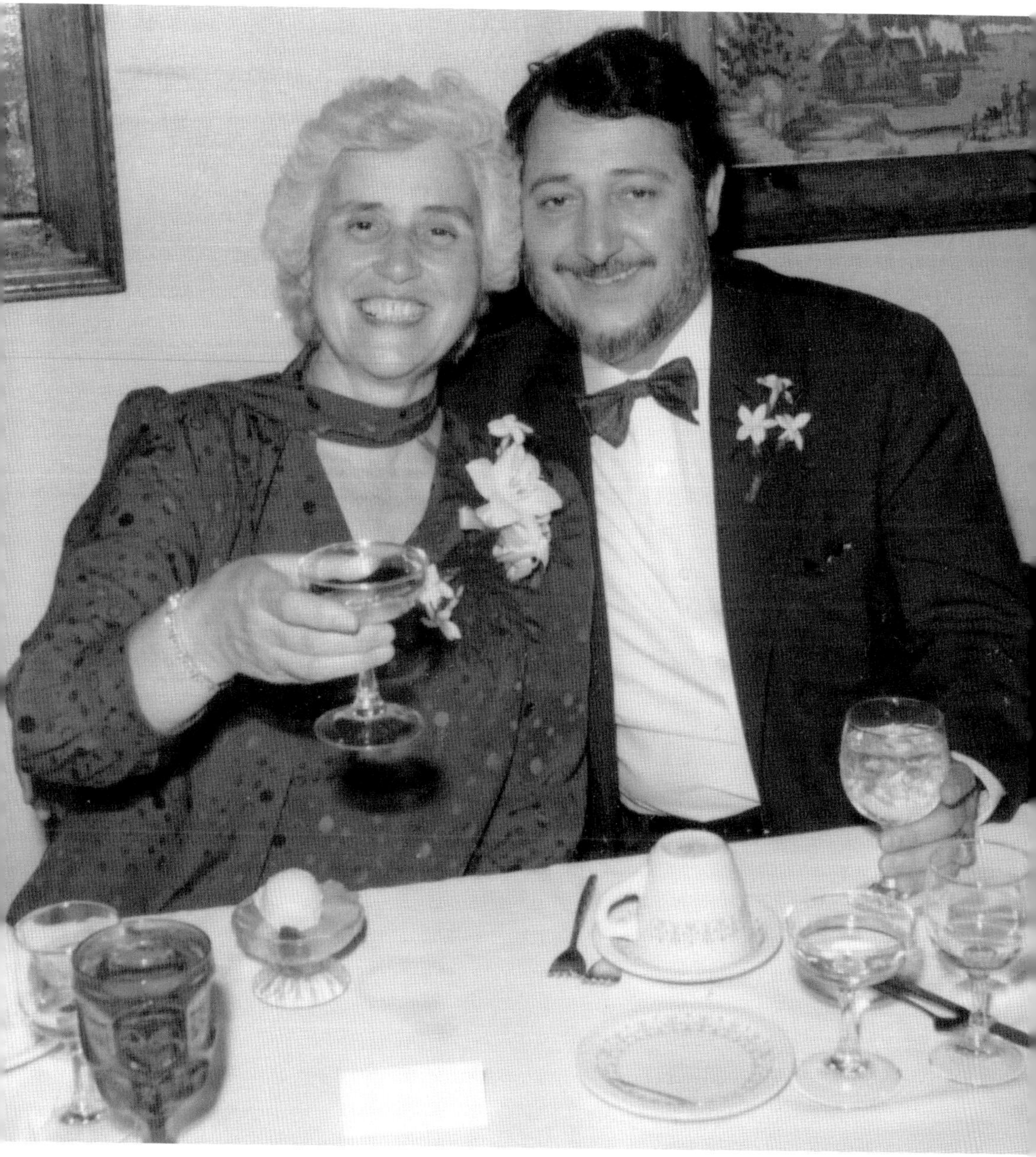

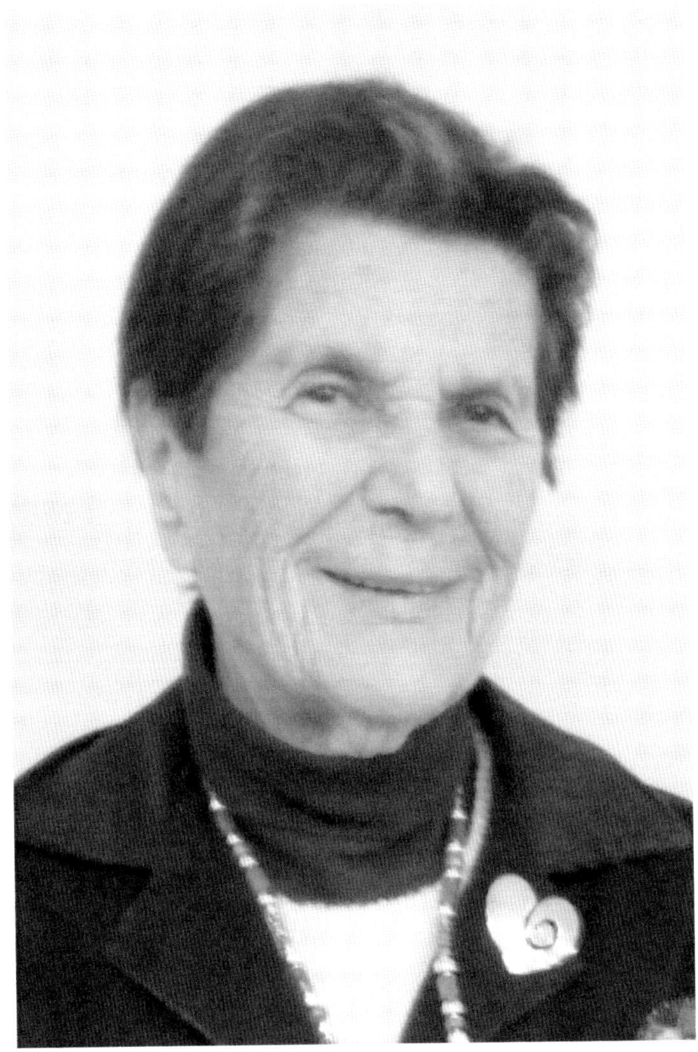

Shirley (Edelman) Pick (1921–2010)
Pick was born to Russian immigrants who settled in Windham, Connecticut. After graduating from high school, she enrolled in the nursing program at Beth Israel in Boston, where she met her husband, Dr. Walter Pick. They married in 1943, and Dr. Pick served at military hospitals during World War II. Dr. Pick set up a pediatric practice in Fitchburg and was an affiliate with the Burbank Hospital. The Picks established their residence on Ellis Street in 1948. After earning a bachelor's degree in 1968 and a master's degree in 1972, Pick taught reading at Montachusett Regional Technical Vocational School for 12 years. She was best known for her volunteer work. Pick served as president of the League of Women Voters and was a literacy volunteer, teaching English to new immigrants for more than 25 years. She helped organize the North Central Court Mediation Services and served as a mediator, its first president, and a board member for a number of years. In 2004, Pick brought together a large group of her peers to create Adult Learners in the Fitchburg Area (ALFA), a program that offers five-week courses for elders on a variety of topics, a lecture series, and day trips to places of interest. At the January 2008 Fitchburg State graduation, Pick was awarded the President's Medal in recognition of her extensive service to the Fitchburg community. Since her death in 2010, ALFA has added a Shirley Pick spring lecture series to honor her memory and her love of learning. (Courtesy of Fitchburg State University.)

CHAPTER SIX

Education and Health Leaders

I am more than the sum of all my experiences,
As my nerve and muscle and brain
Are more than the air and the food and the drink
That sustain me.

—Excerpt from *What am I?* by John Thompson

Fortunate to have many citizens interested in education, Fitchburg developed a school system that included a high school attended by local residents as well as students from neighboring towns. In the 1890s, an innovative superintendent of schools led the lobbying for a normal school to be located in Fitchburg and ensured that it would have an ongoing relationship with the city school system. The normal school grew and expanded its programs over the years. In 2010, under the leadership of Dr. Robert Antonucci, it became Fitchburg State University. Burbank Hospital and the Burbank Nursing Program were also started in the 1890s by a generous trust Gardner Burbank left to his wife, Sarah. Another private benefactor, Fay Bigelow Crocker, established a maternity hospital known as the Lucy Helen. The city had many highly regarded doctors, some of whom practiced in the area for 50 years. Several of the legendary locals in other chapters were also instrumental in the support of schools and hospitals. The people of Fitchburg have long enjoyed the benefits of a fine education and modern health care.

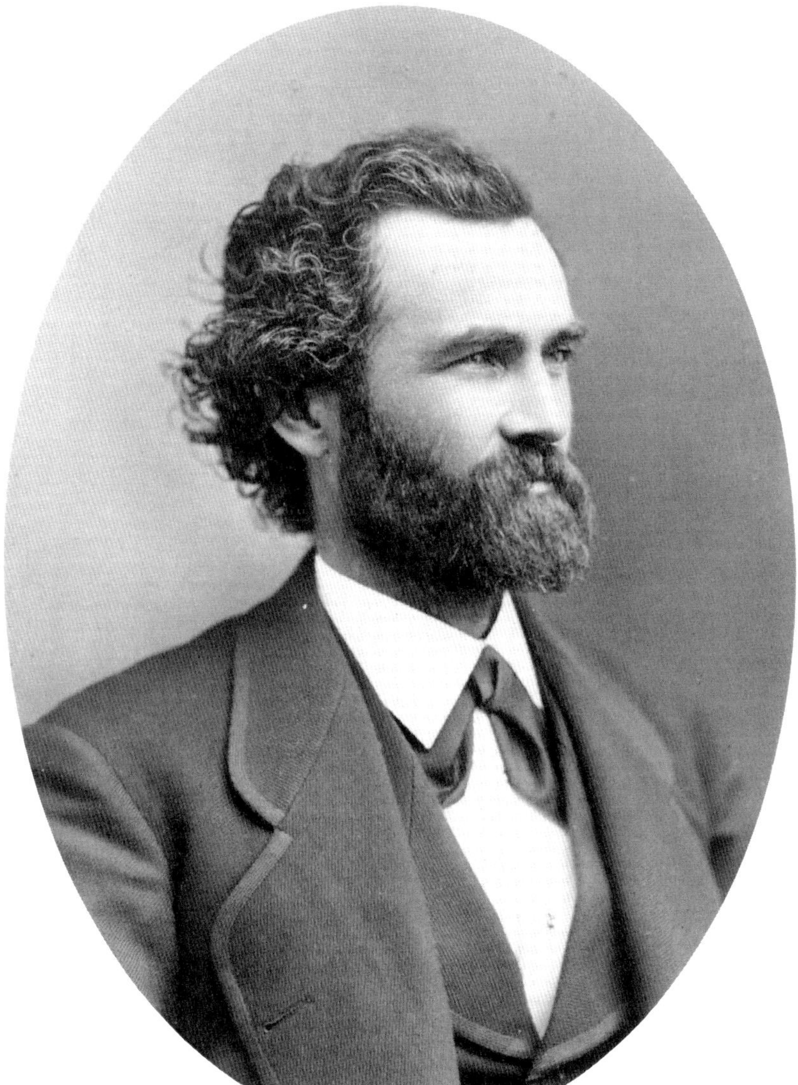

Joseph Edgerly (1838–1922)

Edgerly was born on October 12, 1838, in Barnstead, New Hampshire. At age 10, he worked as a bobbin boy in the Amoskeag Mills. He began teaching in 1857 in Boston, New Hampshire, where he had 45 to 50 students whose ages ranged from 4 to 21. In 1862, he tried to enlist as a volunteer for the Army during the Civil War. He was refused, so he joined the Army Postal Service. In 1864, he entered Dartmouth College, graduating in 1867. He served as superintendent of schools in Manchester from 1867 to 1875, when he became the superintendent of schools in Fitchburg, a position he held until his retirement in 1916. Edgerly led the call for a normal school to be located in Fitchburg in the 1890s because he recognized the need for qualified teachers and wanted to ensure that they had instruction that would prepare them. He also promoted the practical arts movement, making Fitchburg a leader in educating students for jobs after schooling had been completed. Edgerly was well loved by students and teachers and was honored with a pageant, dances, songs, and readings at the Lowe playground for his retirement. (Courtesy of Fitchburg State University.)

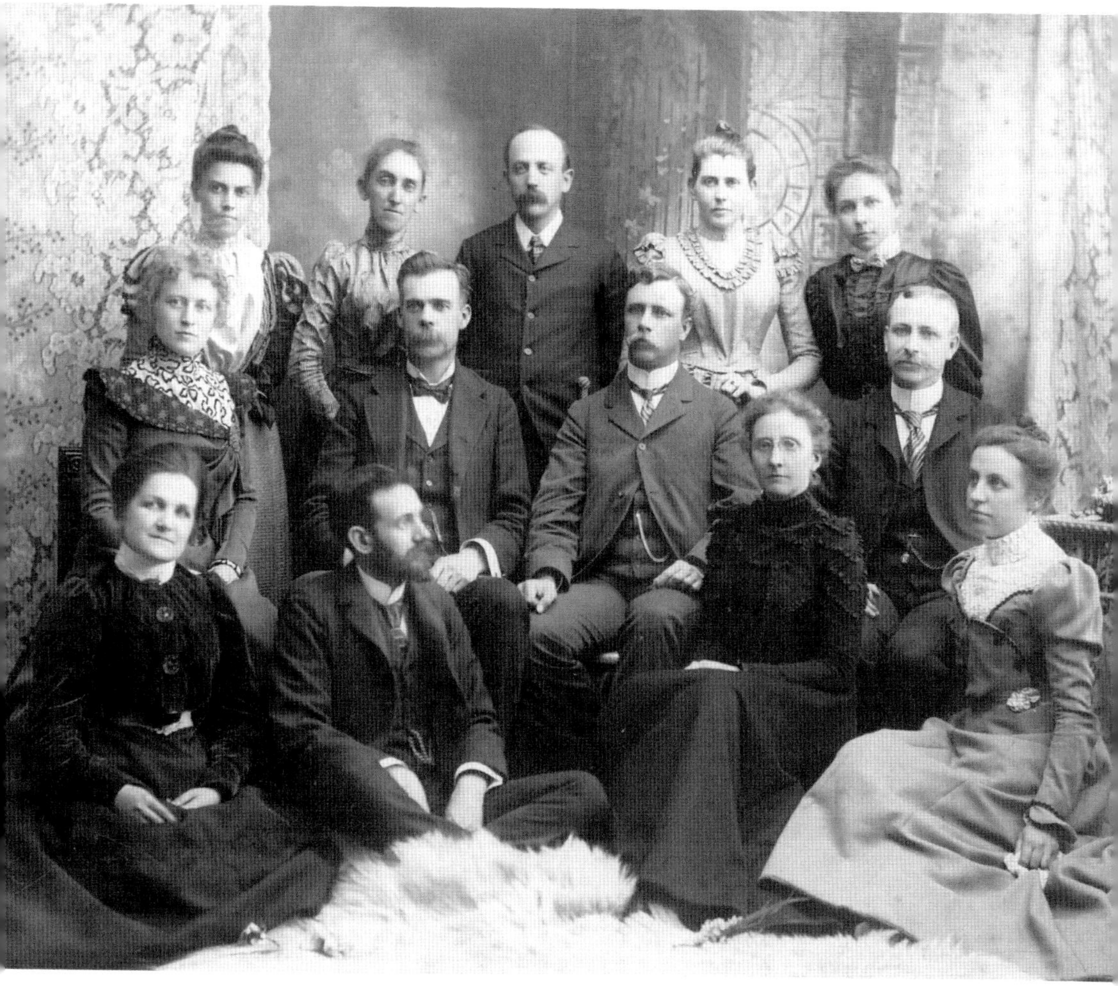

John Gilbert Thompson (1862–1940)

Aiding Edgerly in his goal to establish a normal school in Fitchburg was John Thompson, who was the first principal of the Fitchburg Normal School. Born on June 23, 1862, in New Bedford, Massachusetts, Thompson was a prolific writer, teacher, and superintendent of schools in Leominster before he accepted the position of principal, or president, in 1894. In collaboration with Edgerly and the City of Fitchburg, he established a practice school where students observed and instructed actual classes. He also helped establish a practical arts training program, which brought male students to the normal school. Thompson wrote numerous texts as well as a collection of poetry titled *A Quarter Century of Years and Poems*. He served as principal for 25 years, giving the normal school a solid foundation for the future. The original building for the Fitchburg Normal School was named in honor of Thompson and remains a central part of the university today. Thompson is pictured in the second row, third from the left.

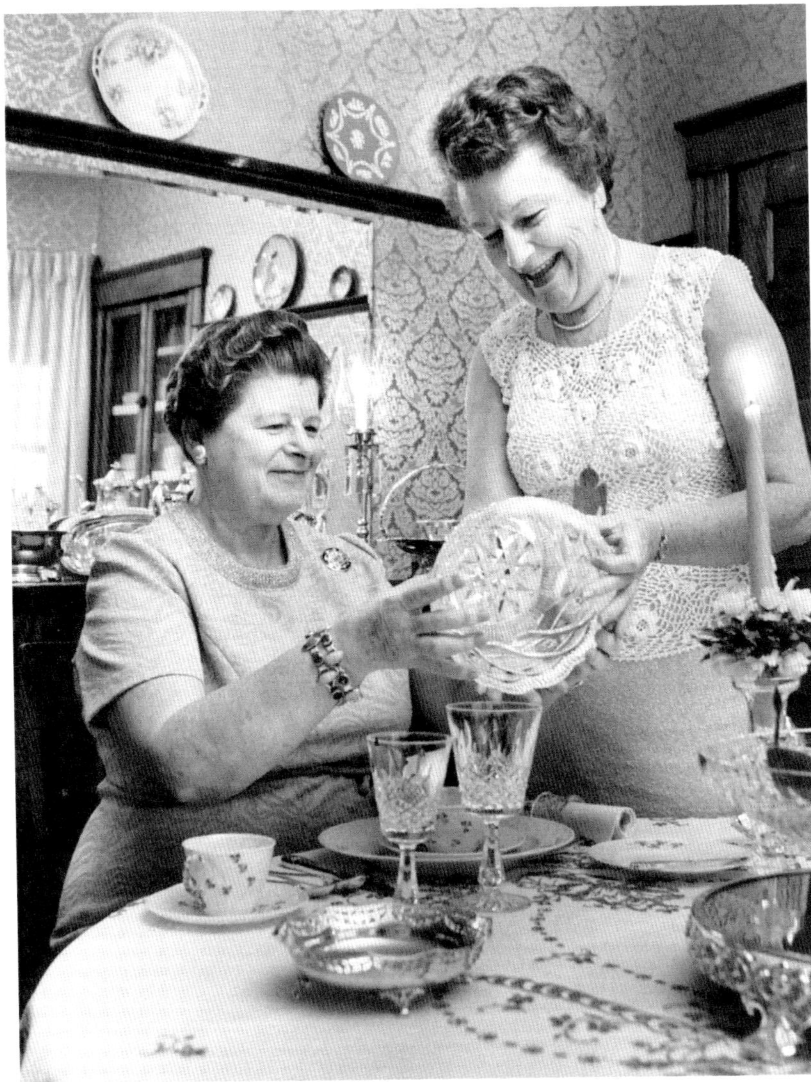

Dr. Margaret E. Kielty (1904–1994)

Educator, author, consultant, and lecturer, Dr. Kielty (left) was the force behind the Americanization and adult education programs in the Fitchburg Public Schools. When she graduated from college in 1926, she began teaching English to immigrants, and since there was no curriculum to prepare them for citizenship, she established a program for Americanization. This evolved into a variety of adult education courses that continued beyond her 1974 retirement. Immigrants learned about the adult education courses when they came to her with questions about naturalization or citizenship. In 1963, she established a high school equivalency program, which by 1972 had graduated more than 500 students between the ages of 18 and 74. Dr. Kielty was a graduate of Trinity College, Fitchburg Normal School, and Boston University. Born and raised in Fitchburg, her father, Peter B. Kielty, taught her to respect everyone regardless of ethnicity. He owned a pharmacy on Water Street and learned to converse with customers in Italian, French, and Polish. He even taught his daughter how to count in Chinese, which she claimed she never forgot. Dr. Kielty was honored many times locally and nationally for her service to immigrants as well as for her contributions to public education. In 1980, she was awarded an honorary degree from Fitchburg State College and, two years later, was honored for her service to the elderly by having a room named for her at the senior center.

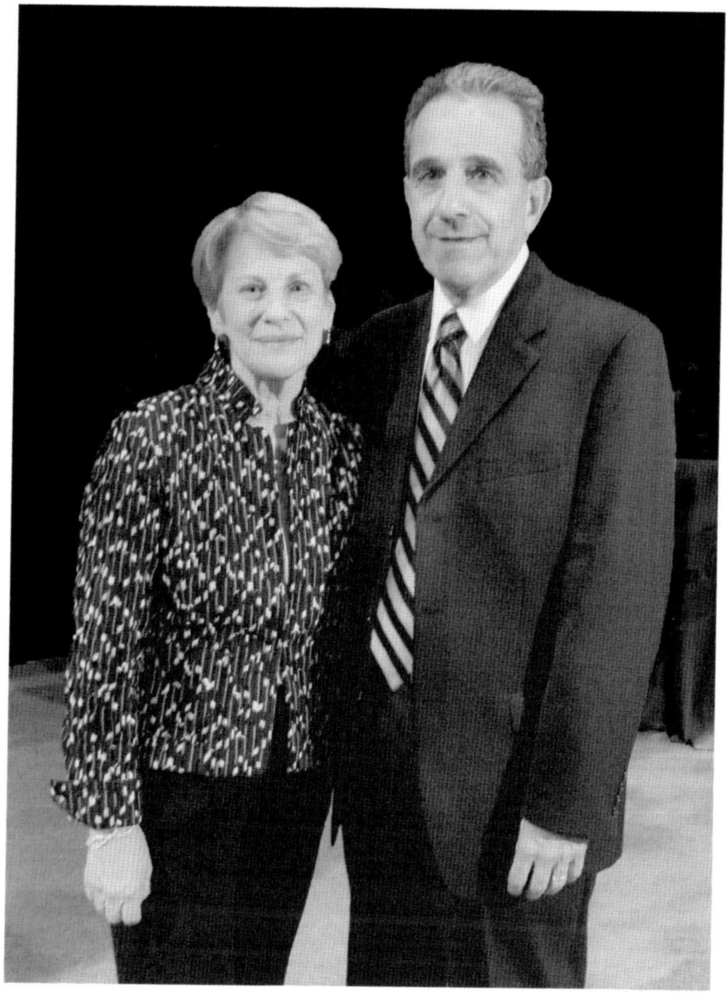

Dr. Robert V. Antonucci (1945–present)
Dr. Antonucci was born in the neighboring community of Leominster. He graduated from Leominster High School in 1963 and enrolled as an education major at the State Teachers College at Fitchburg in the fall. After receiving his bachelor's degree in 1967, Dr. Antonucci completed his master's degree in 1971 at the renamed Fitchburg State College. His doctorate in education was earned at Boston University. Dr. Antonucci served as assistant superintendent of schools in Leominster, superintendent of schools in Falmouth, and commissioner of education in Massachusetts before returning to his alma mater in 2003 to become president. His major objective when he returned was to make the school the best in the state college system, a goal that many believe he has achieved. Dr. Antonucci arrived in challenging economic times when morale was low, enrollment was declining, and the physical plant, program equipment, and technological infrastructure all needed significant upgrades to support and enhance academic programs. Now, 10 years later, the college is identified as a university, a new science building has opened, and the academic programs have been strengthened. The Hammond Building, which was sometimes described as the "fortress on the hill" by city residents when Antonucci arrived, now has an open and inviting entrance toward the city neighborhoods and symbolizes the university's increased involvement in the city. Jeanne Antonucci, his wife, who also earned a bachelor's degree and a master's degree at Fitchburg State, plays a significant role in the university community and local charities, further strengthening the reputation of the city's major educational institution. (Courtesy of Fitchburg State University.)

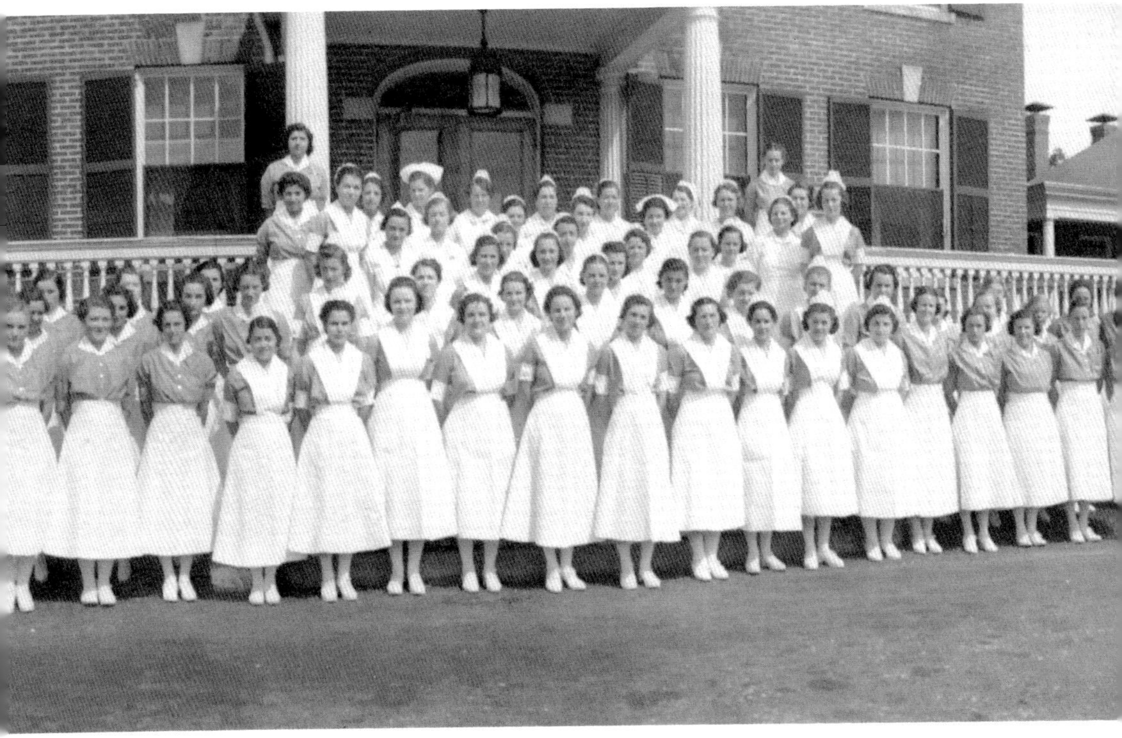

The Burbank School of Nursing

The Burbank School of Nursing, begun in 1894, was a two-year program that combined coursework taught by the doctors and hands-on training. In 1896, the first two nurses completed the program. In 1929, a full-time nurse-training instructor, Grace Gummo, was hired. She adapted their curriculum to gain accreditation by the New York Board of Registration, making Burbank one of the 20 elite nursing schools. During the Depression, the National Board of Nurse Training ordered Burbank and other hospital training schools to reduce student enrollment. In 1937, Gummo was hired as the director of nursing, a position she would hold for the nearly 30 years. Gummo was an innovative leader, always politically astute and on the forefront of the changes in nursing curriculum. In 1943, Burbank and the State Teachers College at Fitchburg initiated a program that combined 2.5 years of academic coursework with 2.5 calendar years in practice at Burbank Hospital. In 1954, the joint program was fully accredited by the National League of Nursing. In 1962, Gummo and Burbank Hospital joined with Fitchburg State Teachers College in petitioning the state board of education to seek legislation that would enable the college to take over full administrative and educational responsibility of the program, which was approved. In 1964, the combined program ceased to exist, though the diploma program at Burbank remained until 1982. Today, the Fitchburg State Nursing Program offers an undergraduate degree in nursing as well as an online master's degree in forensic nursing, and Fitchburg State nurses practice at sites throughout Massachusetts.

Burbank Hospital

Upon his death in 1888, Gardner S. Burbank placed in trust, with his wife, Sarah, $500,000 for the establishment of a hospital, with the stipulation that the funds be transferred to the City of Fitchburg upon her death. In 1890, a corporation known as Burbank Hospital was formed with 15 members constituting the board of trustees. In 1891, Sarah proposed that if the city procured the funds to build, she would pay the interest on the debt during her lifetime. Later that year, a 400-acre property known as Nichols Farm was purchased. For a time, the manor house served as a temporary hospital. The hospital received its first patient on July 19, 1894. Concurrent with the opening of the hospital, a two-year nursing program was implemented. Sarah donated another $50,000 for the construction of a nurses' home, which was authorized by the trustees and built in 1910. In 1950, a new nurses' home was built and is now the Highlands Life Care Center, which opened in 1988. No evidence of the original four cottage-style hospital buildings exists today, and the site is now occupied by the Simonds-Sinon Regional Cancer Center. The manor house was converted to the Cottage Birthing Center in the 1980s, and in the 1990s, it stood vacant and in a state of disrepair. The building is now used for the WIC (Women, Infants, and Children) program. The granite hitching post, bearing the initials "LN" for Lyman Nichols, remains as silent witness to its early origins. In 1993, Burbank and Leominster Hospital consolidated to form Health Alliance.

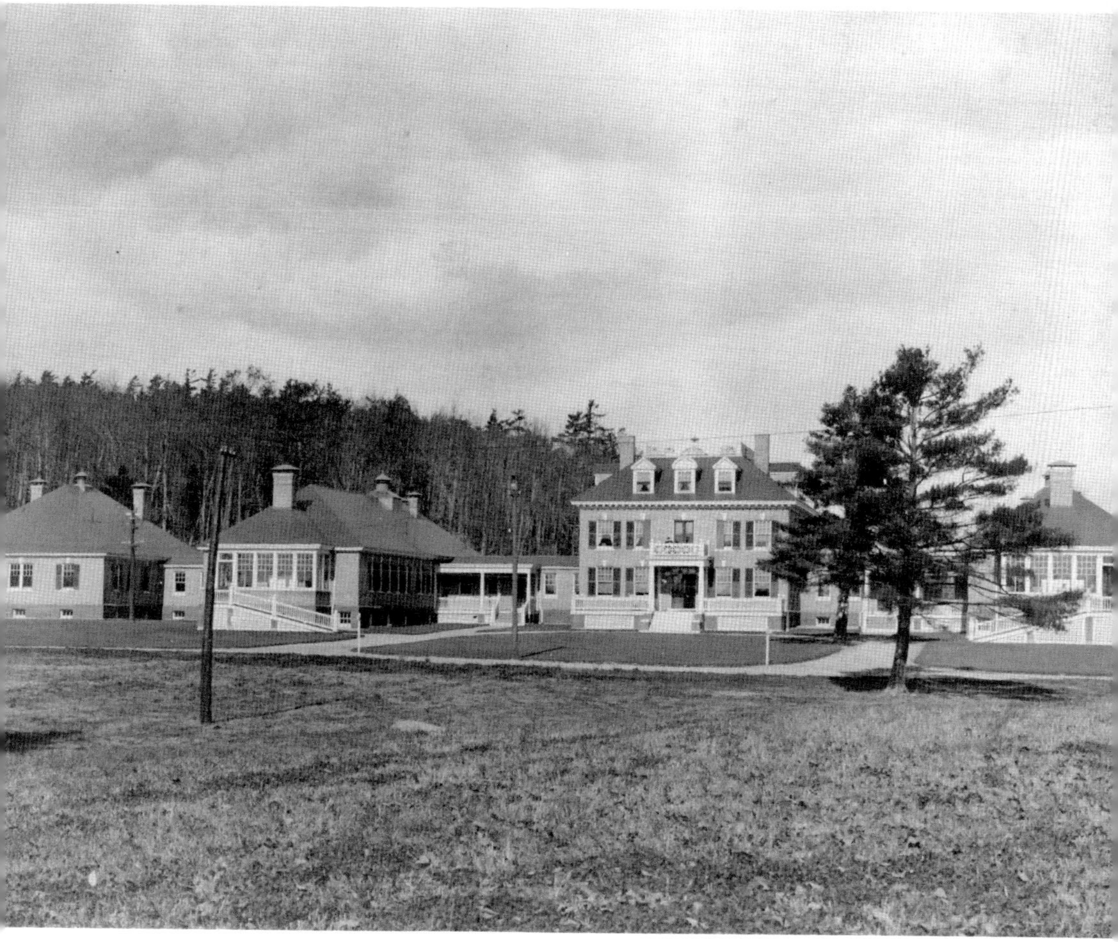

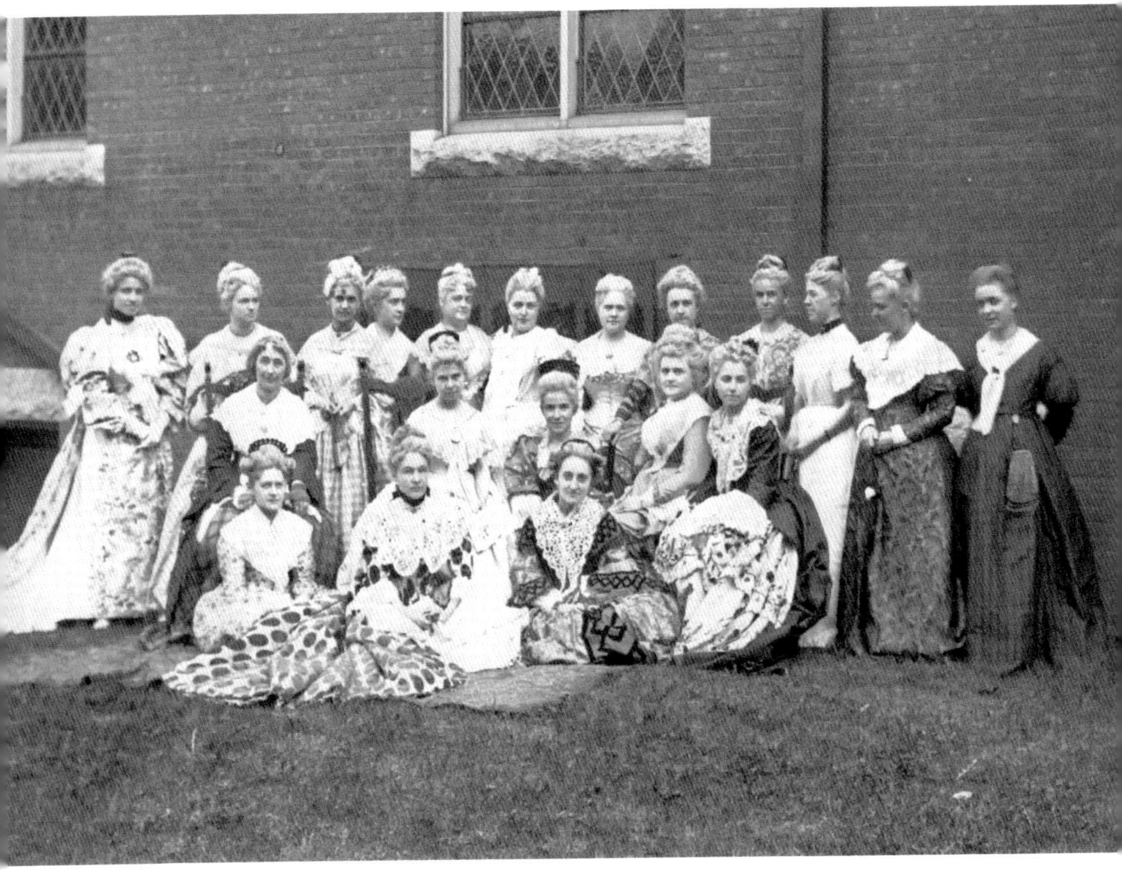

Fay Bigelow Crocker (1869–1956)

Fay Bigelow (standing far left) married Charles T. Crocker II, embracing her role as a civic leader. The Crockers had three children—Tom, Bigelow, and Darthea. The couple opened their home as an emergency hospital during the 1918 influenza epidemic and also founded the Lucy Helen Memorial Hospital—named in honor of Fay's mother, Lucy, and Charles's mother, Helen—on Main Street to provide modern maternity care. In 1926, Crocker became the first woman to sit on the board at Burbank Hospital. After the Lucy Helen Hospital closed in 1954, she converted the building into a hostelry for the Girls Friendly Society of the Christ Episcopal Church. Crocker and Helen Stratton cofounded the Stratton Theater, one of the oldest continuously operating community theaters. Applewild, the Crocker family home on Prospect Street, became a school by the same name.

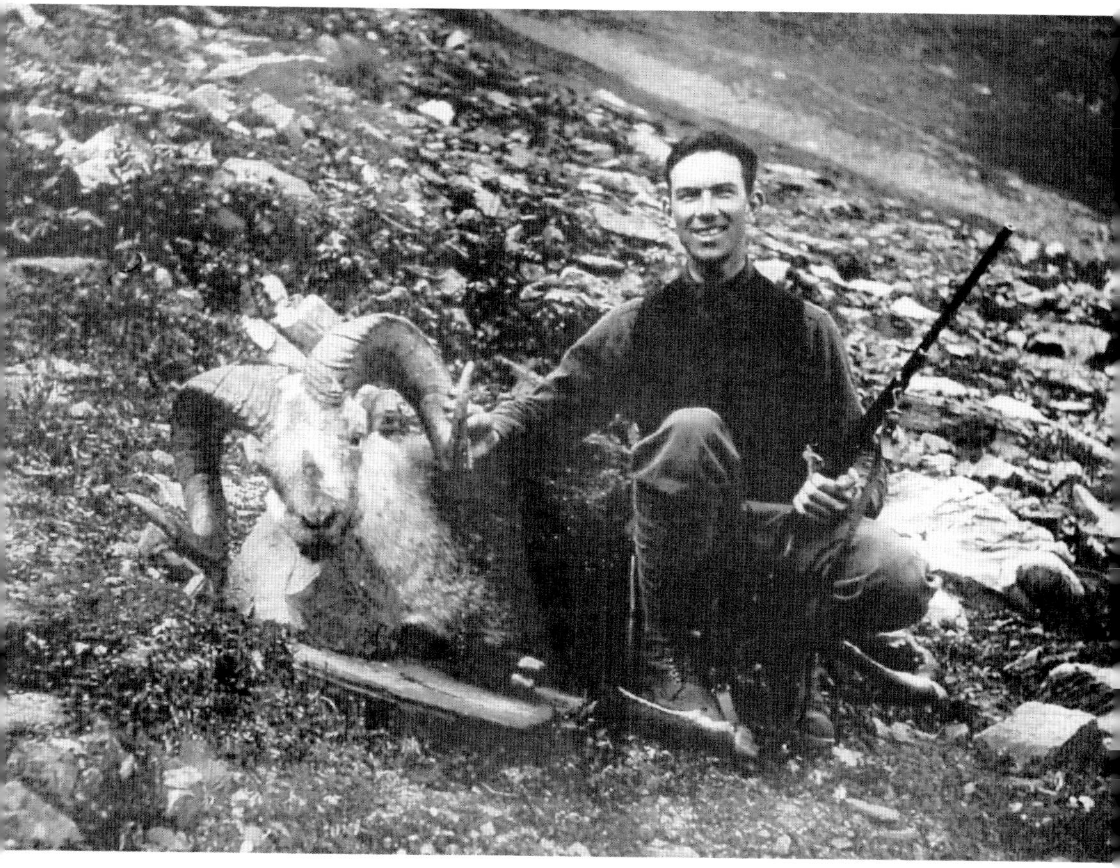

Richard Bullock (1892–1981)
Bullock was born in Fitchburg and joined a long line of successful family businessmen. Bullock's parents were well known in Fitchburg for their involvement in railroads and banking. Richard was born in the family home on Prospect Street, where he lived for his entire life. He attended Harvard University and graduated in 1915. At age 23, Bullock took a two-month-long trip to British Columbia, where he hunted big game; the heads of moose and rams were later hung on the walls of his home. After his adventures, Bullock returned home to work at one of his father's banks. In 1926, he was appointed as the directing trustee of Burbank Hospital, a position he held for more than 30 years. It was at Burbank Hospital that he met his wife, Nancy, a nurse. Richard and Nancy were married and had four children. (Courtesy of Kathleen Flynn.)

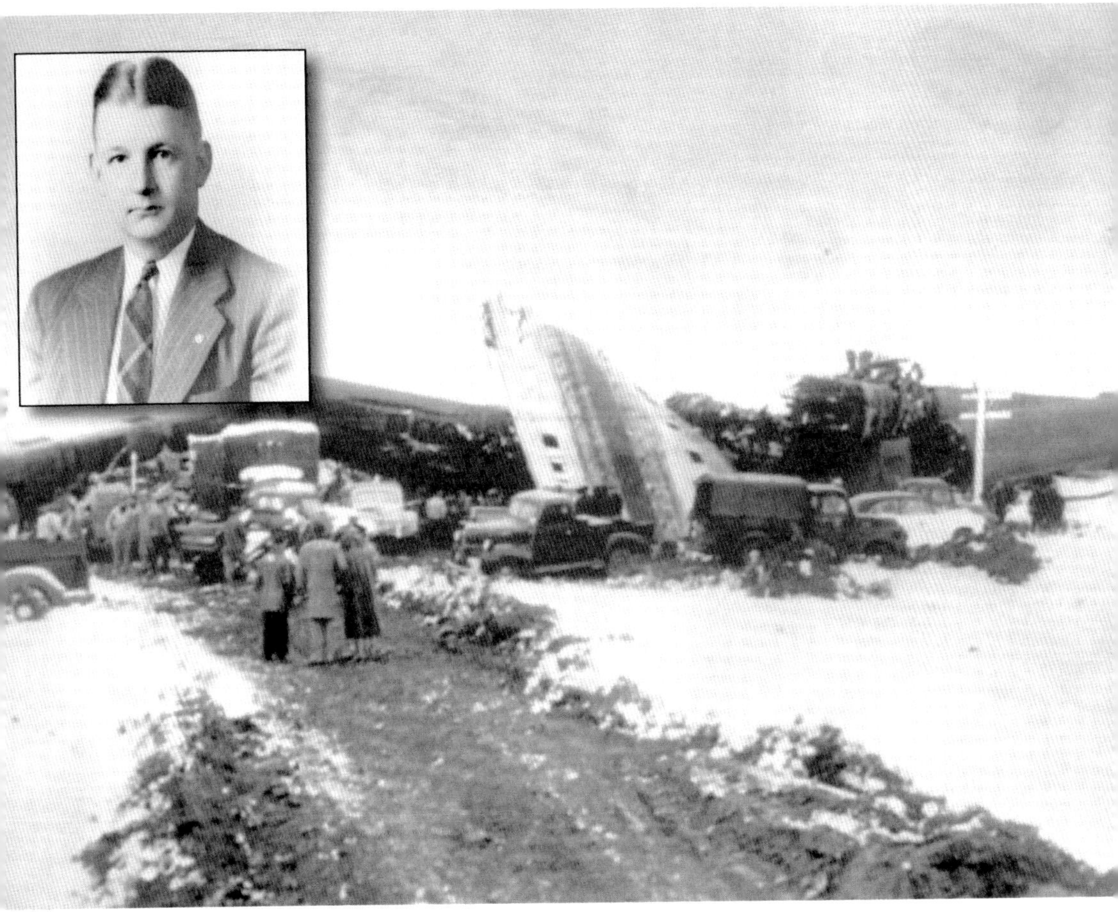

Dr. Rudolf (1907–1951) and Aileen Bachmann (1907–1951) and Dr. Robert Thomson (1912–1951)
All three were tragically killed in a train accident on November 13, 1951, when they were returning from the annual medical convention for the College of Surgeons in San Francisco. The City of Los Angeles train in which they were traveling was rear-ended by a City of San Francisco train in a blinding snowstorm in Evanston, Wyoming. Dr. Bachmann was 44 and Dr. Thomson was 39 at the time. Dr. Bachmann was a prominent surgeon who also had a large general practice. He had come to Burbank Hospital after completing his medical degree and had served as medical examiner for the Third Worcester District, from 1942 until his death. Dr. Thomson, known for specialization in cancer surgery, received his medical degree in 1938. He served in World War II for 18 months and came to Burbank in 1946. The funeral for the Bachmanns was held on November 19, 1951, at the Calvinistic Congregational Church with more than 1,000 people in attendance. The honorary and active pallbearers were primarily doctors from Fitchburg, among other cities. Recognizing that the entire community was suffering from the loss of the Bachmanns, the chamber of commerce sponsored a five-minute radio message from Rev. Robert N. Foster that was played in all Main Street stores during the service. Reverend Foster noted, "All of us—the store clerk, the business executive, the school-age youngster—have suffered loss beyond estimate. We therefore pause as one." Dr. Thomson's remains were recovered on the day of the Bachmann funeral. His funeral was held on November 26, 1951, and followed a similar format to that of the Bachmanns. Rev. George B. Ratcliffe, from Thomson's hometown of Milton, assisted with the service and commented on his younger years. The Bachmanns and Dr. Thomson are buried at Forest Hill Cemetery in Fitchburg.

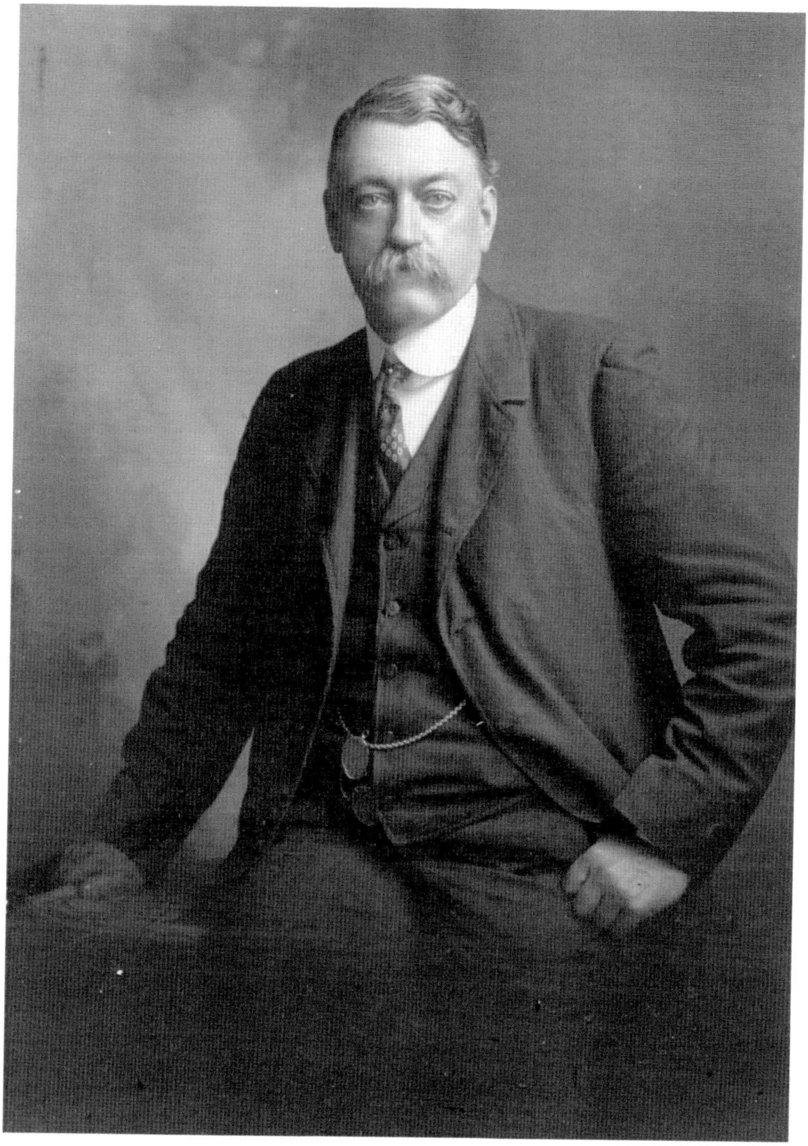

Dr. Frederick H. Thompson Jr. (1875–1966)

Born in Fitchburg, Dr. Thompson Jr. was the son of Dr. Frederick H. Thompson Sr. (1844–1939), who began his practice in Fitchburg in 1874, serving as the city physician and a member of the city board of health, as well as one of the founders of Burbank Hospital. Both father and son were graduates of Harvard Medical School. Dr. Thompson Jr. set up his practice on Prichard Street in 1902. Per a requirement of state law, he was appointed as the first school physician, a position in which he served for 25 years. During the influenza epidemic of 1918, he was in charge of a hospital addition set up to treat flu cases. Isolated from October to December, he and several nurses worked in the Davis House on View Street, where flu victims were brought for treatment. He recalled caring for 150 patients, 50 of whom died. When Dr. Thompson Jr. came down with influenza himself, his father treated him with mustard-saturated cloths, which cured him. Dr. Thompson Jr. reminisced about the many changes in medical practice over his lifetime and that of his father when he was named General Practitioner of the Year in 1961. Both began their practices with horse and buggy and without sulfa drugs or antibiotics, such as penicillin, which later became available.

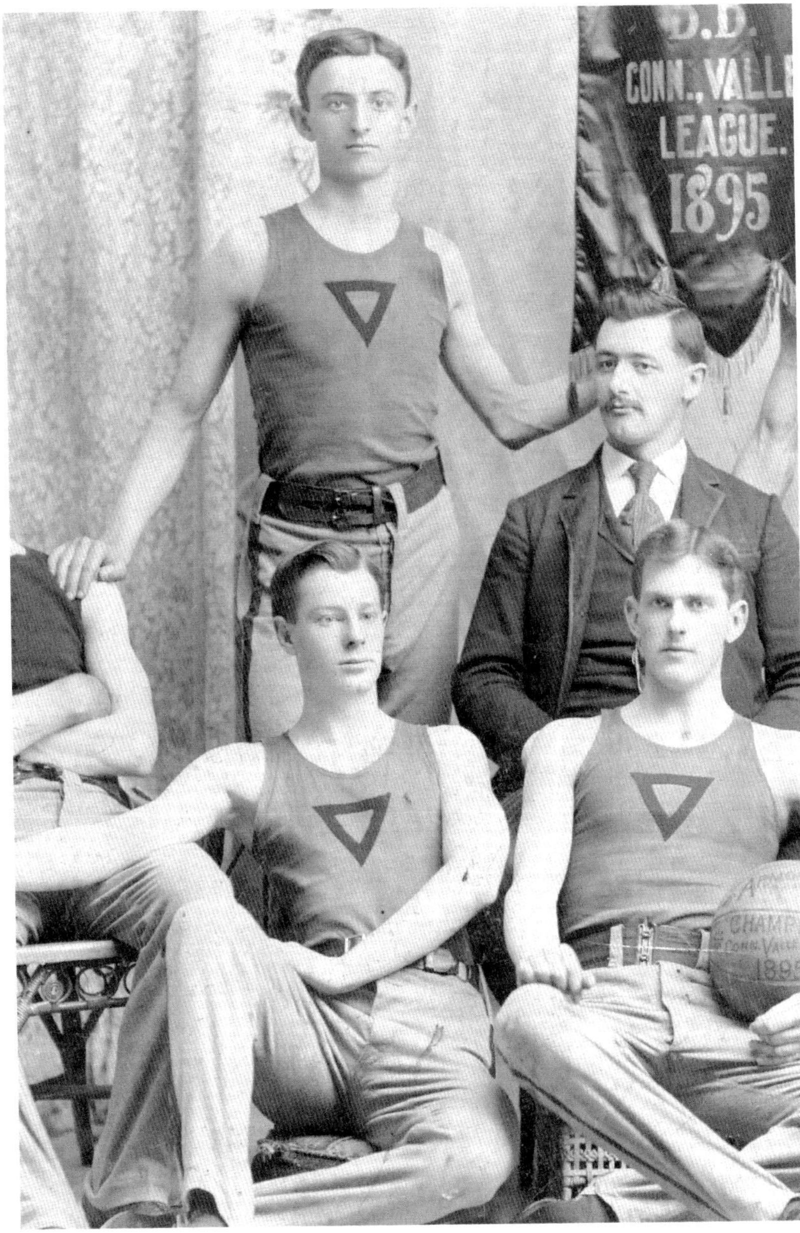

Dr. Curtis H. Jennings (1876–1934)

Dr. Jennings (seated, left) was born to Calvin and Ann Maria Jennings in Brookfield, Massachusetts. Upon graduating from Springfield High School in 1895, he entered the Western Reserve Medical University. His education was interrupted in 1898 when he enlisted in the US Navy during the Spanish-American War. After the war, Dr. Jennings completed his medical training at the University of Baltimore Medical School and graduated in 1902. In 1905, he moved to Fitchburg, where he established Burbank Hospital's first radiology department. When the United States entered World War I, he reenlisted and, in 1918, was named assistant surgeon of the Naval Hospital in Newport, Rhode Island. Celebrated for his skill in X-ray diagnosis, Dr. Jennings was considered one of the leading radiologists in the United States. He passed away in 1934 due to years of exposure to X-ray radiation.

CHAPTER SEVEN

Arts and Entertainment Leaders

Rollstone mountain, thee we hail,
Girded with thy granite mail!
Many a legend, story and song
Round thy steadfast grandeur throng.

—Excerpt from *Rollstone* by Martha A. Tolman

The citizens of Fitchburg ensured a strong arts community by supporting institutions that provided spaces and opportunities for various artists to grow and share their talents. The Fitchburg Art Museum, Fitchburg State University, Saima Park, Whalom Park, and Stratton Theater, among other art and dance studios, all provided the small city with first-class culture. The citizens pledged their support to bands and singing groups, with dance, drama, and music teachers helping new generations become, and remain, involved in the arts. Sculptures and paintings abound in the city, with photography documenting the people, places, and events that have become part of its history.

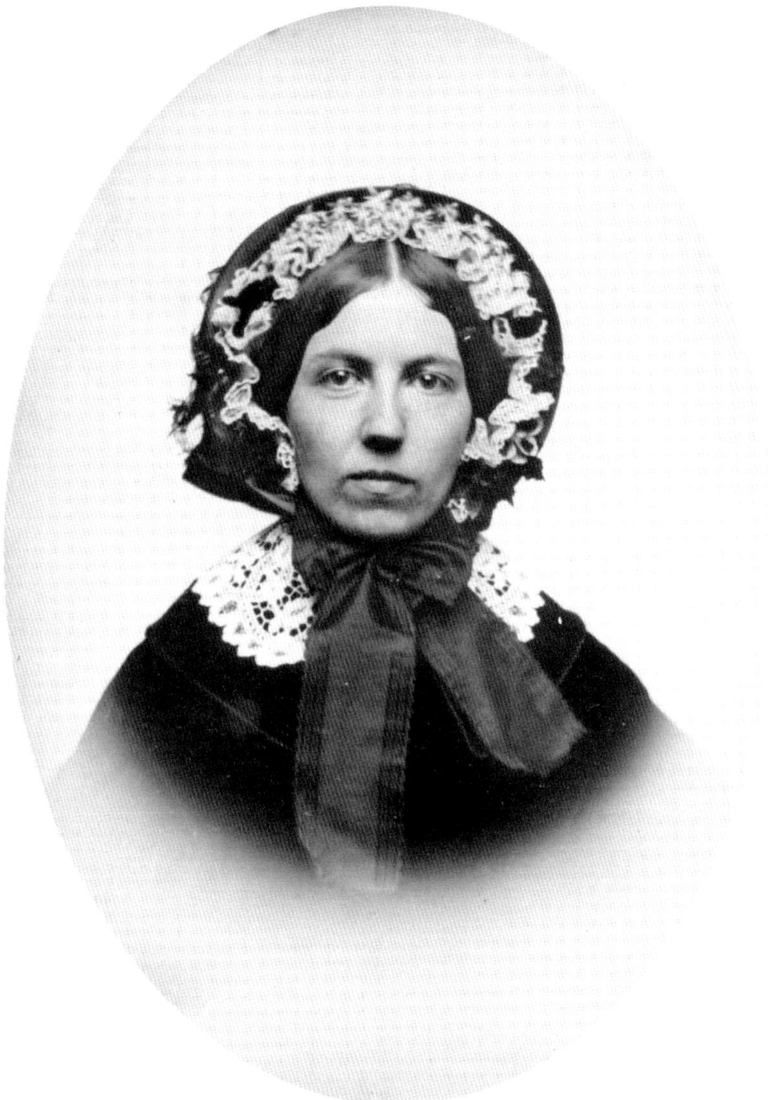

Caroline Atherton (Briggs) Mason (1823–1890)
Mason was born in Marblehead, Massachusetts. She began writing at an early age, but her first successful poem "Do They Miss Me at Home?" was originally published in the *Salem Register* in 1844, the same year she graduated from the academy. That poem, along with some of her other poetry, were turned into hymns. Perhaps her most important legacy to Fitchburg was her poem featured throughout this book, "Ode to Fitchburg," the memorization of which was required for 19th-century Fitchburg schoolchildren. Caroline and the Briggs family moved to Fitchburg in 1852. She married lawyer Charles Mason in Fitchburg in 1853. The Masons lived in a home overlooking the city, and they had one son, Atherton, who went on to become a physician in Fitchburg. Her first collection of poetry, *Utterance or Private Voices to the Public Heart*, was published in 1852. The final collection of her work, *The Lost Ring and Other Poems*, was published posthumously in 1890. She also wrote short stories and articles for the *Atlantic Monthly*, among other journals of the day. Mason often wrote under the pseudonym of Caro. Reportedly, she was also a prolific correspondent to local newspapers, where her missives were signed as "C.A.M." She supported the abolition of slavery, the establishment of women's rights, and the prevention of cruelty to animals.

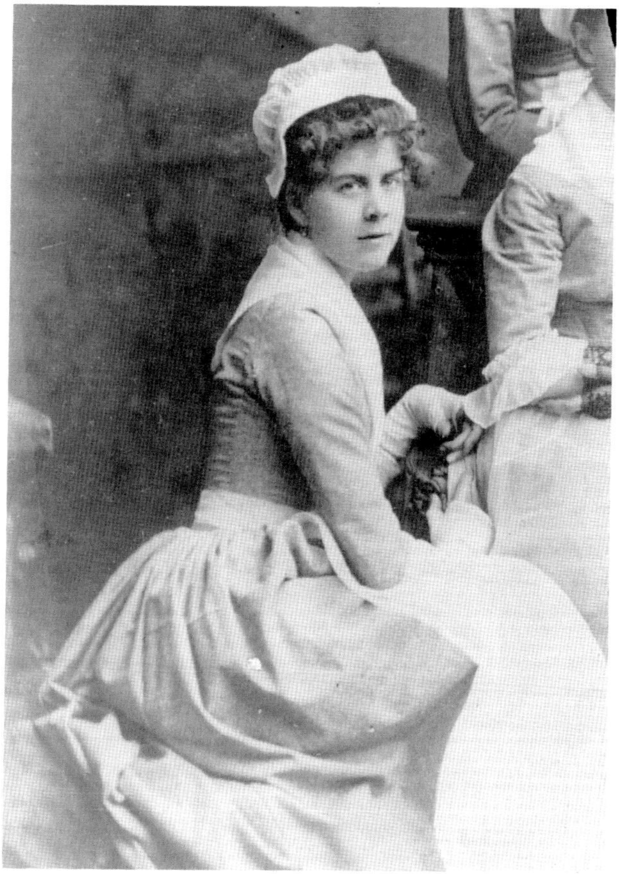

Eleanor Norcross (1854–1923)

Norcross was born Ella Augusta to Amasa Norcross, the city's first mayor, and Susan Augusta Norcross, famous for her work with the Ladies' Soldiers Aid Society. Her young brother Nelson died of scarlet fever during the Civil War, and her mother died of consumption a few years later. These sad deaths left Eleanor, as she was later known, and her father as a small family that remained close throughout their lives. After graduating from Fitchburg High School, Norcross attended Wheaton Female Seminary, then helped with her father's mayoral campaign before enrolling at the Massachusetts Normal Art School in Boston to become an art teacher. She obtained her teaching certificate and began to teach drawing in Fitchburg. When her father was elected to the House of Representatives, Norcross accompanied him to Washington, DC, where she acted as his hostess. During this time, she also attended classes in New York City at the Art Students League, where she took painting courses from William Merritt Chase, a popular artist and teacher who suggested that Norcross go to Paris to study under Belgian artist Alfred Stevens. Thus, Norcross left for Paris, where she lived for 40 years. While in Paris, she exhibited her paintings, enjoying the city's culture and that of the rest of Europe as she traveled. Following his retirement, her father spent winters in Paris with her until his death in 1898. Norcross's paintings consisted of mainly portraits and, later, interiors; both were noted for their use of light and color, along with delicate brush strokes. Two of her most famous paintings feature her father. Throughout her artistic career, Norcross had hoped to open an art museum in Fitchburg and had been collecting accordingly. When she died from kidney failure, her will provided for a $100,000 trust to be used as her two Fitchburg friends, and executors, deemed appropriate. In accordance with her wish to establish an art museum in her hometown, the executors hired female architects to remodel an old stable that would become the Fitchburg Art Museum in 1929.

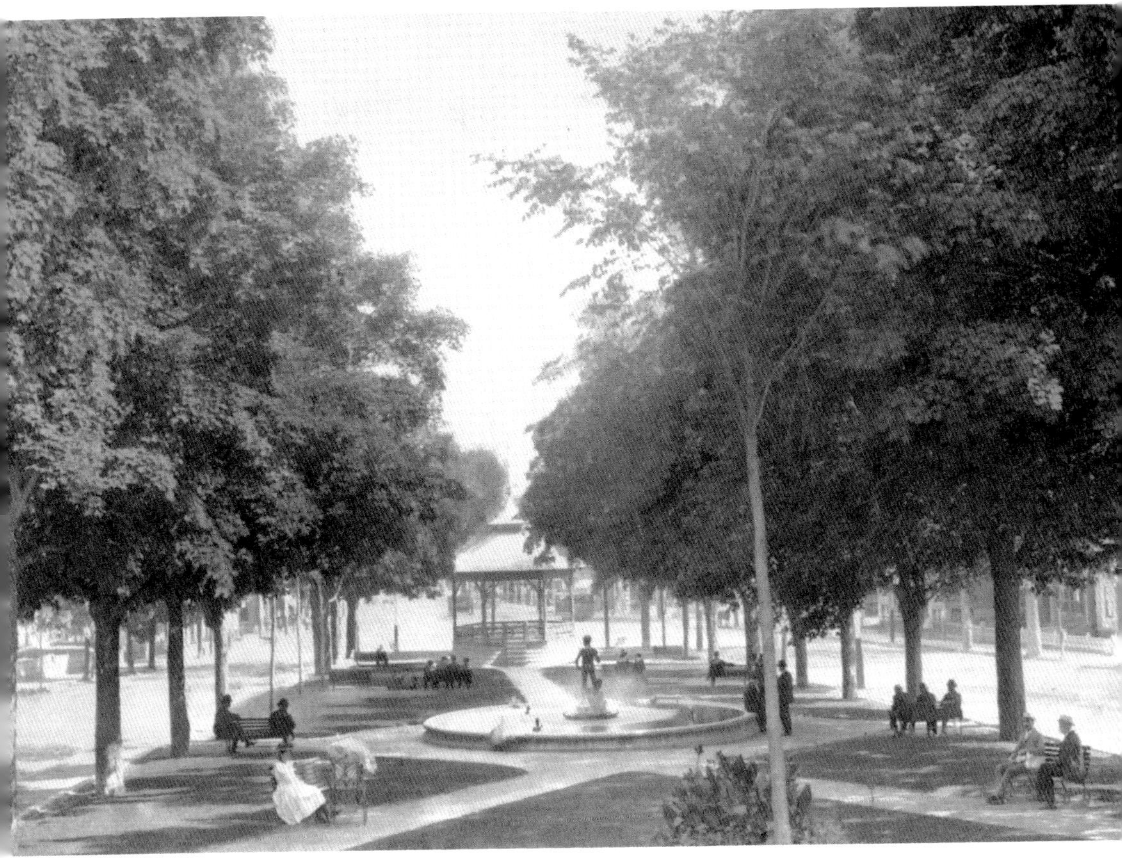

Samuel Herbert Adams (1858–1945)

Adams was born in Concord, Vermont. Herbert, as he wanted to be called, was the son of Samuel M. and Nancy A. (Powers) Adams. By the tender age of three, Adams was already exhibiting his love for art. His family moved to Chestnut Street in Fitchburg when Adams was five to be closer to his father's work as a pattern maker. Though Adams apprenticed in his father's machine pattern-making trade, he dedicated every spare minute of his time to the arts. At the age of 18, he was listed in the local directory as a taxidermist, a necessary skill for form and sculpting. In 1877, Adams entered the Massachusetts Normal Art School, where he met his wife, Adeline Valentine Pond. After formal schooling, he returned to teach art in the Fitchburg Public Schools. Two years later, Adams and his wife moved to Paris, where he gained his first honorable mention for the marble bust of Adeline. It has been noted that one can see the "sparkle in her eyes, the promise of a smile, and remarkable softness in the cheeks of the bust." In 1889, Adams was commissioned to create the 68-inch *Boys and the Turtles* sculpture seen on the Fitchburg Common. Later, he also sculpted *Winged Victory*, the World War I monument on the common. Between those years, more than 400 works graced cities across the nation. The US Senate and Library of Congress in Washington, DC, hold dozens of his works. Adams was commissioned to finish the 3.5-ton bronze doors for the Library of Congress when his good friend Olin Warner, who had originally been commissioned to create them, died suddenly. During Adams's lifetime, he completed more than 200 major public works of art and thus is considered one of the most important American sculptors.

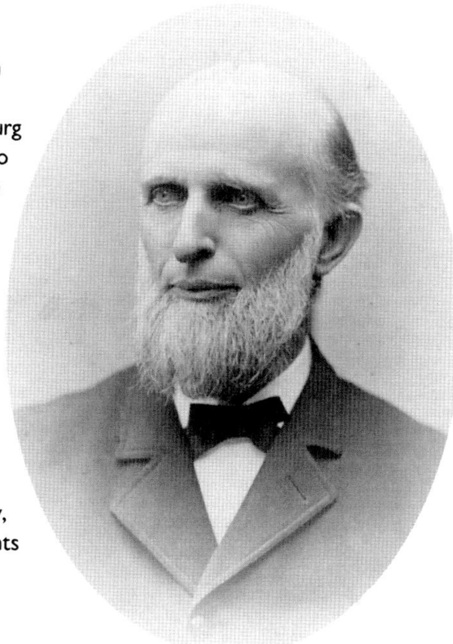

Joseph Carr Moulton (1824–1914)
Moulton settled in Fitchburg in 1848, moving his studio several times before finally settling on Main Street. In his lifetime, he took more than 40,000 photographs of various types as the medium changed over time. Known for his portraits and Civil War cabinet cards of soldiers leaving for war, he also photographed ordinary, and not-so-ordinary, events in the city.

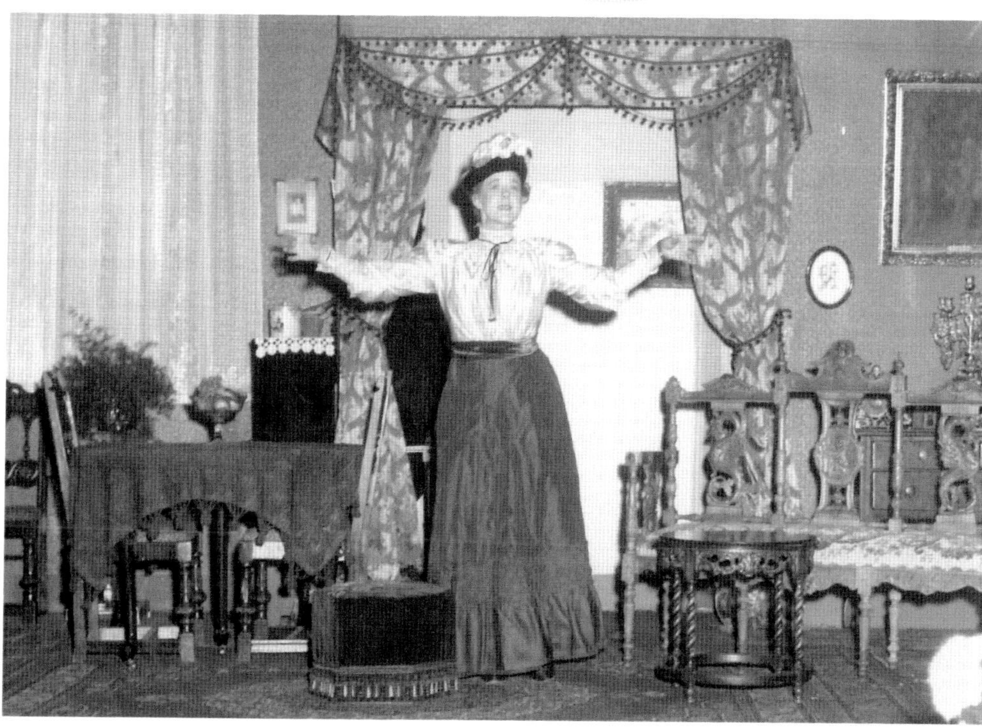

Miriam Lehto (1913–2003)
Lehto was born to Finnish immigrants in Fitchburg and was raised to speak both Finnish and English. Accordingly, she performed and directed both Finnish and English plays at Saima Park and the Stratton Theater, where she was active for 71 years. In 1992, the government of Finland awarded Lehto the Finnish Lion for her promotion of Finnish culture.

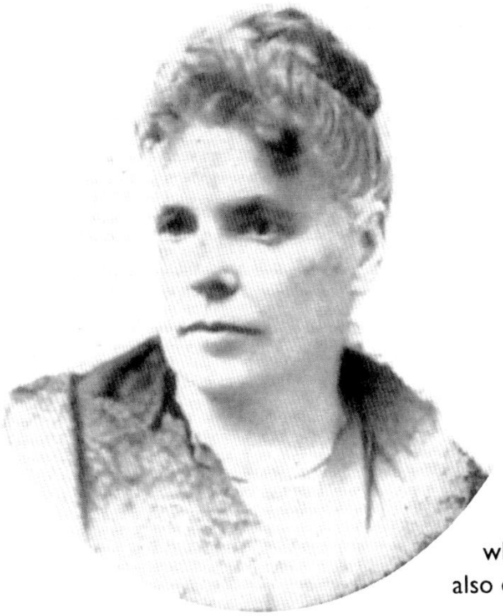

Sybil Augusta Dean Fairbanks (1839–1929)
Considered the artist of Dean Hill, where she lived, Fairbanks diligently recorded epitaphs and dates from the Dean Hill Cemetery tombstones. Fairbanks exhibited artistic talent as a child and later studied with impressionists John Joseph Enneking and F. Childe Hassam, along with Eleanor Norcross in Paris. After returning, she opened an art studio on Garnett Street, where she gave instruction and painted landscapes and portraits.

Zaydee Dejonge Harris (1898–1995)
Harris directed the Fitchburg Art Museum for 30 years. Born in New Jersey, she grew up in Fitchburg and studied at the School of Fine Arts, Crafts & Decorative Design in Boston, then in Europe. In 1942, Harris (facing the children) established an art department at Cushing Academy, where she taught for 26 years. Beginning in 1943, she also directed the art museum until her retirement.

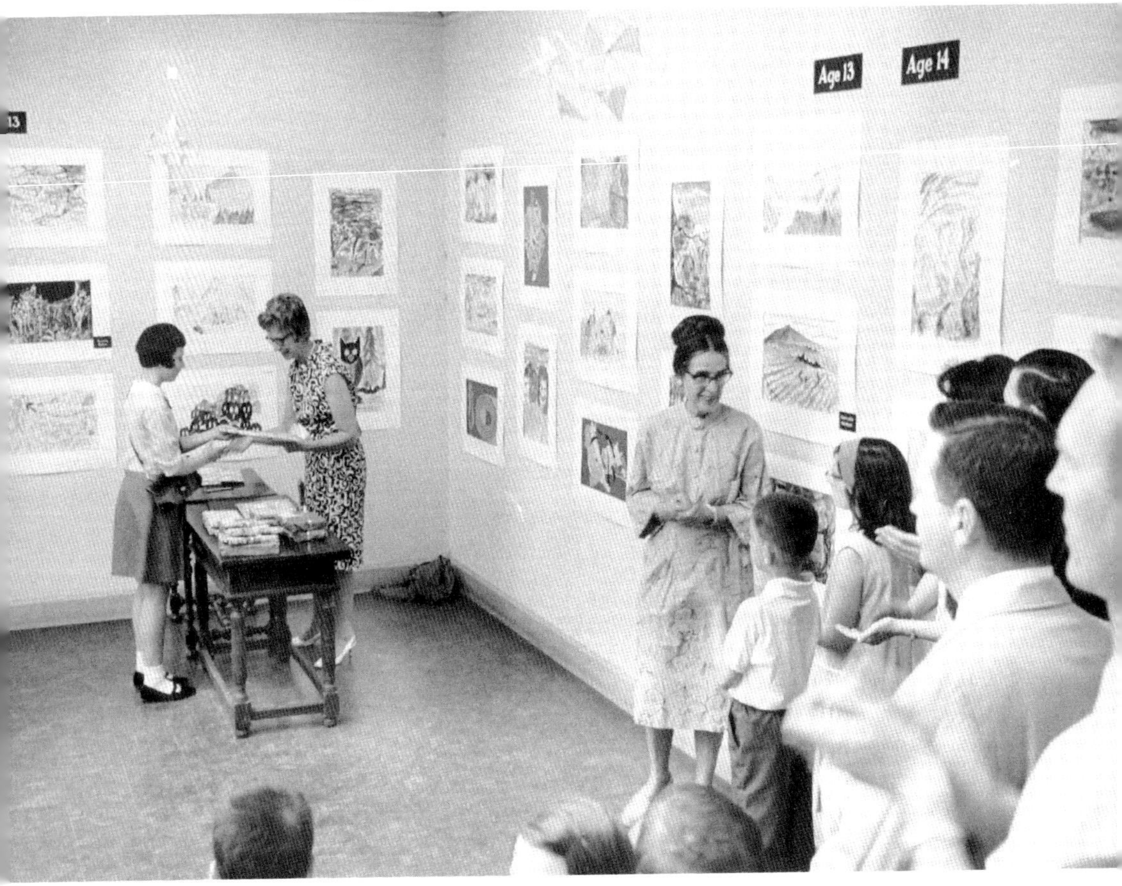

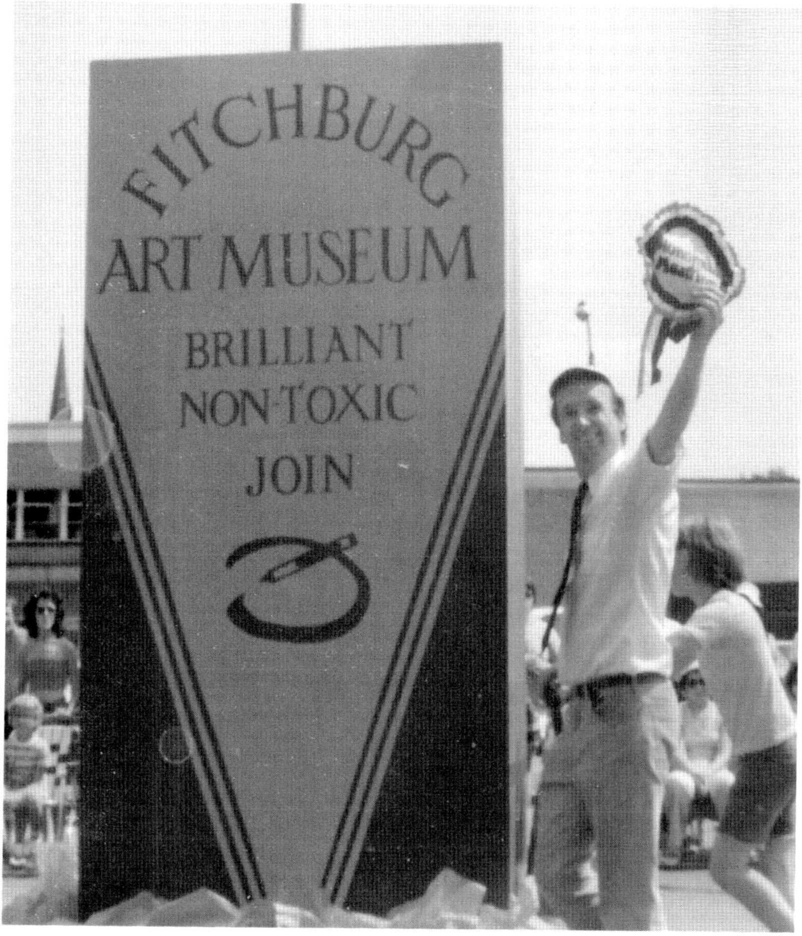

Peter Timms (1942–present)
The Fitchburg Art Museum is vastly different from when Peter Timms accepted the director position in 1973. What was primarily an art center, a single building with three galleries, has become a world-class museum under his directorship. When he retired in December 2012, he held the record as the longest-serving museum director in New England history. Timms, originally from Philadelphia, developed an interest in museums as an outgrowth of his archaeology training. When he applied for the Fitchburg position, he was performing graduate work at Harvard University. Immediately after his hiring, he and his wife, Romayne, an artist, left Cambridge, and he called on museum directors in the Boston area who came to his aid. Susannah Fabing, formerly of the Fogg Museum at Harvard University and later a Fitchburg Art Museum trustee, helped bring groups she called "Visiting Committees" together. These were working groups who met with the trustees and provided guidance to Peter in running a museum. Over his more than three decades, however, Peter proved that he could indeed run a museum, as evidenced by the many changes and additions he initiated: the building itself grew from 10,000 to 40,000 square feet; the numbers of annual visitors grew from 1,100 to 25,000; the budget increased from $50,000 to $800,000; and endowments grew to $17 million. The museum offers many classes, lectures, and special events and continues to have an excellent partnership with the city's schools and youth. He credits his no-nonsense approach as a museum director to his years as a Marine, serving in Vietnam in the mid-1960s. He has no regrets, and when he marched in the Fourth of July parade pictured above, he certainly had no idea how high he and the museum would soar. Peter and Romayne have three children and reside in Ashburnham. (Courtesy of Peter Timms.)

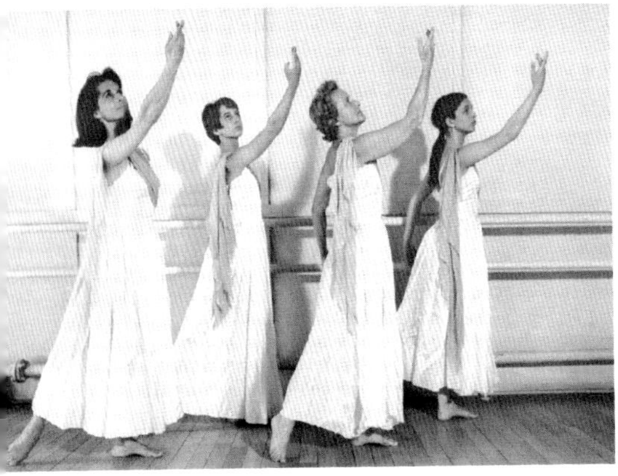

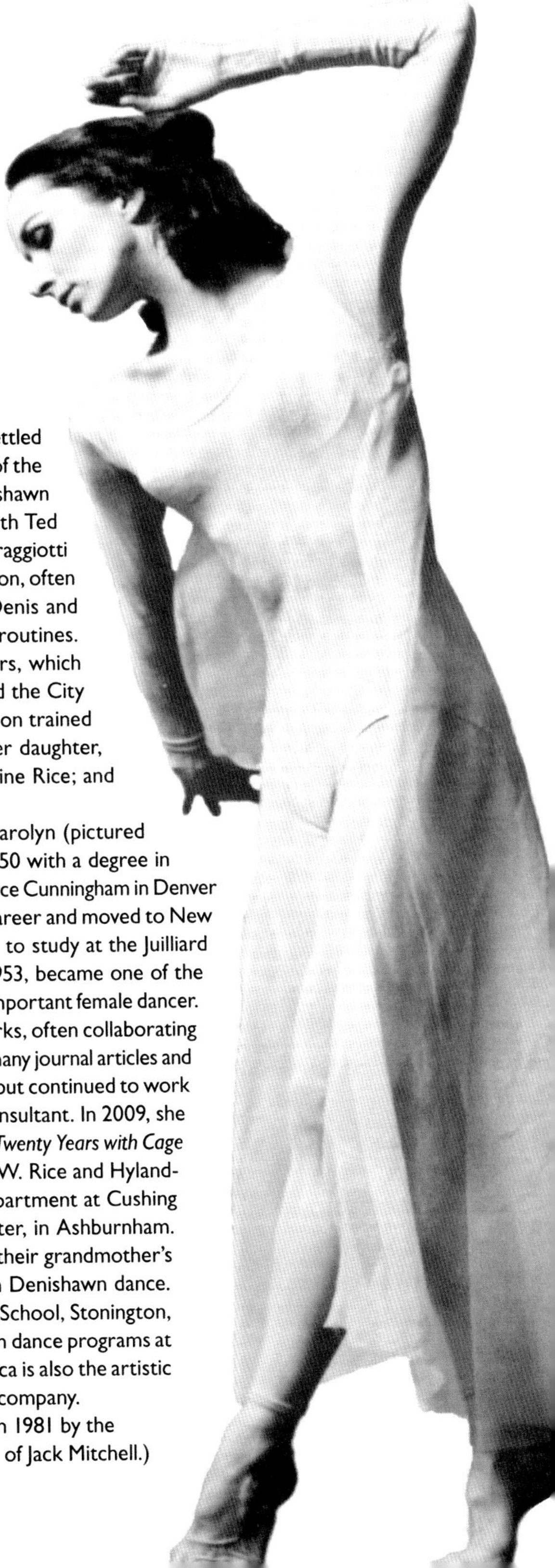

Marion Stevens Rice (1904–1995)

Originally from Hingham, Massachusetts, Marion settled in Fitchburg and founded the Marion Rice Studio of the Dance, where she taught and performed the Denishawn technique for more than 60 years. She studied with Ted Shawn, Ruth St. Denis, Miriam Winslow, and the Braggiotti sisters at the Braggiotti-Denishawn School in Boston, often performing and producing works by Ruth St. Denis and Ted Shawn as well as her own choreographed routines. She created the Marion Rice Denishawn Dancers, which performed at dance festivals at Jacob's Pillow and the City College of New York, among other venues. Marion trained many dancers and choreographers, including her daughter, Carolyn Rice Brown; daughter-in-law, Mona Irvine Rice; and granddaughters, Robin and Rebecca Rice.

A performer, writer, lecturer and teacher, Carolyn (pictured at right) graduated from Wheaton College in 1950 with a degree in philosophy. After attending a master class with Merce Cunningham in Denver in 1951, she decided to pursue a full-time dance career and moved to New York with her husband, composer Earle Brown, to study at the Juilliard School. She studied with Cunningham and, in 1953, became one of the founding members of his company and the most important female dancer. For the next 20 years, she danced in 40 of his works, often collaborating with Cunningham and John Cage. She has written many journal articles and received several awards. Carolyn retired in 1973 but continued to work with the Cunningham Company as an artistic consultant. In 2009, she published her memoir, *Chance and Circumstance: Twenty Years with Cage and Cunningham.* Mona, wife of J. Parker Rice (F.W. Rice and Hyland-Rice family businesses), founded the Dance Department at Cushing Academy as well as her studio, the Dance Center, in Ashburnham. Their daughters, Robin and Rebecca, have kept their grandmother's legacy alive by continuing to teach and perform Denishawn dance. Robin founded the dance program at Pine Point School, Stonington, Connecticut, and Rebecca developed the modern dance programs at MIT, Boston Ballet, and Dana Hall School. Rebecca is also the artistic director of Rebecca Rice Dance, a professional company.

January 18 was declared "Marion Rice Day" in 1981 by the mayors of Fitchburg and Leominster. (Courtesy of Jack Mitchell.)

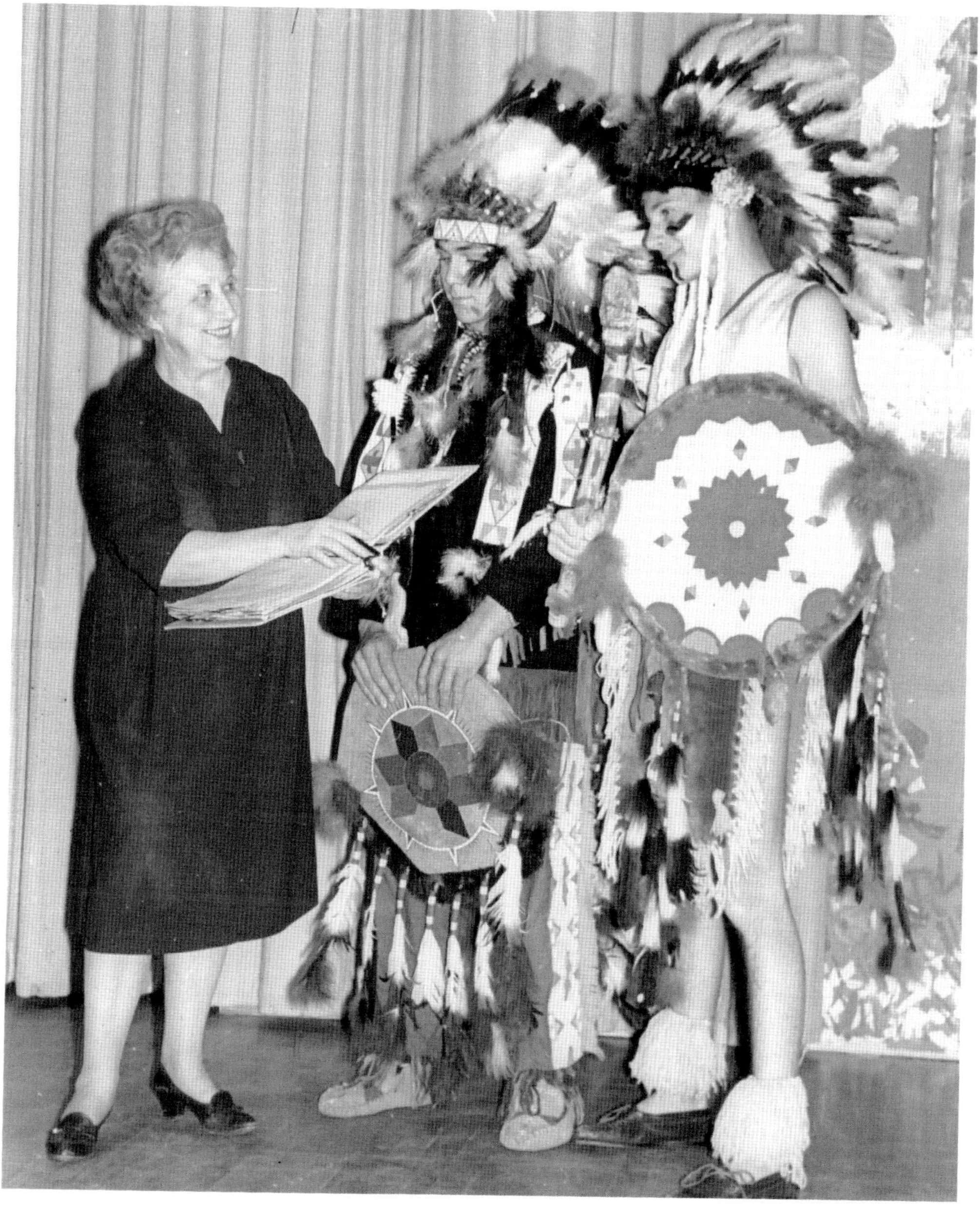

Martha Daly (1904–1993)

An amateur theater promoter, Daly was born in Attleboro and grew up in Fitchburg. In 1934, Daly joined the Workshop, also known as the Stratton Players. She directed her first play four years later, when the Stratton Players converted the barn on Wallace Avenue into the Stratton Theater. Her extensive background in set design was helpful when she had to choose plays with simple sets. Daly directed 64 plays, often with husband John, an electrician, as lighting director. During one of these plays, *The Fantasticks* in November 1963, Stratton canceled a performance after President Kennedy's assassination. She always had a knack for encouraging the best from performers. During World War II, Daly served the Red Cross as an entertainer. She was also an avid golfer, bridge player, and member of the Actors Equity, Women's Club, Fitchburg Art Museum, and Fitchburg Historical Society.

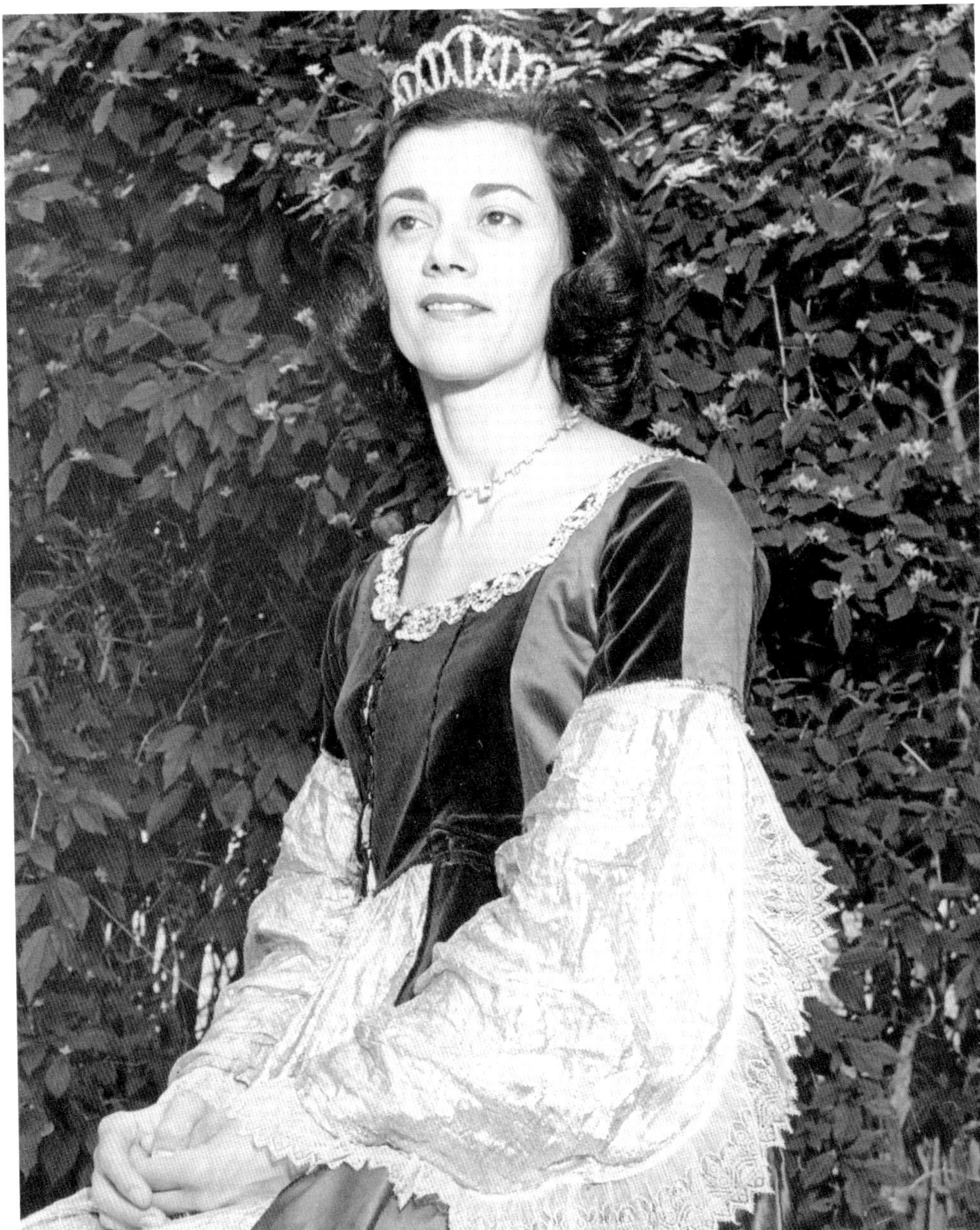

Janet Mirijanian Cragin (1932–present)
A moving force in the city's cultural life, Cragin was born in Fitchburg. She graduated from Fitchburg High School and studied at the American Academy of Dramatic Arts in New York City. Cragin continued her education at the Fitchburg State Teachers College. For 36 years, Cragin was a teacher and the drama director at Applewild School. Since October 1962, she has been a member of the Stratton Players. Her first role was Rebecca in *Our Town* in 1963, and she has acted in or directed more than 100 Stratton Theater productions. She is a founding member of the Fitchburg Cultural Alliance, established in 1976, and in a recent honor by the alliance, annual scholarships named for Cragin are given to young people in the Fitchburg Public Schools.

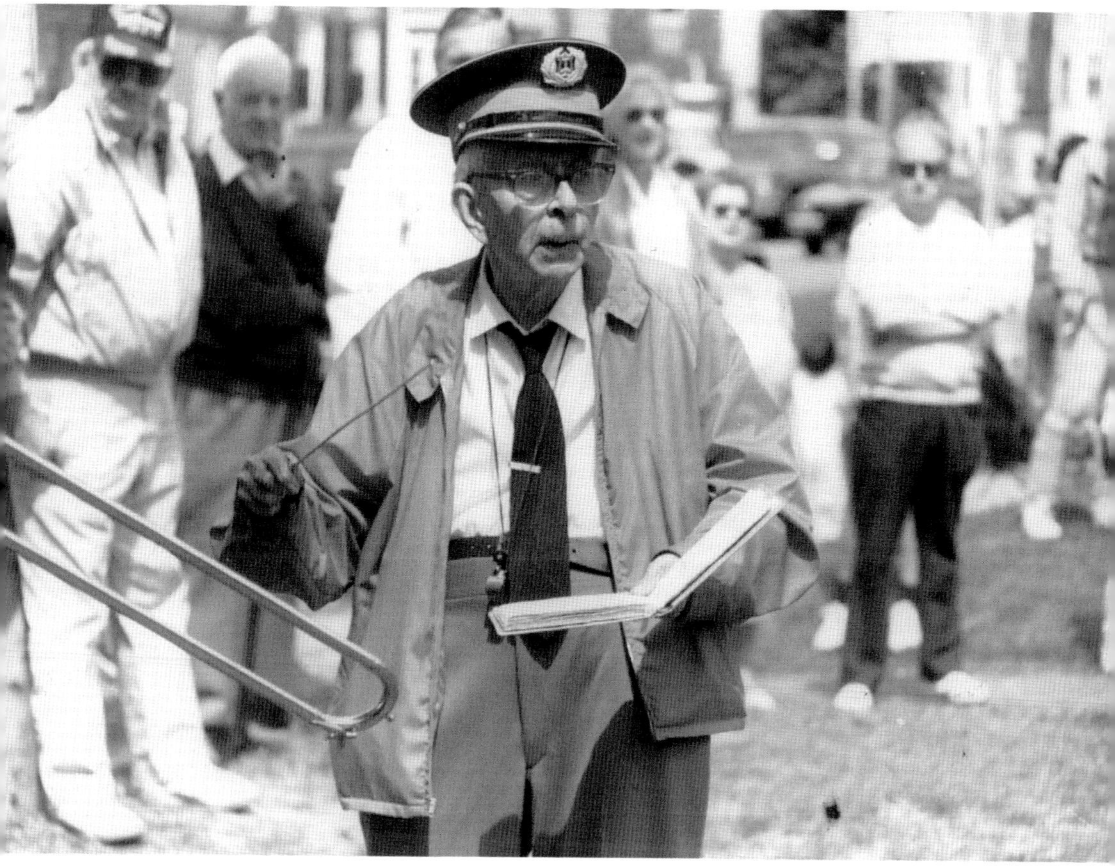

George S. Talcott (1904–1990)
Talcott was born in Worcester, and his family moved to Fitchburg as he entered sixth grade. That same year, he joined his first band, organized from the student body of the practical arts building at the Fitchburg Normal School. In 1924, he entered the Fitchburg Normal School and was assigned to assist J. Edward Bouvier in directing the new Fitchburg High School band, which he continued for 27 years. He became the band director for Fitchburg Public Schools until he retired in 1971. Talcott served in, founded, and led several bands across Massachusetts, including the American Legion Band, the Westminster Town Band, the Lunenburg Town Band, and the Townsend Military Band. After his retirement, he continued to direct various bands in central Massachusetts until he passed away in 1990.

Jacques Aubuchon (1924–1991)

The son of Arthur and Flora Aubuchon, Jacques Aubuchon was born in Fitchburg. His proficiency in French led to his being an interpreter during World War II with the French Forces Signal Center Language Team. In 1948, Aubuchon followed his first love of acting and attended the American Theater Wing for Advanced Studies. Aubuchon became a character actor, appearing in more than 300 television shows, 30 movies, and 10 stage productions. One of his best-known roles was Chief Urulu on *McHale's Navy.* Hometown fans followed Aubuchon's career, with articles that referred to him as "Fitchburg's own" and identified his appearances in film, television shows, and on stage.

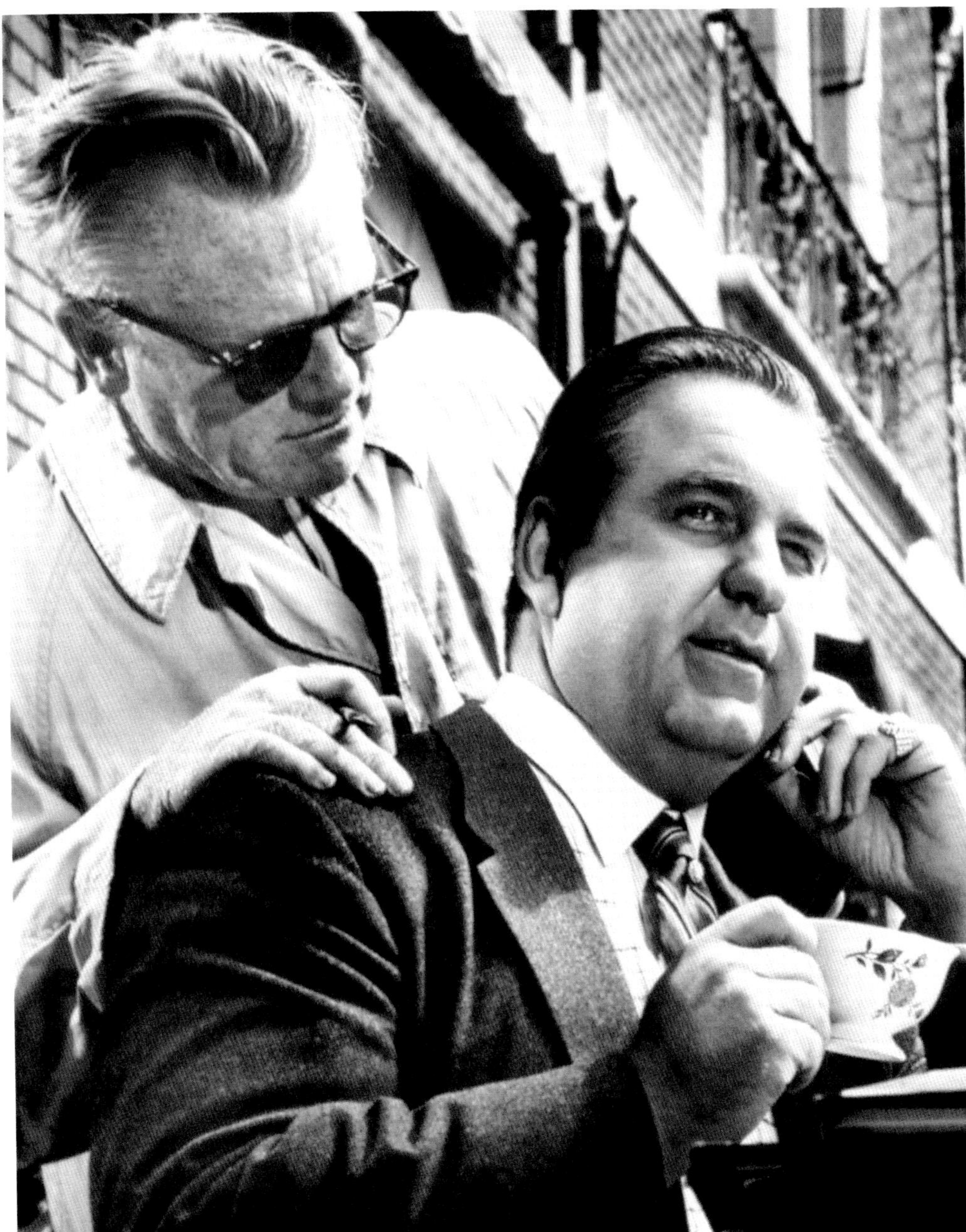

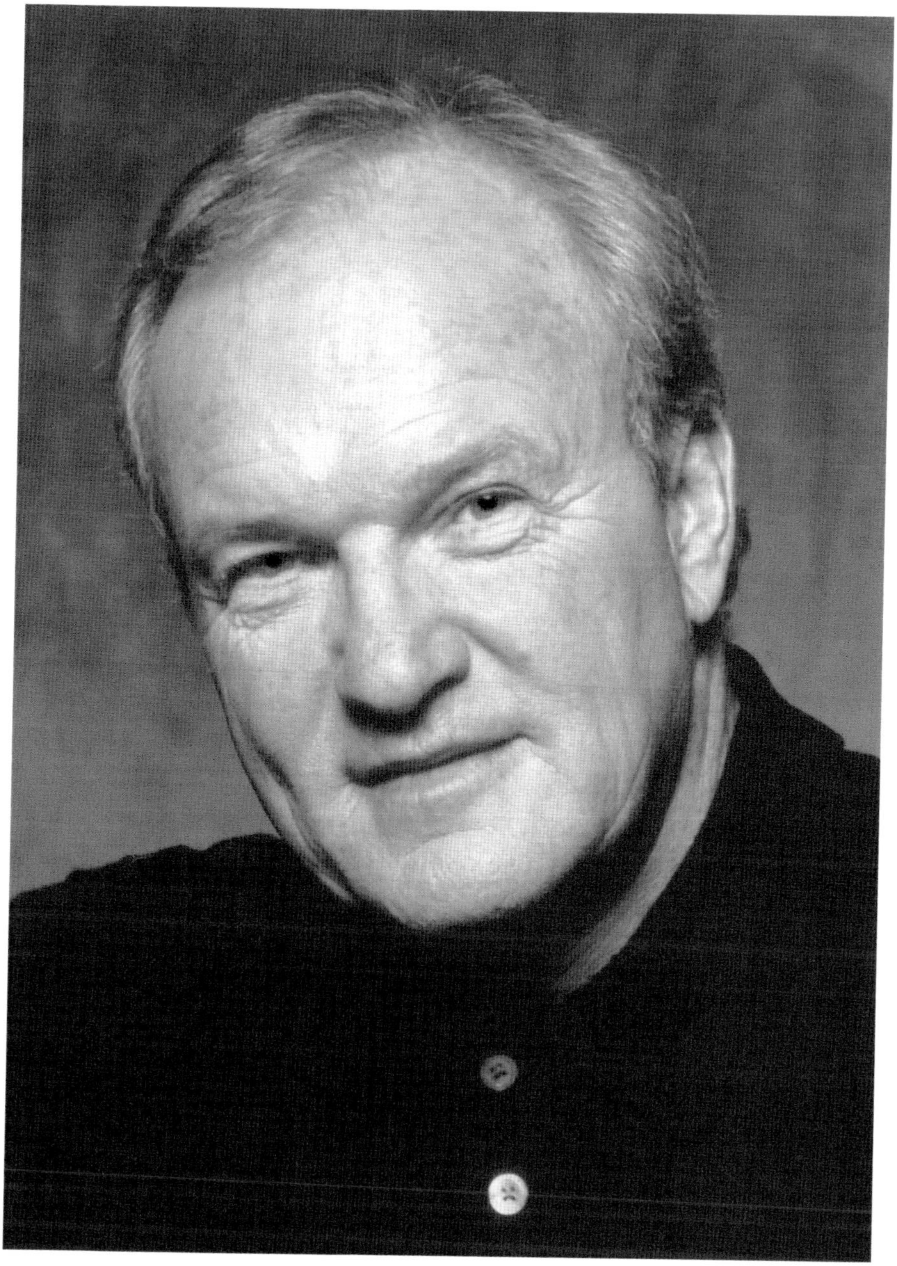

Michael "Mike" Barnicle (1943–present)
Barnicle was born in Worcester and raised in Fitchburg. After graduating from Boston University in 1965, he began writing for the *Boston Globe* in 1973 and wrote for the paper for 25 years, during which time he became well known for both his political insight, on local and national issues, and his features on the struggles of everyday families. His reporting helped the *Boston Globe* earn a Pulitzer Prize for Public Service in 1975. In 1998, Barnicle became the subject of controversy when he was accused of plagiarizing and using false information in his columns. The scandal led to his resignation, but he continues to write for the *New York Daily News* and the *Boston Herald*. In addition to newspaper work, Barnicle has also been featured on television news programs, appearing regularly on MSNBC. (Courtesy of Washington Speakers Bureau.)

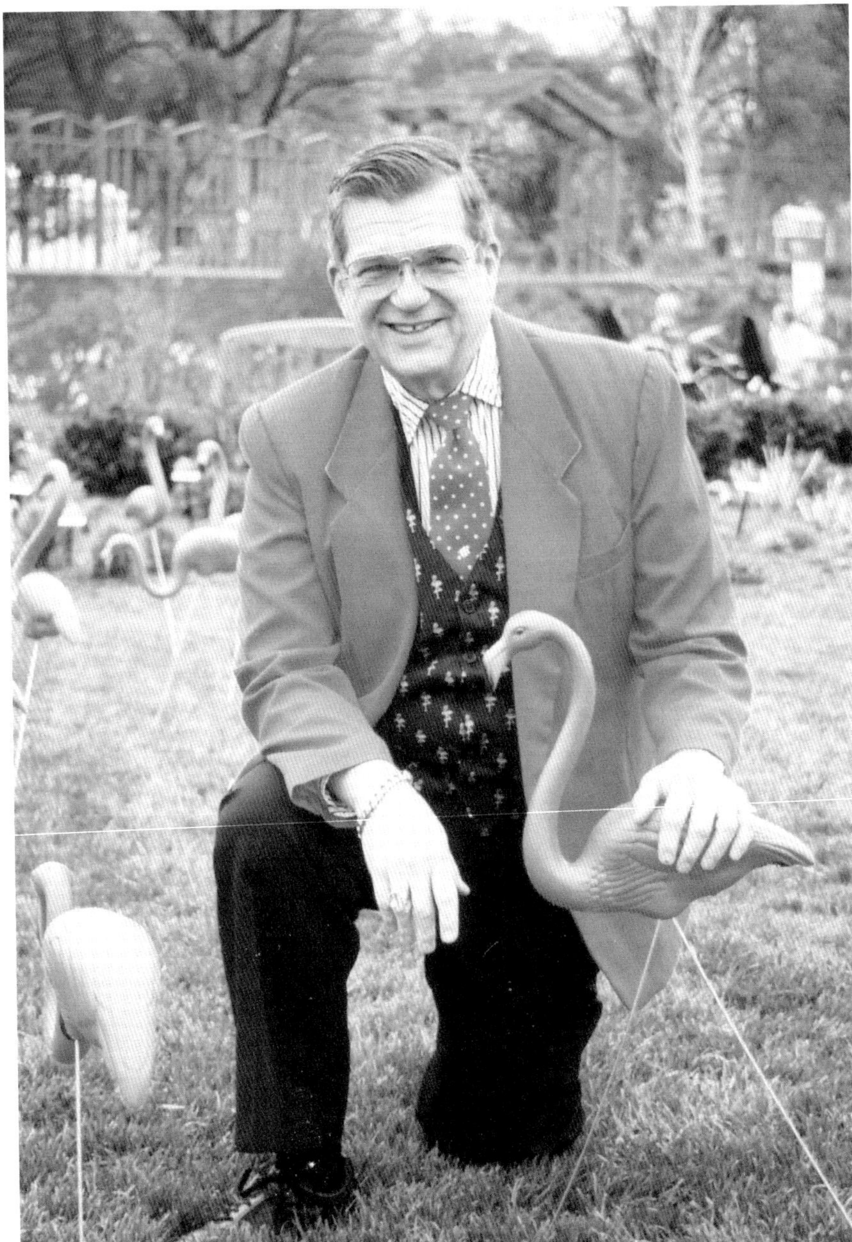

Donald "Don" Featherstone (1936–present)
Featherstone, who attended the School of the Worcester Art Museum, is an artist living in Fitchburg with his wife, Nancy. At Union Products in Leominster, he created the designs for 750 molded lawn ornaments. At first, he designed a duck, using a live model, Charlie, who was released to Coggshall Park upon his retirement. Featherstone's most beloved creation is the plastic pink flamingo, the original mold of which was inscribed with his signature. When the company removed his signature in 2001, consumers boycotted the unsigned flamingos until his signature reappeared. Currently, the Cado Manufacturing Company in Fitchburg produces the flamingos. Disney's recent film *Gnomeo & Juliet* (2011) used Featherstone's original design to create the flamingo character, appropriately named "Featherstone."

CHAPTER EIGHT

Athletic Leaders

Alma Mater so true, we'll think oft of you
While climbing life's road to fame.
Mid sorrows and joys
Seeking virtue and poise
We'll endeavor to honor thy name.

—*Labor Omnia Vincit* by Gladys Crouch, class of 1926

Fitchburg has always been known for producing great athletes. Born in the 1870s, two baseball legends left Fitchburg in the early 1900s and made it into baseball record books. In 1902, James Joseph "Nixey" Callahan pitched the first no-hitter in American League history, and in 1919, Patrick Joseph "Pat" Moran, as manager of the Cincinnati Reds, defeated the Chicago White Sox to win the World Series. From 1913 to 1938, Clarence Amiott, as coach and athletic director, guided his high school players to great heights like the 1926 national basketball championship while instilling strong values in them as part of his winning philosophy. John Chalmers, a Rhodes Scholar, and Carl Fellows, recognized as the US Naval Academy's finest athlete in 1935, excelled under Coach Amiott. Among Fitchburg's accomplished athletes are Olympians Erkki Koutonen and Erika Lawler, as well as Carmelita Landry Bernard and Arthur M. Longsjo Jr., who are both in the National Speed Skating Hall of Fame. She won the North American Speed Skating Championship in 1941 and 1942, and Longsjo holds the distinction of being the first American to participate in the Winter and Summer Olympics in the same year (1956). Longsjo is also in the United States Bicycling Hall of Fame.

The athletes of Fitchburg include Randy Thomas, who was once ranked the No. 5 marathoner in the world and Ronald "Ron" Bouchard, who held the NASCAR Rookie of the Year title in 1981. Each athlete here has shown great character, perseverance, and determination, not only in their respective sport but also in their lives.

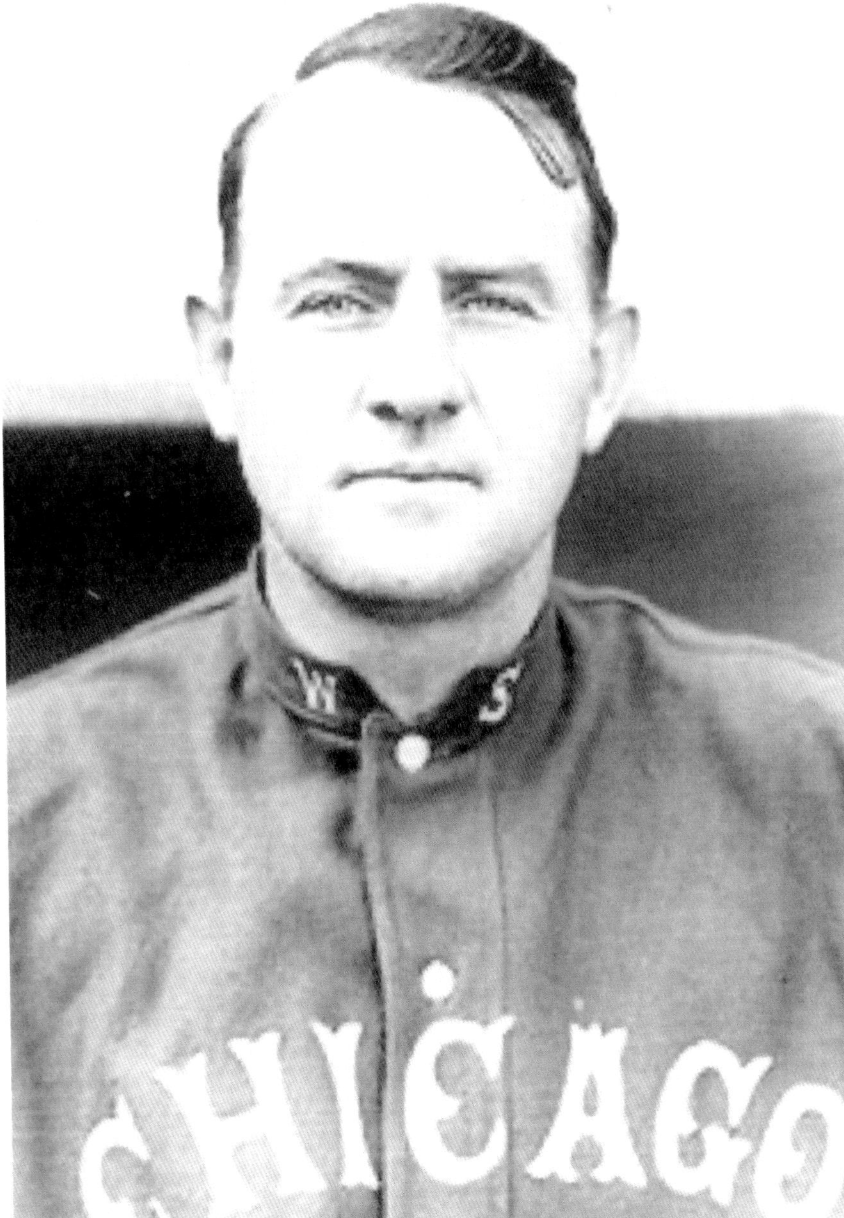

James Joseph "Nixey" Callahan (1874–1934)
Callahan was born in Fitchburg. At the age of 14, he dropped out of school and became a sewing machine boy to help his widowed mother. In his spare time, he played baseball. At 19, Callahan was signed by the Philadelphia Phillies as a pitcher and an outfielder. On September 20, 1902, while pitching for the Chicago White Sox, Callahan threw the first no-hitter in American League History. He later became the manager of the White Sox, from 1903 to 1904 and, again, from 1912 to 1914. He finished his career as the manager of the Pittsburgh Pirates. Callahan is buried at St. Bernard's Cemetery in Fitchburg.

Patrick "Pat" Moran (1876–1924)

Moran was born in Fitchburg. He became a National League catcher and, later, a manager for Major League Baseball. Moran played for the Boston Beaneaters, the Chicago Cubs, and the Philadelphia Phillies. In 1915, he became the manager of the Cincinnati Reds. He led them to win the World Series in 1919; however, it was marred by the fact that eight members of the White Sox conspired with gamblers to "throw the game," which became known as the Black Sox Scandal. Moran later died of Bright's disease. So revered was he that several of the Cincinnati players came to Crocker Field in 1925 and played in a game against a team of local all-stars to raise money for a memorial. Today, the Pat Moran Memorial still stands in West Fitchburg, honoring one of its own.

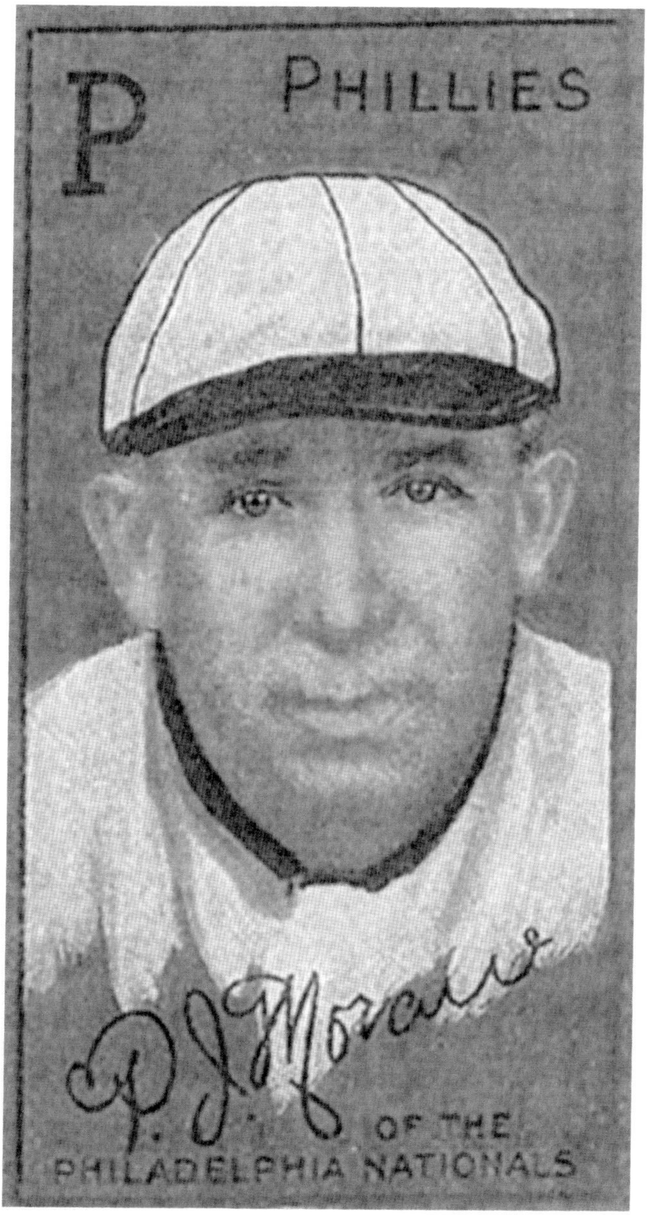

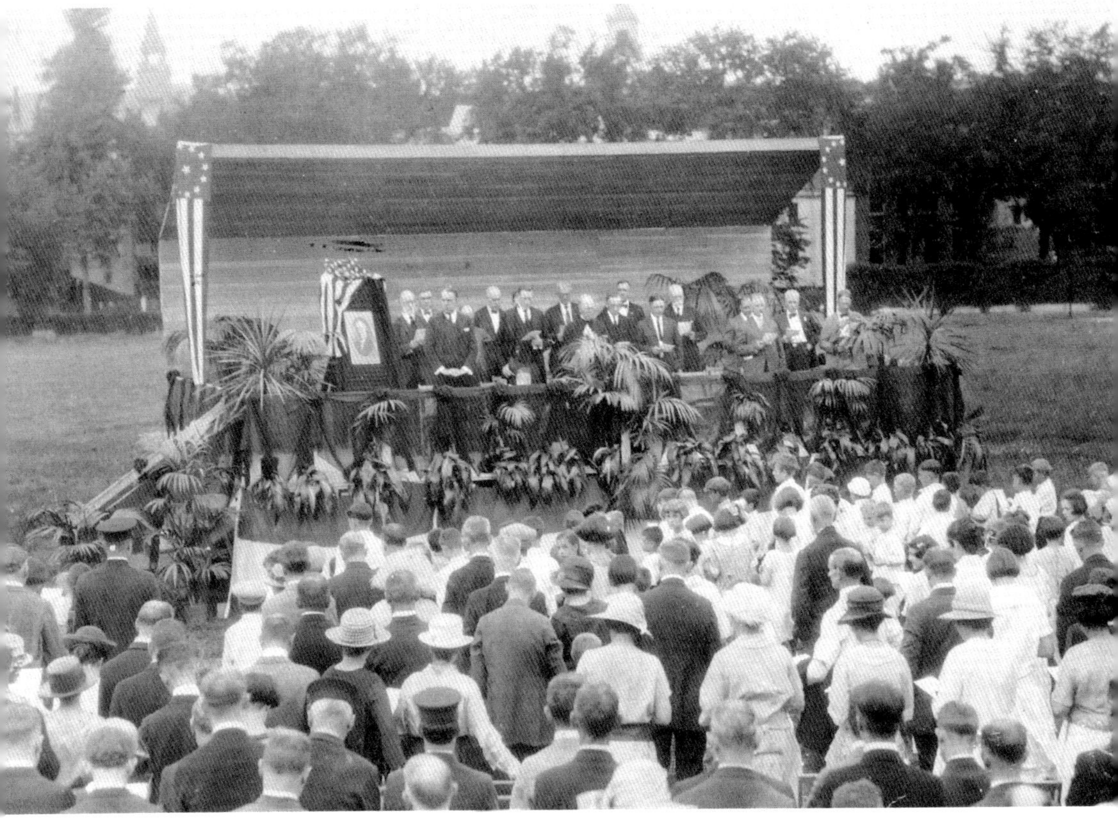

Crocker Field

Alvah Crocker II, a successful Fitchburg industrialist who felt a deep responsibility to the people of his community, began building the Crocker Field in 1917 after his wife, Charlotte, told him that the children did not have a place to play ball in town. Crocker visited the principal of Fitchburg High School and offered to build a field for the children near the river. He gave the principal, Charles T. Woodbury, $38,000 as a down payment. When the students heard the news, they marched from the school to the Crockers' home, singing songs and shouting their thanks to him. Crocker hired the Frederick Law Olmsted & Sons Landscaping Firm of Boston to do the work, as Frederick Sr. was known for designing Central Park in New York City. It took two years during World War I to build the field at a cost of $250,000.

Clarence N. Amiott (1891–1942)

Amiott is considered the most important person in Fitchburg High School sports. Two years after graduating from Fitchburg High School, Amiott was hired as the athletic director and head football coach. By 1924, Coach Amiott had developed a line of outstanding teams. That October, his football team played powerhouse Proviso High in Illinois and defeated them. On the way home, they were invited to the White House to meet Pres. Calvin Coolidge. Two years later, Coach Amiott and his basketball team returned to Illinois, where they won the National Championship. Amiott won 77 percent of his basketball games and 72 percent of his football games in his 25-year career. He was forced to retire at 48 due to heart problems. Amiott died in Florida and was buried there with full military honors.

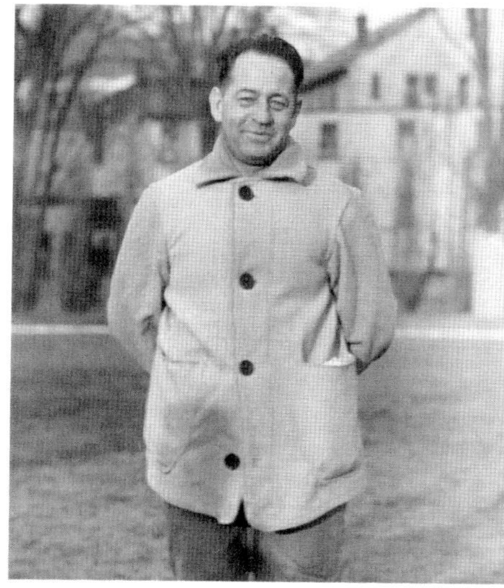

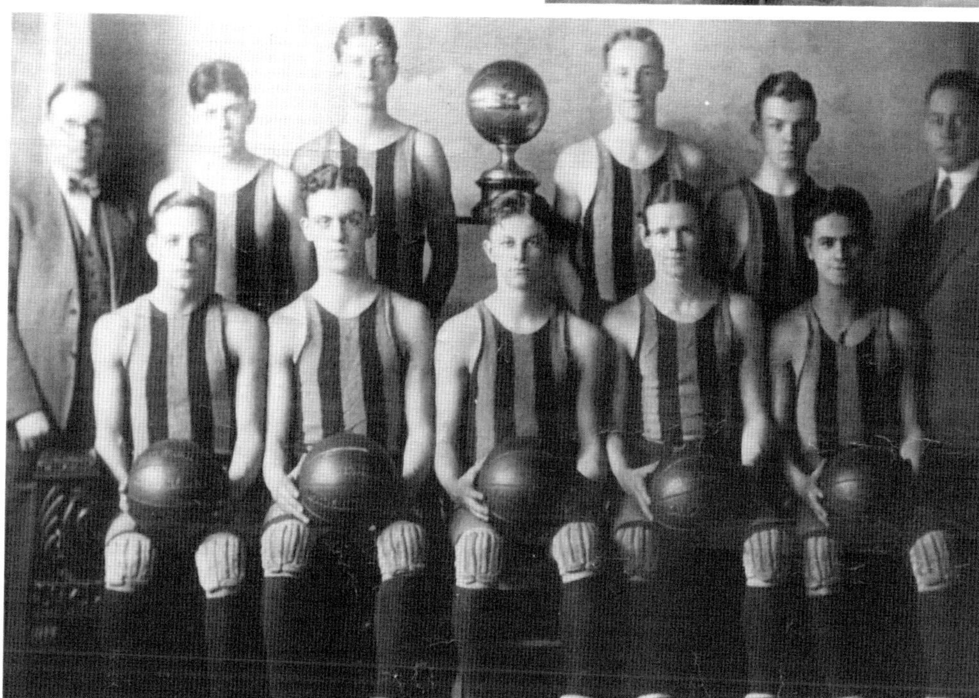

1926 Fitchburg High School Basketball Team

Coach Amiott led the Fitchburg High School basketball team all the way to the national championship in 1926. The team, made up of boys whose parents had emigrated from Europe, represented each ethnic group of Fitchburg. Some of Coach Amiott's best players were Lauri Myllykangas, the Finn; Johnny Oliva, the Italian; Anastos Fanos, the Greek; Dan Quinn, the Irishman; and David Allan, the Nova Scotian. Amos Alonzo Stagg established the Chicago National Tournament, where 40 teams were invited to play. In Chicago, Fitchburg defeated four teams before finally defeating Fargo, North Dakota, 25-14 to become the national champions. The team was given a gold-plated trophy and the five game balls from each tournament win. In 1974, the surviving players allowed the basketball used in the final game against Fargo to be given to the Naismith Memorial Basketball Hall of Fame in Springfield, Massachusetts, where it remains today.

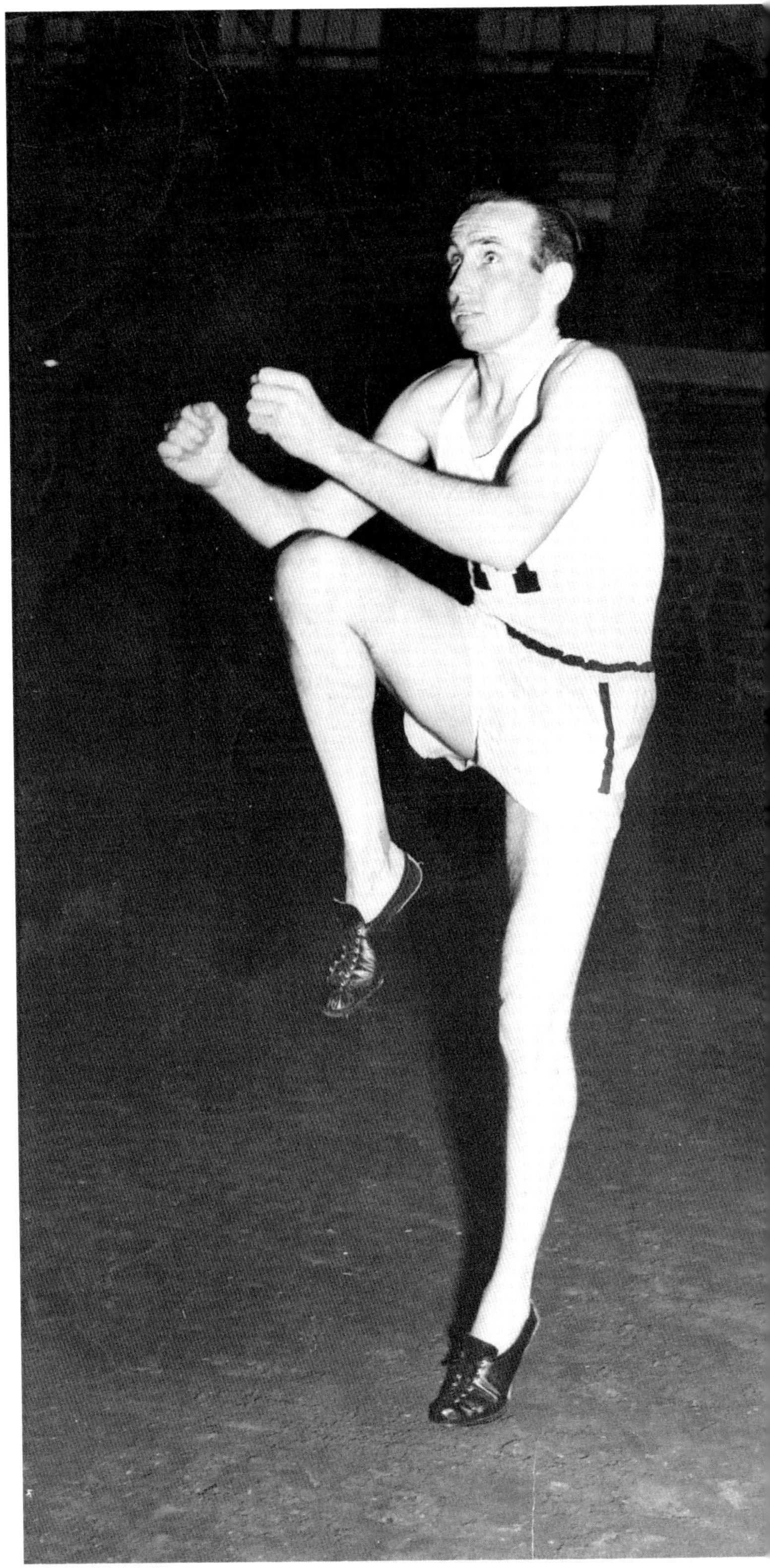

Erkki Koutonen (1927–1987)
Koutonen was born in Finland in 1927 and came to Fitchburg at age 11. Before graduating from Fitchburg High School, he was drafted into the Marines. While serving in the Pacific, he received his high school diploma and his US citizenship papers. Koutonen went to the University of Michigan in 1947 and qualified for the 1948 US Olympic Team when he came in first at the national championship in Illinois. Koutonen participated in the hop, step, and jump, which would later be called the triple jump. After the London Olympics, he finished his degree at the Fitchburg State Teachers College. He went on to teach industrial arts and coach track-and-field at Fitchburg High School for 30 years, until his death in 1987. Koutonen was inducted into the Massachusetts Track & Field Coaches' Hall of Fame in 1977. (Courtesy of John Koutonen.)

Carmelita Landry Bernard (1917–2002)

Bernard was born in Canada and moved to Fitchburg when she was six years old. A year later, her face was badly burned as she watched a friend drop a lit match into a gas tank. Doctors managed to salvage her face from disfigurement and save her left eye, but she lost complete sight in her right eye. At the age of 11, she took up skating. By 17, Bernard had begun speed skating and won the New England championship that year. In 1941 and 1942, she won the North American Speed Skating Championships. In all, she won 16 titles and 23 championships. She retired in 1944 and married Edward Bernard. In 1969, she was inducted into the National Speed Skating Hall of Fame, and in 1972, the Carmelita Landry Bernard Skating Arena in Fitchburg was named in her honor.

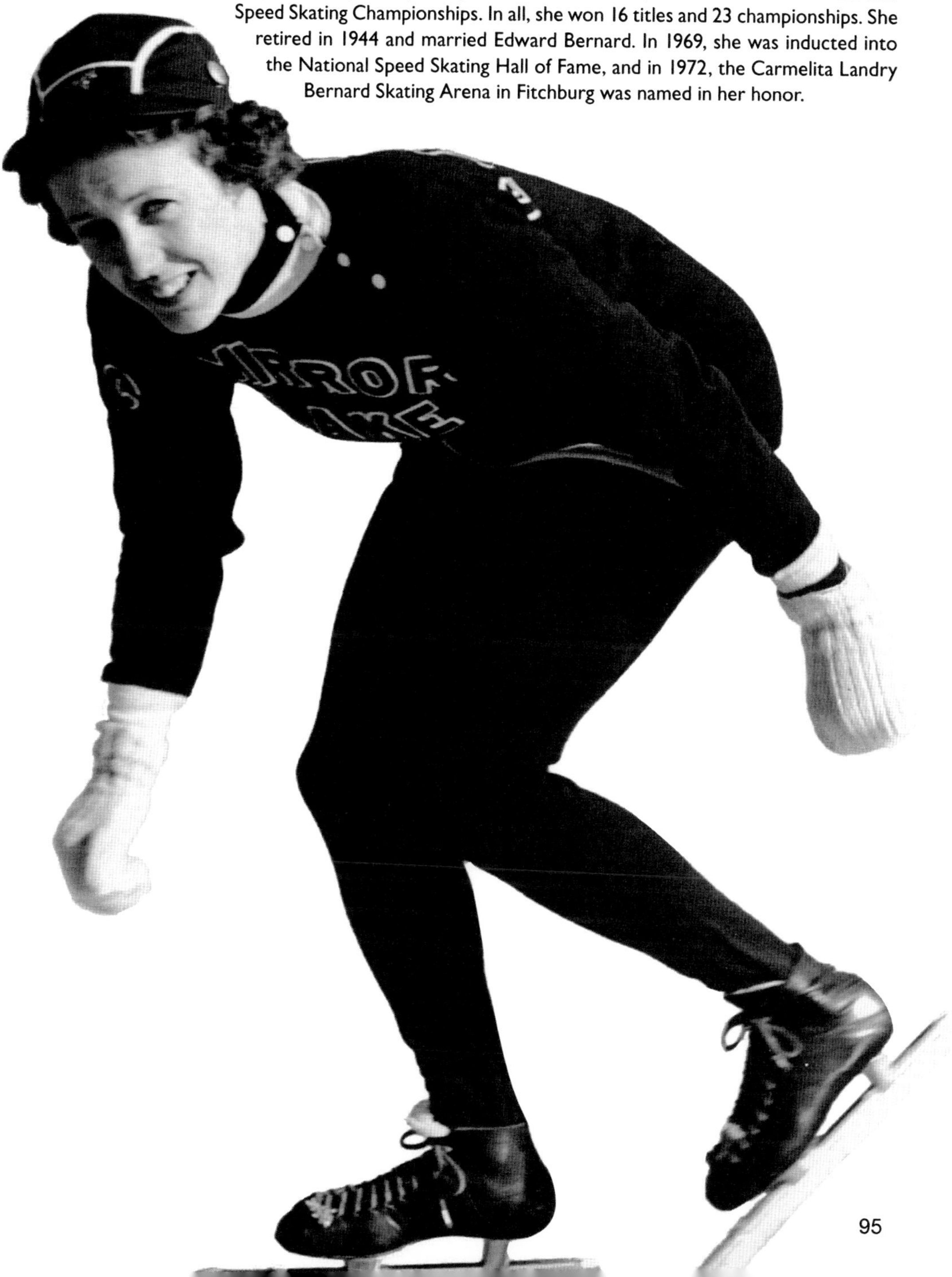

Arthur M. "Art" Longsjo Jr. (1931–1958)

Longsjo was born in Fitchburg, where he spent most of his youth racing on frozen ponds, but when he turned 21, he divided his attention between skating and cycling, both of which became his passion. Longsjo won the first bicycle race he entered, the Massachusetts state championship, in 1953. In 1956, he held the distinction of being the first American to ever compete in both the Summer and Winter Olympics in the same year. Longsjo won the 5,000-meter race at the US national championship in St. Louis to qualify for the 1956 Winter Olympics in Cortina, Italy; however, he became ill before the race and finished outside the medal finals. That summer, he competed in the 4,000-meter team pursuit event in the Melbourne, Australia, Olympics for the United States, but his team did not place. Longsjo spent most of 1957 recovering from a broken leg, but the following year, he came back stronger than ever. That fall, while competing in eastern Canada, he won the 500-mile Tour du Saint-Laurent and the one-day, 165-mile bicycle race from Quebec City to Montreal. While heading back home to Fitchburg after these wins, Longsjo was killed in a car accident in Burlington, Vermont, on September 16, 1958, just six weeks shy of his 26th birthday. He left a young wife, Terry Longsjo. In 1960, with the help of his wife, the people of Fitchburg organized a bicycle race in his honor that continued each year. It grew to become the Fitchburg Longsjo Classic, one of America's oldest continuous races, held annually in July. Longsjo was inducted into the National Speed Skating Hall of Fame in New York in 1970, then the United States Bicycling Hall of Fame in California in 1988. Longsjo is buried with his parents at Forest Hill Cemetery.

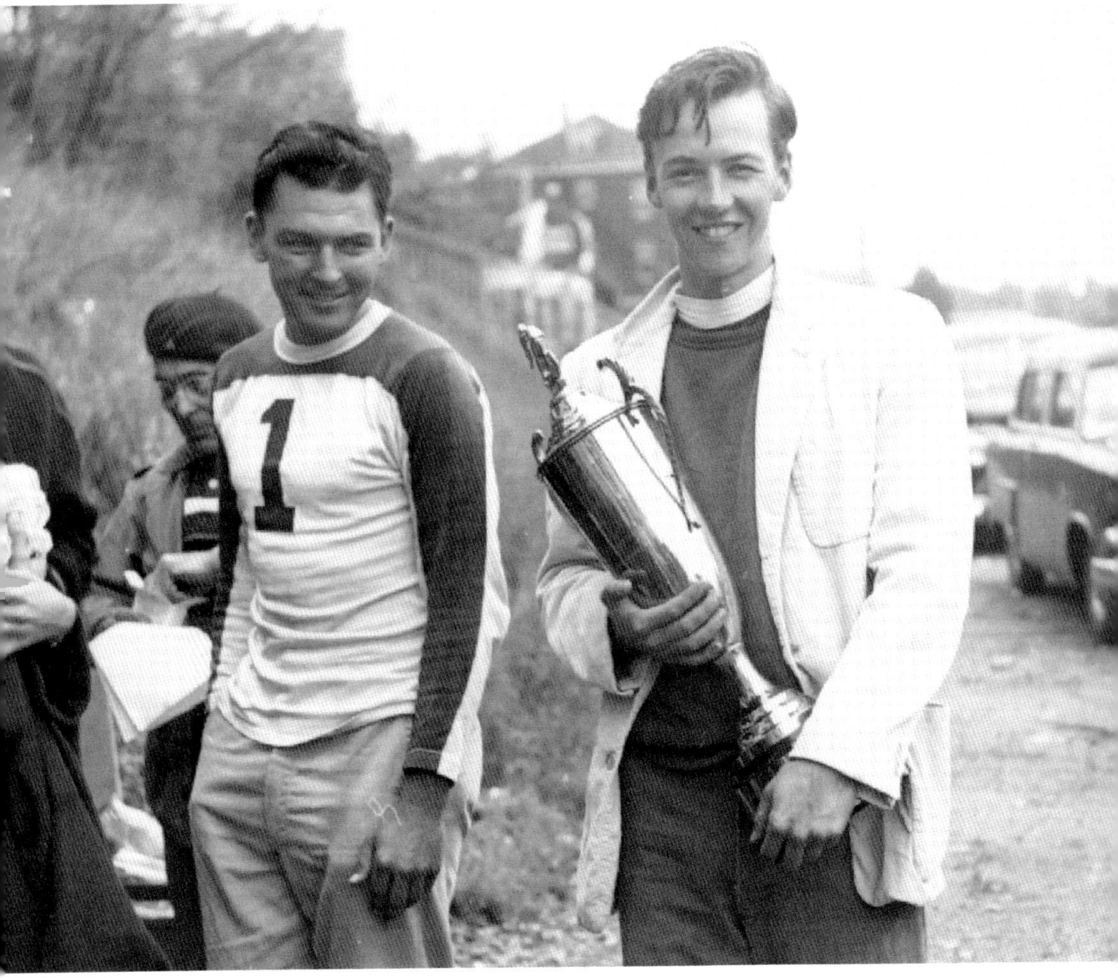

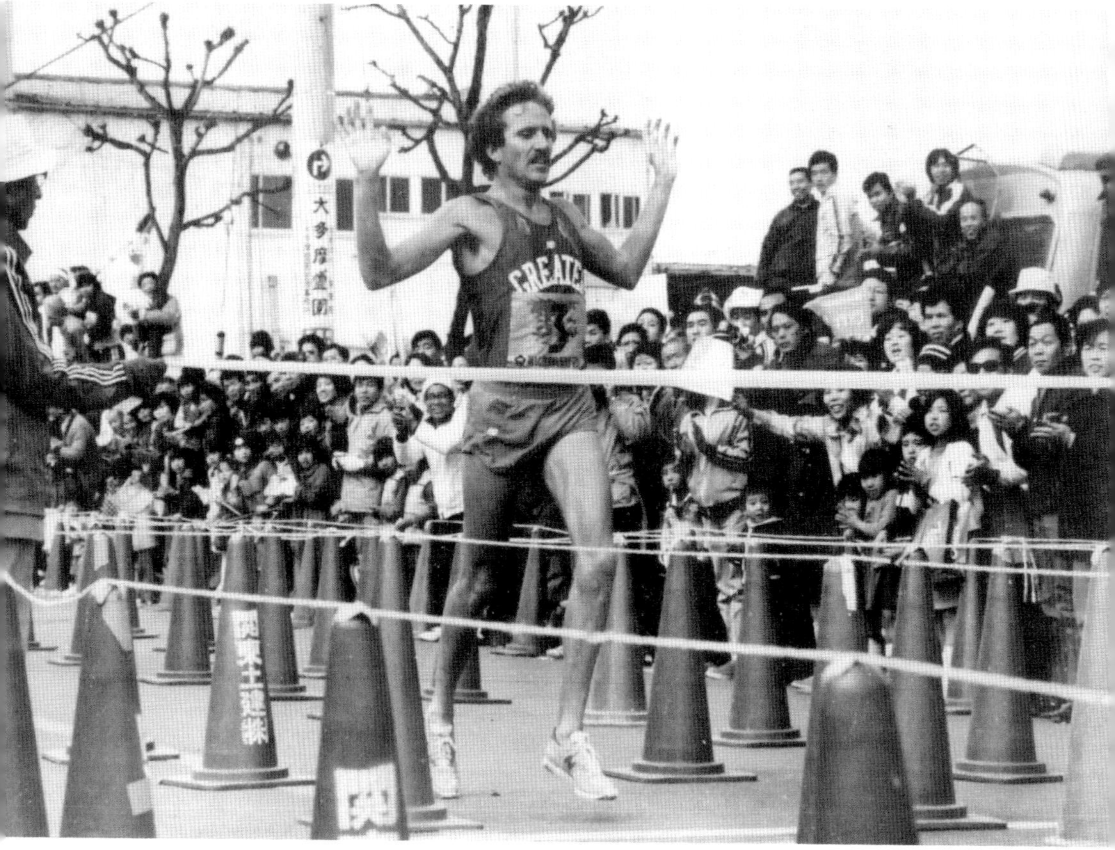

Randy Thomas (1952–present)
Thomas was born in Fitchburg. In 1968, he qualified for the state championship cross-country finals and finished in twelfth place. Thomas went to the University of Massachusetts, where he was named all-American. Between 1977 and 1980, he set the US record in track history for the 10,000 meter (also a world record), the 15,000 meter, the 20,000 meter, the 30,000 meter (another world record), the 10 mile, and the half marathon. In 1978, Thomas finished fifth in the Boston Marathon; he was ranked as the No. 5 best marathoner in the world and as the No. 8 fastest roadrunner. In 1987, he was appointed the head cross-country coach at Boston College, where he has led the women's cross-country team to 13 NCAA Championships.

John Chalmers (1916–2008)

Born in Fitchburg, Chalmers was known for his intelligence on and off the field. In 1933, he was the quarterback of the undefeated Fitchburg High School football team and a star basketball player. Chalmers was an undergraduate at Middlebury College, then became a Rhodes Scholar at Oxford University, and earned a doctorate degree at Cornell. He went on to teach at Kansas State University, where a building is now dedicated to him.

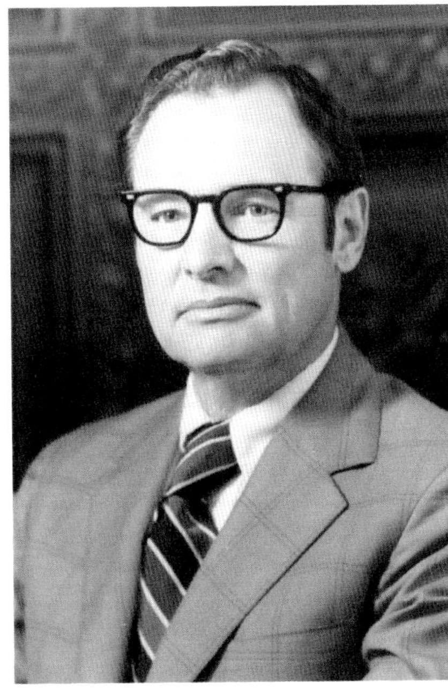

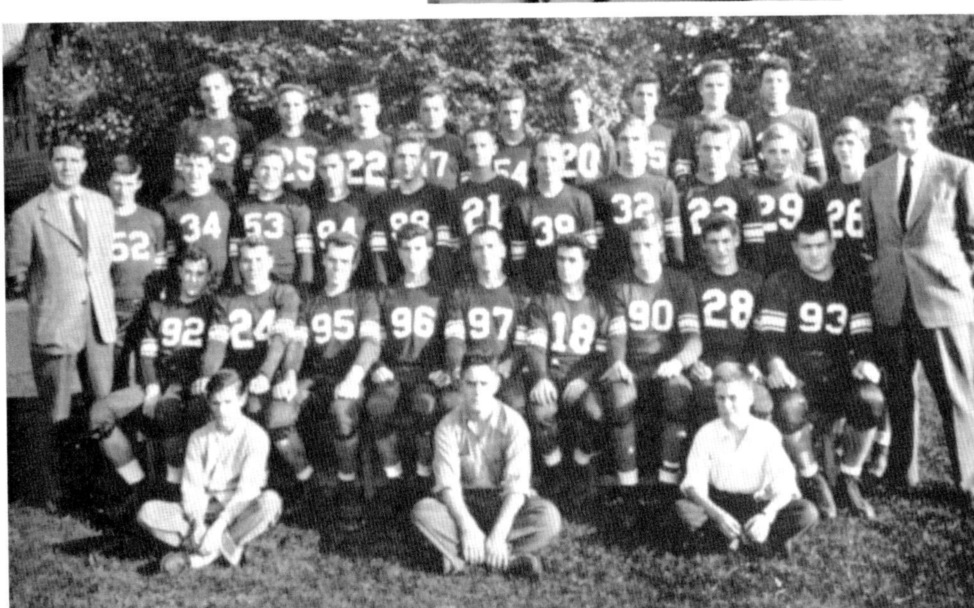

James Davis "Jim" Meredith (1933–1962)

Meredith was born to British immigrants in Fitchburg. He was a standout on the Fitchburg High School varsity football and baseball teams. After graduating in 1950, Meredith (second from the right, back row) went to Boston University, where he starred as a linebacker. In 1954, he enlisted in the Army Airborne Division as a first lieutenant. While training as a paratrooper in Germany, he took a hard landing and broke his leg, then developed cancer, which eventually led to amputation. After his recovery and discharge, Meredith returned to Fitchburg as a teacher and football coach at Fitchburg High School. Coach Meredith was loved by all. In 1962, he was again diagnosed with cancer, and this time, he did not recover. He died at the age of 29 and was buried with full military honors at Forest Hill Cemetery.

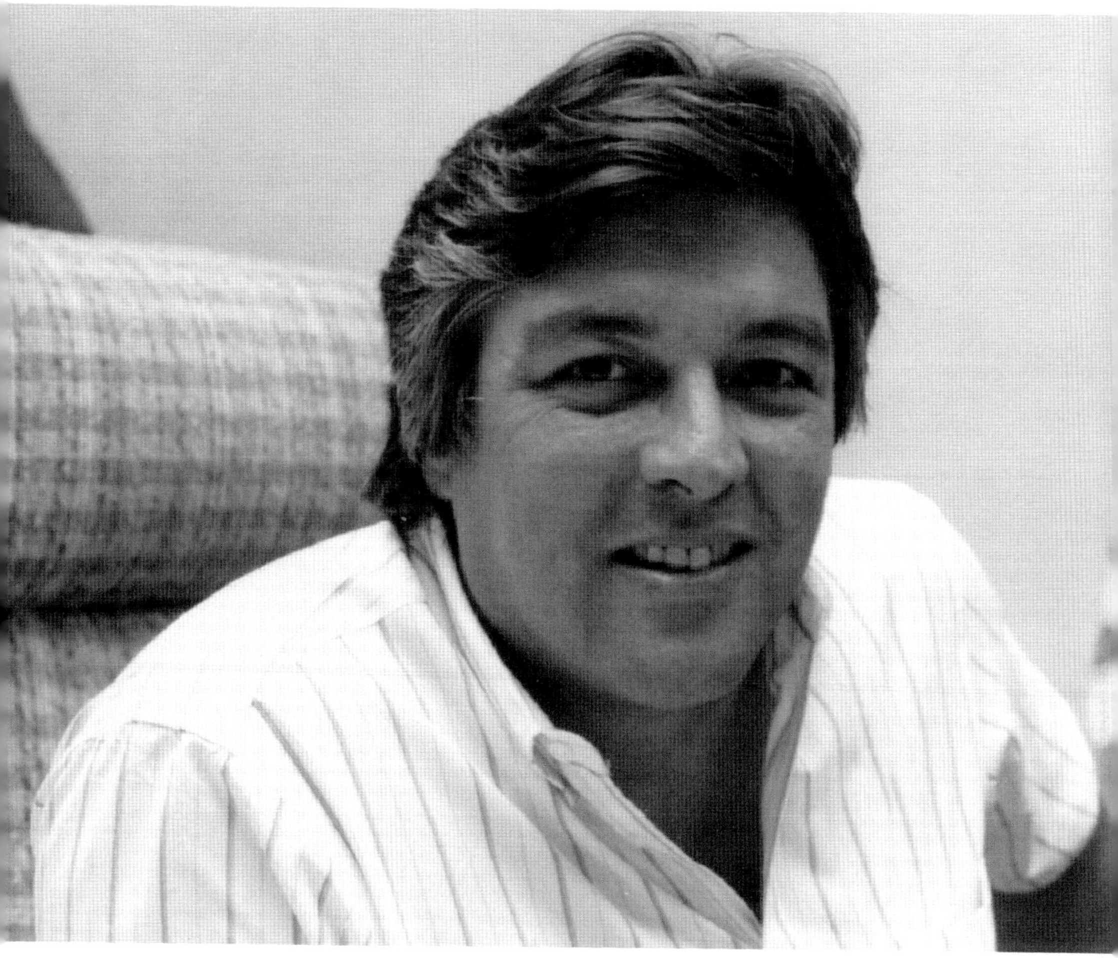

Ronald Robert "Ron" Bouchard (1948–present)
Bouchard was born in Fitchburg and graduated from Fitchburg High School in 1966. His first love was stock-car racing. Bouchard's dad fixed up cars and raced them at Brookline Speedway in New Hampshire. In 1963, Bouchard drove in his first race when his dad's driver got sick. He raced his father's cars, winning five consecutive track championships at Seekonk Speedway, from 1967 to 1971. He had 35 career victories at Stafford Speedway. In 1973 and 1979, he also won the modified championships there. In 1981, he began his NASCAR career and became the NASCAR Rookie of the Year. He also won his first place finish at the 1981 Talladega 500, averaging 156.7 mph. In 1998, Ron Bouchard was inducted into the New England Auto Racers Hall of Fame. Today, he owns Ron Bouchard Auto Stores.

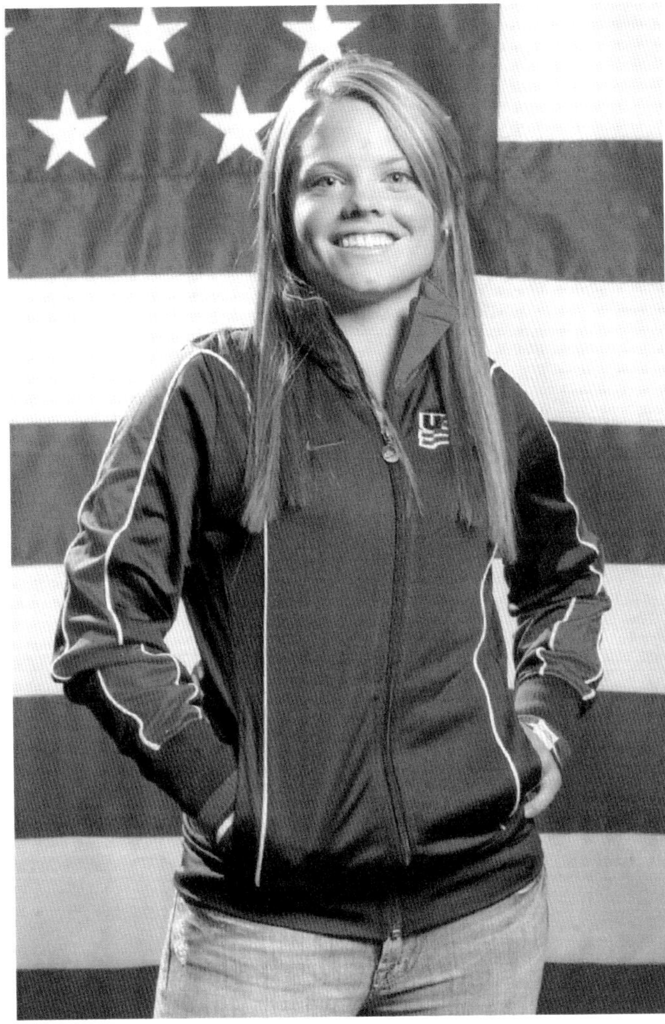

Erika Lawler (1987–Present)
Before Erika Lawler was born in Fitchburg, her aunt Kathy Lawler became a national women's ice hockey star at the State University of New York at Potsdam. In the early 1980s, Kathy set the national men and women's college record for most points. Over her career, Kathy scored 293 goals and 157 assists for a national record of 450 points—a record that still holds today. It is hard to say that her aunt Kathy did not have some kind of influence on Erika. Despite her small size, Erika showed great promise as a young athlete. She attended grade school at McKay Elementary in Fitchburg. Later, Erika attended Cushing Academy, a prep school in nearby Ashburnham, where she starred on the ice hockey rink. While she was at Cushing, Erika won three Bette Davis Awards as the top athlete in her class. After graduating from Cushing, Erika went on to play forward for the women's ice hockey team at the University of Wisconsin in Madison, winning three NCAA Championship titles in 2006, 2007, and 2009. Following her graduation from Wisconsin, Erika was selected to play on the US National Women's Ice Hockey Team, which won the silver medal in the 2010 Winter Olympics in Vancouver, British Columbia. At four foot and eleven inches tall, Erika held the distinction of being the shortest athlete to compete in the 2010 Olympic Games. Though she is currently on the roster for the Boston Blades Professional Ice Hockey Team, a leg injury and surgery kept her from trying out for the 2014 Winter Olympics, held in Russia. (Courtesy of Ann Lawler.)

CHAPTER NINE

Military Leaders

Her sympathies are large and sweet,
And when at freedom's call,
The war flags wave, the war drums beat
She sprang, responsive to her feet
And freely offered all!

—Excerpt from "Ode to Fitchburg" by Caroline A. Mason

Throughout Fitchburg's history, local men and women have bravely served in major wars, with the support of the town and, later, the city, beginning with the Revolutionary War. When the first shot was fired in the battle of Lexington and Concord, two companies of Fitchburg men marched to join them. They were some of the 169 men who fought in the Revolutionary War. Fitchburg men and women have also played prominent roles in the Civil War as well as the more recent war in Iraq. During the Civil War, four women became nurses, while more than 100 worked at home to meet the demand for supplies of those in battle or in prisoner-of-war camps. One Fitchburg soldier, Orlando Boss, won the Congressional Medal of Honor for bravery in the Battle of Cold Harbor. During World War I, the city provided soldiers, officers, and nurses who had trained locally at Camp Devens, and during World War II, an entire local family enlisted in the various services, while other families carried on military traditions of other relatives. In Korea, Vietnam, Iraq, and Afghanistan, local soldiers have served their city and country with honor, sometimes losing their lives in the process.

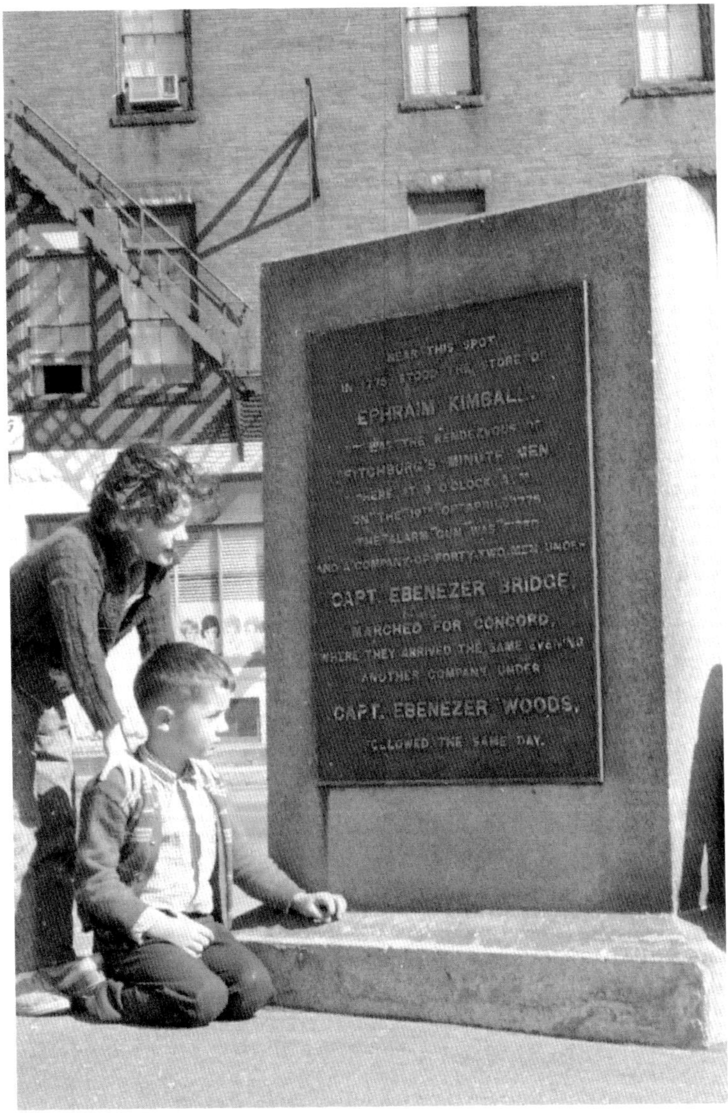

Minutemen from Fitchburg

A militia of 42 local farmers answered the call on April 19, 1775, marching to Lexington as Patriots under Capt. Ebenezer Bridge and Lt. Joseph Fox. Within hours, a second company of 29 men left town under Capt. Ebenezer Woods. Most returned after three days of service, but several rejoined as Continental soldiers during the American Revolution. One man, John Gibson, died in service and is commemorated with a bronze plaque in front of the statehouse in Boston. His father, Isaac Gibson, and his uncle Reuben Gibson both served as well. Imagine their reactions on that April morning. News of the war reached Fitchburg at 9:00 a.m. There was no way of knowing that the battles at Lexington and Concord were already history. Each man grabbed his musket and met downtown to begin their 42-mile trek. It was not uncommon to walk about 20 miles a day in that era, but these men made the trip in less than 12 hours! Finding their services were not needed, they slept on the Lexington Green, and the next day, they marched to Boston, seeking further service. None was needed, so they returned to Fitchburg. A total of 169 men would serve their country during the war. Records show these brave souls served in Boston (the Battle for Breed's Hill), Vermont, and New York.

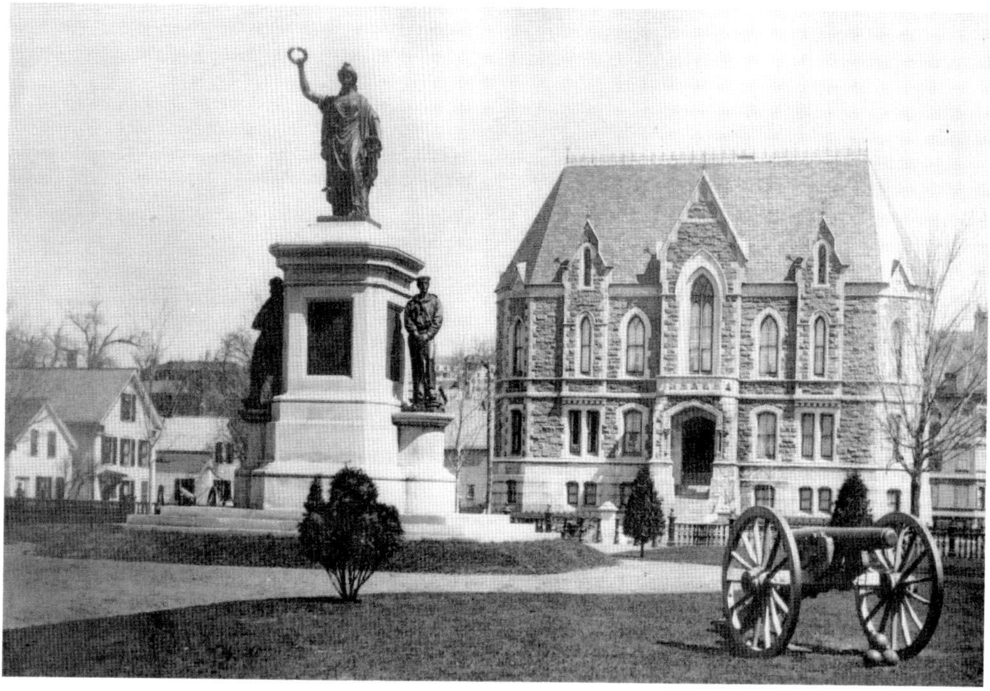

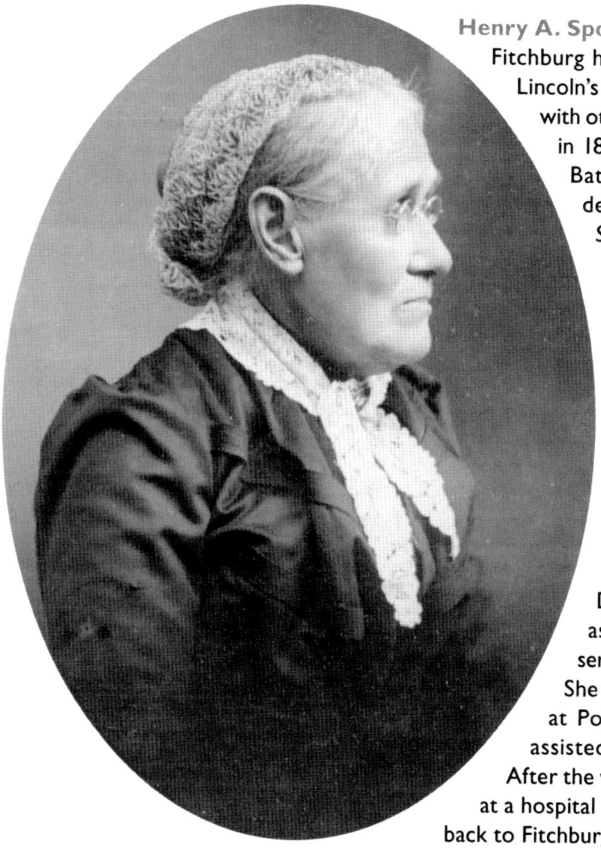

Henry A. Spooner (1829–1888)

Fitchburg hat-maker Henry A. Spooner answered Lincoln's call at the start of the Civil War, training with other Fitchburg Fusiliers, who left Fitchburg in 1861. Their first skirmish occurred at the Battle of Ball's Bluff. Spooner supplied a detailed report and map to the *Fitchburg Sentinel*, which printed the news on November 9. He also wrote letters home, providing vivid accounts of the horrors of war. Pictured is Fitchburg's Civil War monument.

Martha Goodrich (1820–1910)

Dorothea Dix trained Goodrich to serve as a nurse during the Civil War. Goodrich served in Washington, DC, then at Antietam. She volunteered to treat the Confederates at Point Lookout Prison in Maryland and assisted surviving prisoners in Andersonville. After the war, Goodrich became the head matron at a hospital in Pittsfield until she retired and moved back to Fitchburg, where she died.

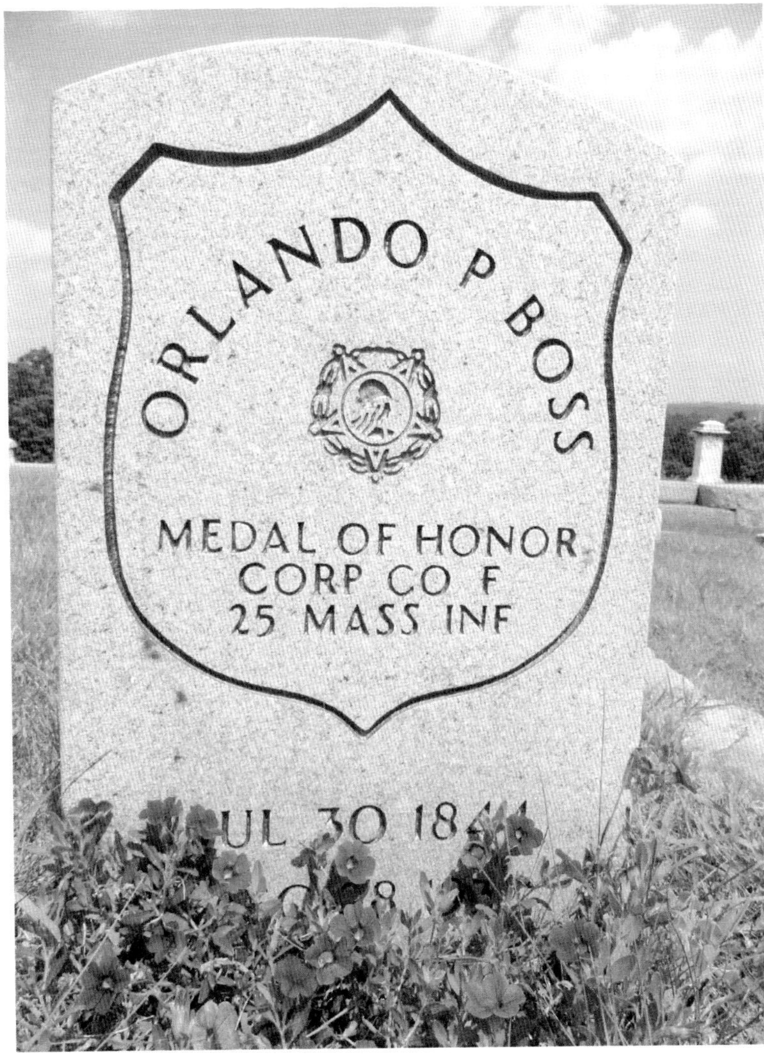

Orlando Boss (1844–1931)

Of all the servicemen and women from Fitchburg who served in US wars, only one man was ever awarded the Congressional Medal of Honor—Orlando Boss. The son of George H. and Catherine L. Boss, Orlando was 18 when he enlisted and mustered on September 16, 1861, in the 25th Massachusetts Volunteer Militia. Boss fought through 12 battles before the horrendous Battle of Cold Harbor, where more than two-thirds of the 25th were lost. Fighting side by side with other Fitchburg men, including William E. Battles, George B. Proctor, William E. Willis, William H. Partridge, John Simonds Jr., J.C. Spaulding, and John Brown, Boss found himself in a foxhole under heavy enemy fire, with his lieutenant critically wounded and calling for help a short distance away. Against orders, he ran to the lieutenant's side, picked him up, and returned to his foxhole. For this, Boss was awarded the Congressional Medal of Honor. Boss served as provost guard from March 14, 1862, to May 9, 1862. He was promoted to corporal on August 13, 1863, and discharged on October 20, 1864, at the completion of his meritorious service. He returned to Fitchburg and married Jennie Hodgman on February 15, 1867. Boss became a machinist and worked at both Putnam Machine and Union Machine until retirement. He also became a commander of Post 19 of the GAR (Grand Army of the Republic). He died on December 28, 1931, at age 88, and is buried at the Laurel Hill Cemetery in Fitchburg.

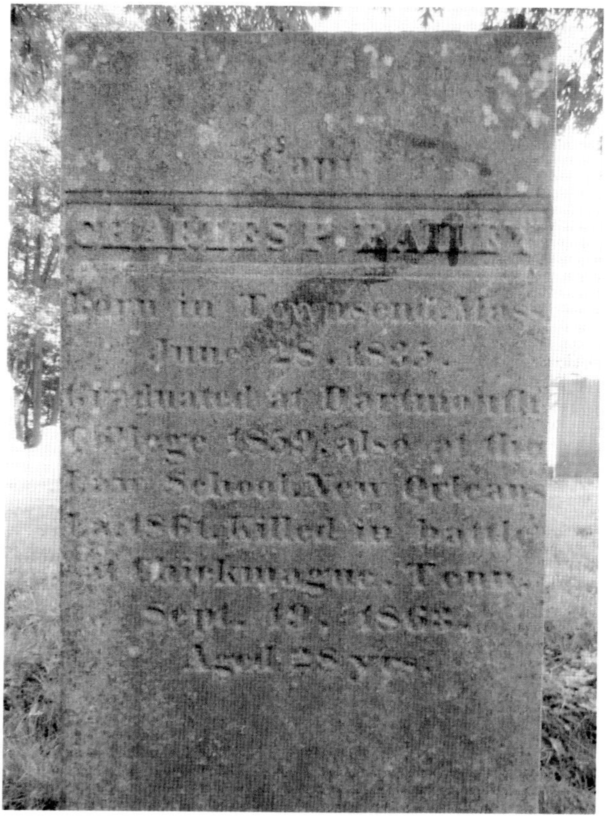

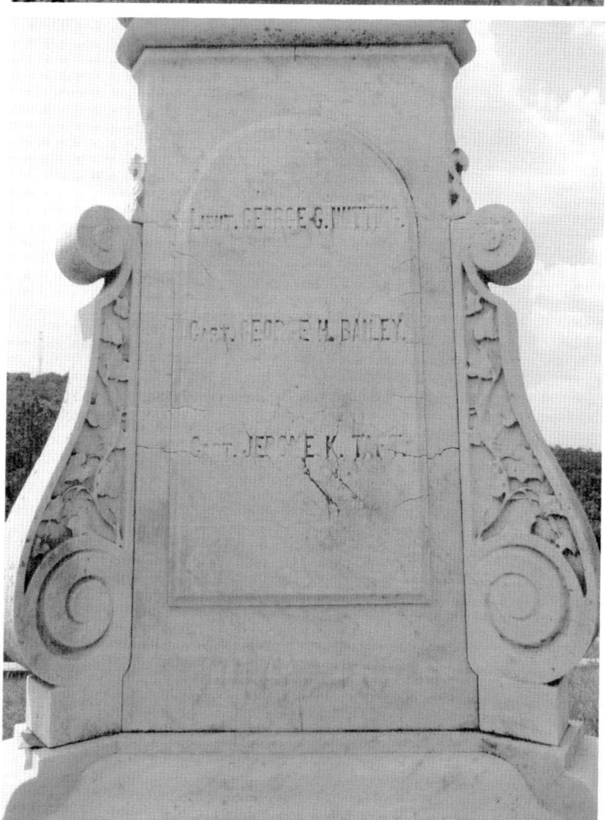

Charles (1835–1863) and George (1833–1863) Bailey

The Bailey brothers, raised in Fitchburg and graduates of Fitchburg High School, fought on opposite sides in the Civil War. After graduating from Dartmouth College, Charles went to New Orleans to live and to study for the bar. He joined the Washington Artillery of New Orleans and was sent to the Army of the Tennessee. Meanwhile, George was sent with other Massachusetts men to Port Hudson, Louisiana, where he was wounded by friendly fire and died in May 1863. Charles lost his life during the Battle of Chickamauga. It is thought that Charles was buried in a common grave at the battlefield, while George was buried at Laurel Hill Cemetery; however, Charles does have a stone at Laurel Hill, which mentions his service but not for which side he fought.

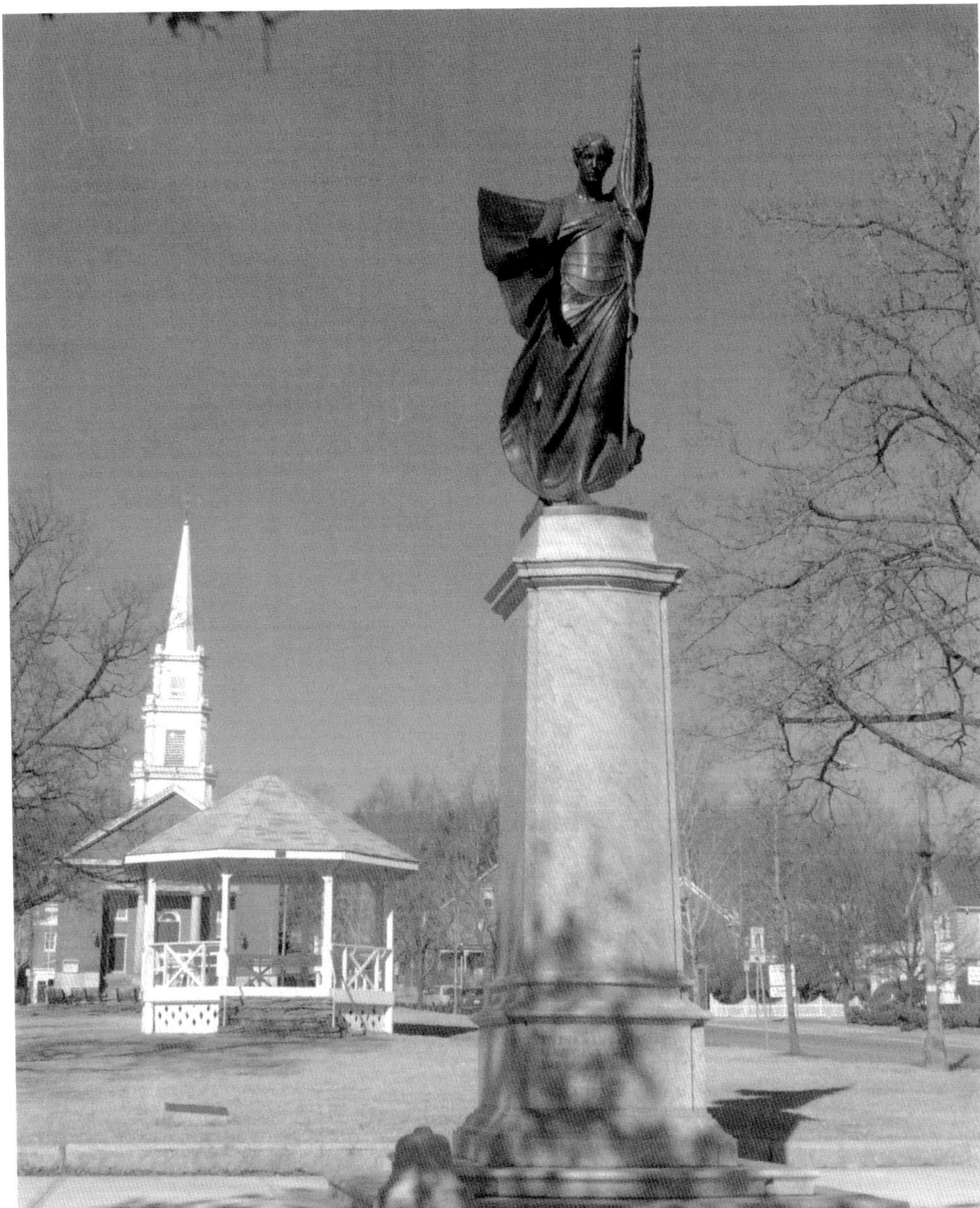

World War I Veterans

The first dedication to the memory of the men and women who died in service during World War I was a living maple tree planted in front of each of their homes, with granite stones and bronze markers, some of which are located in Forest Hill Cemetery, in addition to the 11 found at the entrance to Coggshall Park. In November 1928, Fitchburg dedicated its World War I memorial, funded by donations and designed by Fitchburg sculptor Herbert Adams. The 65 names of the Fitchburg men and women who died during World War I are inscribed on the monument. Approximately 30 of those deaths resulted from pneumonia caused by influenza, an international epidemic during the war. Many of the soldiers were killed in action in France, and the French government awarded certificates to the relatives of 45 soldiers who died there.

Richard A. Bresnahan (1924–2009)

Born in Fitchburg, Bresnahan was the nephew of Brig. Gen. Thomas F. Bresnahan (1892–1971), also born in Fitchburg, who served in World War I and II. Richard was appointed to West Point after a year at Colgate University. In 1946, he was commissioned as second lieutenant in the US Infantry before being assigned to platoon leader and company commander of the 32nd Regiment during the Korean War. In 1969, he commanded the 101st Infantry Division for five campaigns in Vietnam, during which he received the Silver Star of Merit for gallantry in action. In 1971, he became the chief of the Strategic Plans and Policy Division and later served as the chief of staff of the 5th US Army, from 1974 to 1975. Bresnahan retired in 1982 at the rank of major general.

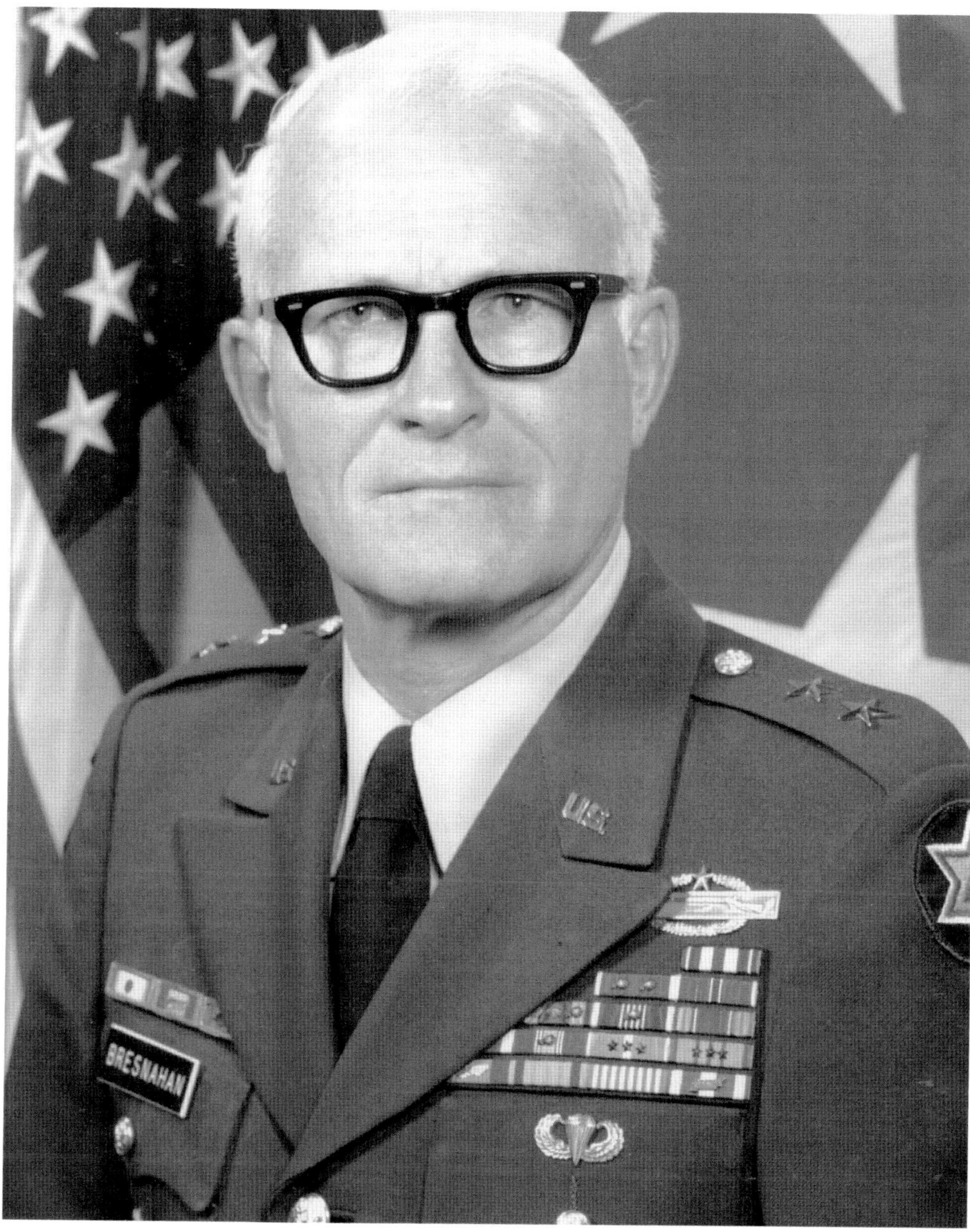

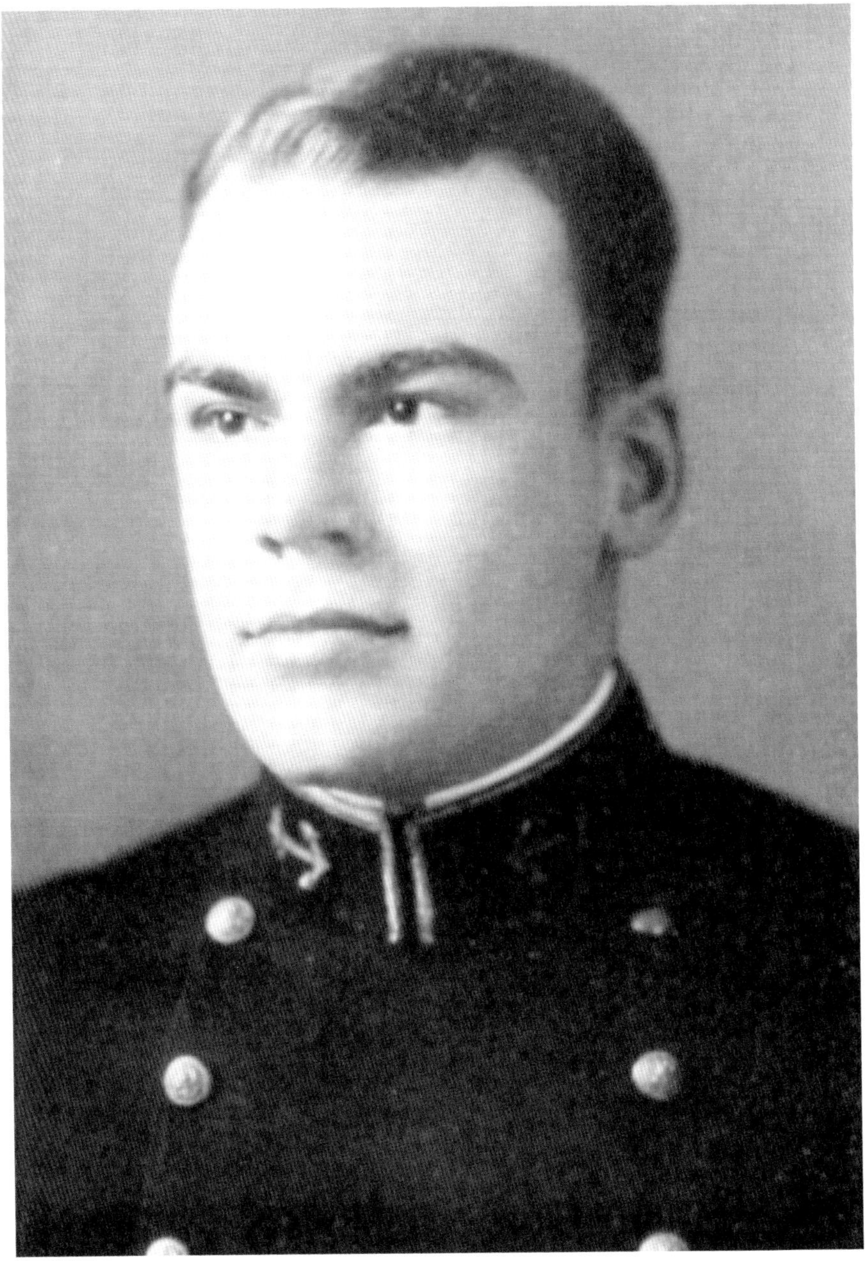

Carl Fellows (1913–1991)
Fellows was born in Fitchburg, where his father, John, served as mayor for two terms in the 1920s. At Fitchburg High School, Fellows exhibited impressive athletic skills, making him a standout in football, basketball, and tennis. Fellows led Coach Amiott's football team to an 11-1 season. As captain of the basketball squad, he led his team to the state championship. Fellows went on to the US Naval Academy, where he excelled in football, basketball, and lacrosse. In 1935, Fellows was presented with the Thompson Sword, the prestigious award given annually to honor the finest athlete in the senior class at Annapolis. During World War II, Fellows commanded two Navy destroyers. After retirement, he returned to Fitchburg in the 1950s and became a paper executive. He died in 1991 at the age of 78.

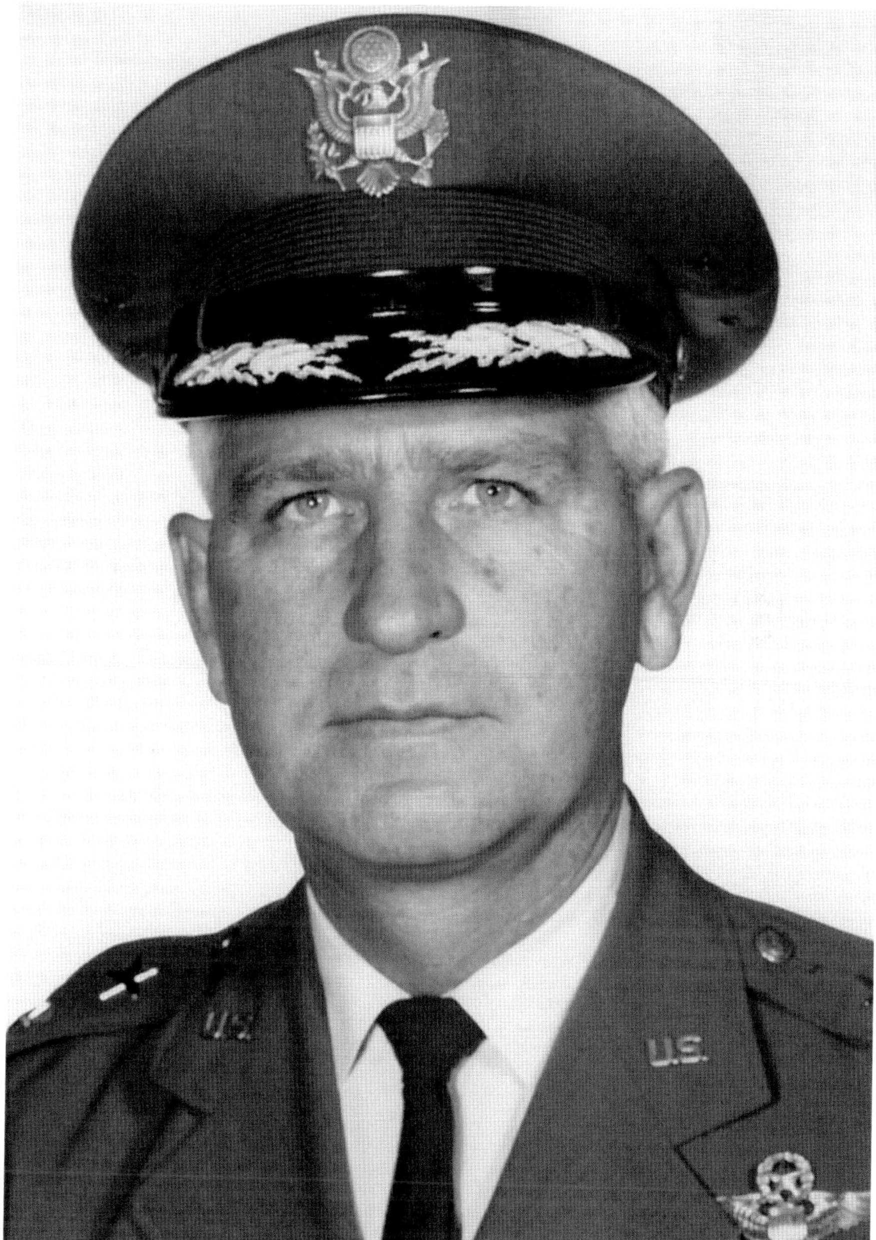

Lt. Gen. Edmund F. O'Connor (1922–present)
O'Connor was born to Irish immigrants in Fitchburg. After graduating from St. Bernard's High School and then West Point, he was commissioned as a second lieutenant and received his pilot wings to fly bombers over Italy. He was also a squadron commander during the Korean War. In 1953, he began working with weapons systems. In 1964, General O'Connor became the director of program management at the George Marshall Space Flight Center of NASA in Huntsville, Alabama, where he was in charge of the Saturn and Apollo launch vehicle programs. For his service in two wars and 36 years in the military, he was highly decorated. Among his awards are the Exceptional Service Medal and the Distinguished Service Medal for his contributions to the Apollo 8 lunar orbital mission and the Apollo 11 lunar landing.

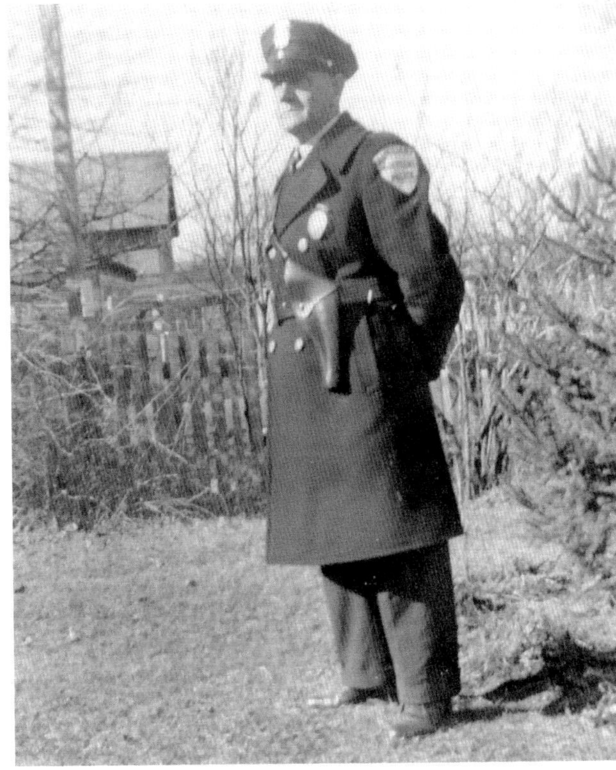

The Demmon Family in World War II

Stunned by the bombing of Pearl Harbor on December 7, 1941, Fitchburg men and women joined US military units to support the war effort. In the George Demmon family, all four siblings enlisted in 1942. Phillip was the first to volunteer, joining the Army Air Force. Stationed in Saipan, he became an instrument and maintenance man on B-29s, where he earned the rank of staff sergeant. Isabel, who had completed her nursing degree at Burbank Hospital in 1940 and worked with the Visiting Nurses Association, joined the Army Nurse Corps. She attained the rank of captain and was stationed in Calcutta, India, until June 1945. Priscilla, Isabel's twin sister, enlisted in the SPARS (Semper Paratus Always Ready), the Coast Guard's unit for women. She earned the rank of storekeeper, first class, and was stationed in Boston, Palm Beach, and Lincolnshire. Arlene, the third sister, joined the WAVES (Women Accepted for Volunteer Emergency Service), the Navy's division for women. Arlene earned the rank of pharmacy mate, second class, and was stationed at Walter Reed Hospital and, later, in Hawaii. George C. Demmon, their father, also served during World War II. He was an auxiliary to the military police of the Army at the Fitchburg Gas & Electric Company from December 17, 1942 to February 14, 1944.

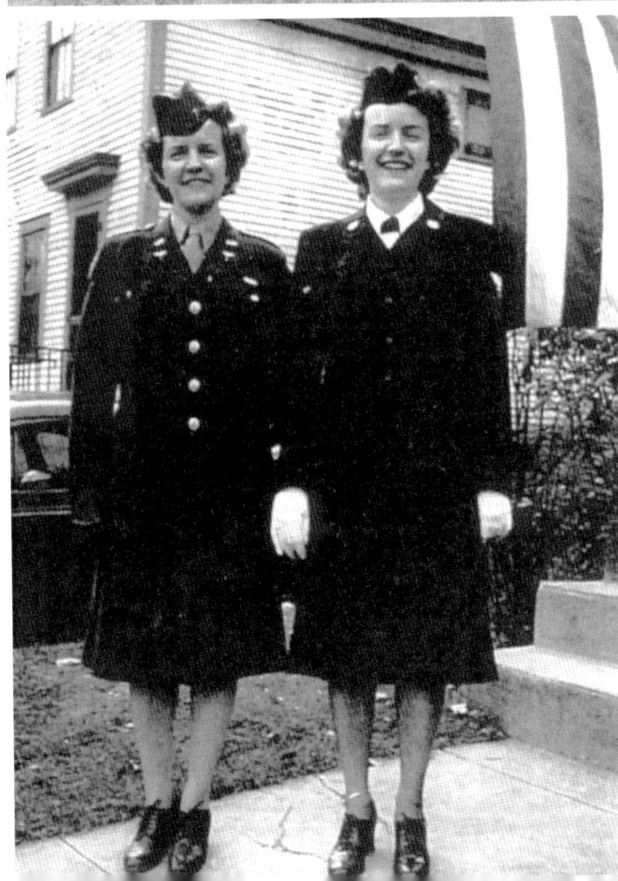

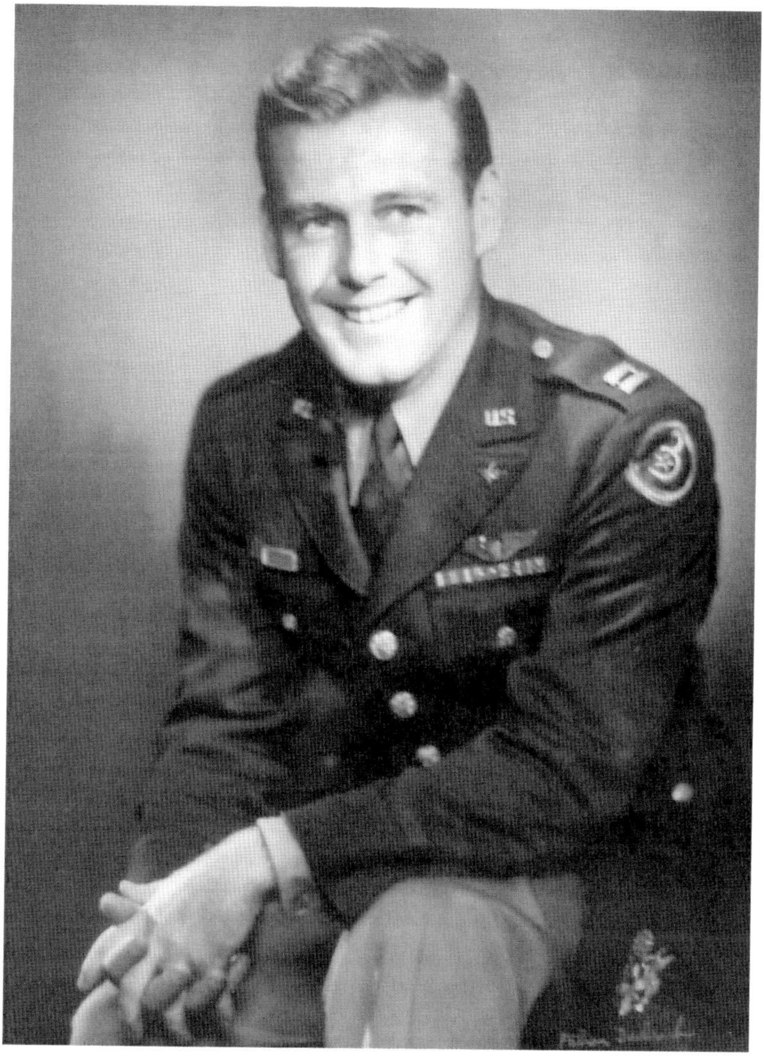

Norman Douglas Tucker Jr. (1920–2005)
Born in Fitchburg, Tucker is described in his high school yearbook as one who "revels in the advanced stages of nonsense." His outlook on life, spring, and young ladies belies his dedicated Army life as a Spitfire pilot. Tucker enjoyed flying since his father bought a Stinson Reliant airplane from the shah of Persia in 1937. While at the University of Vermont, he joined the Civilian Pilot Training program, created by then president Franklin Delano Roosevelt. In March 1942, Tucker enlisted in the Army Air Corps. He successfully completed nine months of pilot-training courses and was promoted to second lieutenant of the 31st Fighter Group stationed in North Africa. As a Spitfire pilot, he flew more than 141 missions over Italy without enduring a scratch or losing a plane, although he once ran out of gas on landing. He received 17 oak-leaf clusters and the Distinguished Flying Cross (April 11, 1944) for extraordinary achievement, bravery, and heroism. As Fitchburg's only "Flying Ace," he was required to down five enemy planes and is credited with having disrupted 20 enemy aircraft and one bomber. He freely admitted to being scared when, in one day, he encountered 50 enemy planes aloft. His "nonsense" turned to wisdom, leadership, and flying skills as he engaged the enemy. At the end of the war, Tucker and his wife, Lucille, returned to Fitchburg to raise a family, becoming leading citizens of the community and owning Speedway stations and Roux Travel Service. (Courtesy of Kit Tucker.)

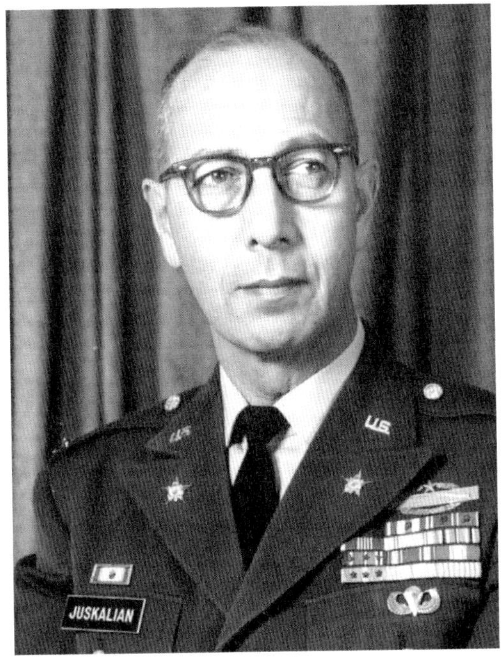

George Juskalian (1914–2010)

Juskalian was born to Armenian immigrants in Fitchburg. When the United States entered World War II, he served in the North African campaign and was captured while saving a fellow soldier. He was a prisoner of war for 27 months before being freed in 1945, when Allied forces seized Nuremberg. He also participated in the Korean and Vietnam Wars. He is buried in Arlington National Cemetery.

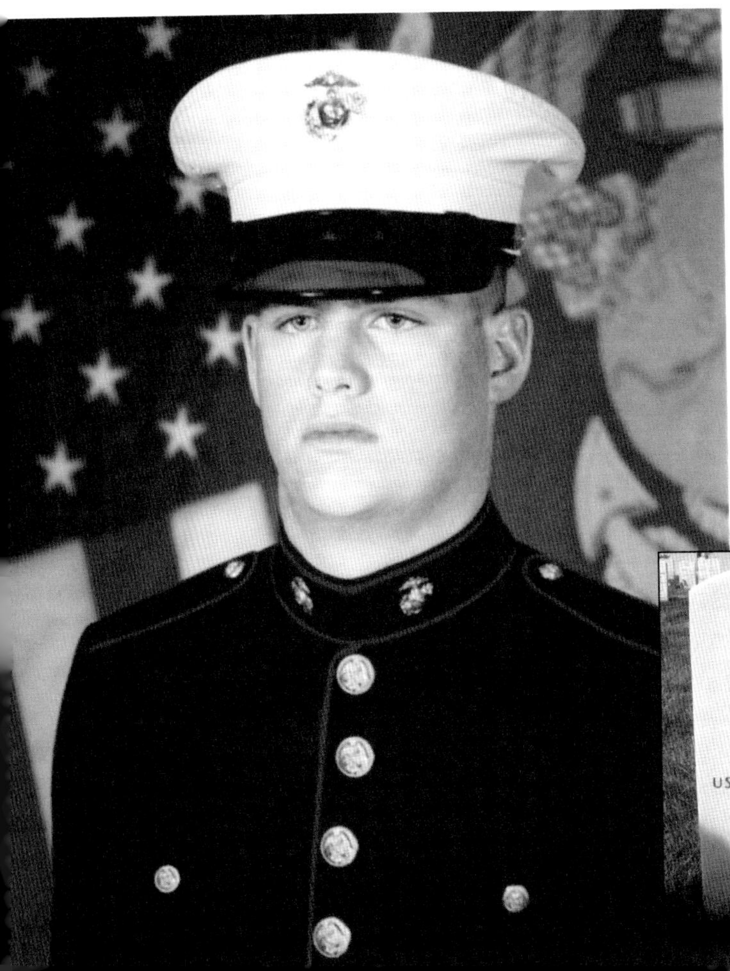

Geofrey Robert Cayer (1986–2006)

Cayer lost his life in Operation Iraqi Freedom. He graduated from Fitchburg High, enlisted in the Marines, and deployed to Iraq in January 2006. A wake was held for him at Fitchburg High School, as well as a mass at St. Joseph's Church, attended by then governor Mitt Romney. Later, Cayer was buried at Arlington National Cemetery. In 2007, a memorial park, located at 2 Boulder Drive, was dedicated to him. (Left, courtesy of Alan Thibault.)

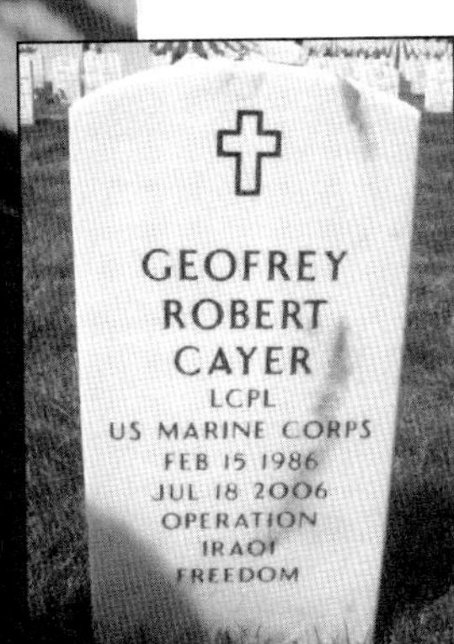

CHAPTER TEN

The People Next Door

Honor and truth her old renown,
Conservative of both
The virtues of the little town,
She holds in legacy to crown
The city's larger growth.

—Excerpt from "Ode to Fitchburg" by Caroline A. Mason

The city of Fitchburg is defined by not only its monuments and buildings but also its people, especially those ordinary individuals who do extraordinary things for their love of community. They are leaders, often unknowingly, who inspire a sense of identity and add to the development of community spirit, pride, and closeness. This chapter highlights some of those individuals who have made, and continue to make, a difference, sometimes in quiet ways, sometimes not. They include newspaper writers, businesspeople, educators, librarians, and humanitarians, all of whom devote their lives to helping children, families, and the elderly. Most important, they represent what makes this city live; they represent our neighbors.

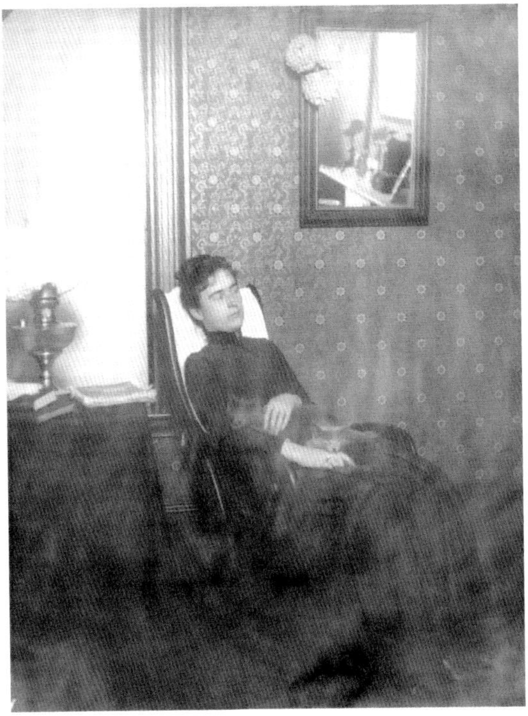

Lucy Fay Griffith (1854–1937)

Griffith inherited the fortune of her father, George Fay, who had been an investor in the railroads and a partner in Crocker Burbank. She joined George Hastings in the establishment of a home for unmarried working girls, Hastings Hall. Griffith also donated the family's Victorian Gothic mansion on Main Street to the Park Gentlemen's Club, which was later renamed the Fay Club in honor of her father's memory.

Susan "Susie" Cushing Dickinson (1860–1926)

The daughter of Joseph Cushing, Dickinson was born in Fitchburg. In 1896, she was one of the founding members of the Union Aid Home for Children, which provided accommodations for homeless and destitute children. When her father died, she donated his residence on Holt Street to the home, which evolved into the Children's Aid and Family Service, Inc.

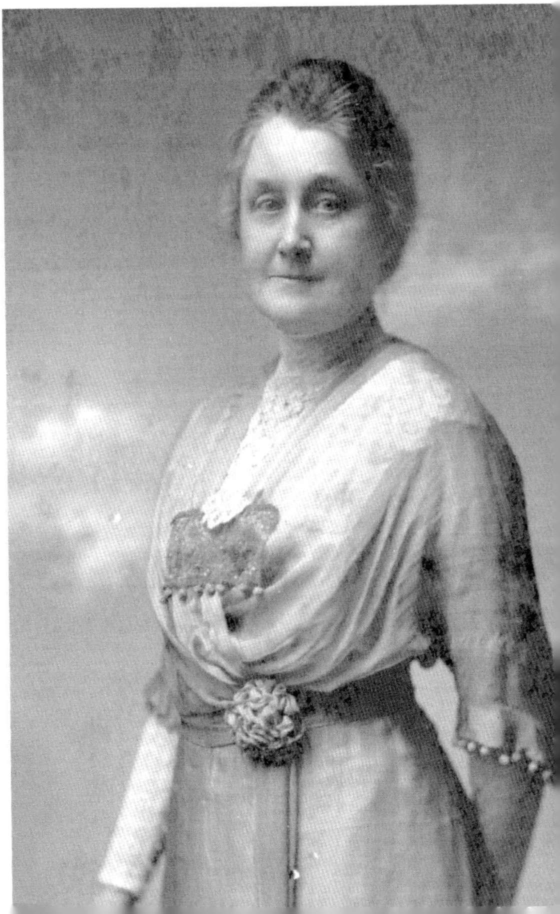

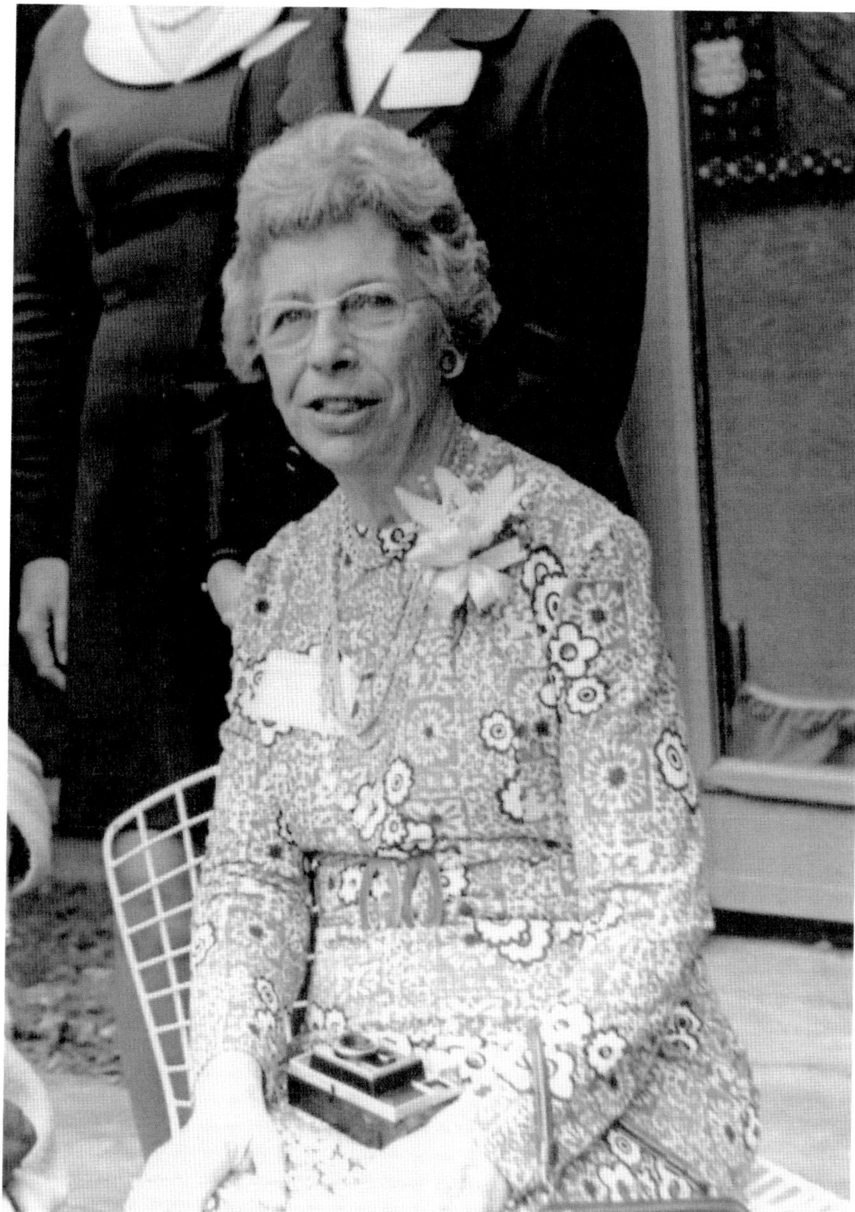

Ruth Hyatt (1906–2000)
Hyatt, who grew up on Martha's Vineyard, became the first female director of the Fitchburg Public Library (FPL), from 1943 to 1961. Hired by Emerson Greenaway as the circulation librarian in 1937, she believed in extending services to the community by providing outreach services to teachers, parents, and children. She incorporated braille material in 1944 and oversaw the Pennies Project, contributions by local schoolchildren for the new youth library, in 1950. Hyatt established the Wachusett Regional Library Group, which laid the groundwork for the Worcester Regional Library System. FPL was among the first in the country to circulate 16-millimeter films (1944) and LP recordings (1948), and under her directorship, bookmobile service began in December 1953. Hyatt retired to a small rural library in Falmouth, Massachusetts, where she eventually died. (Courtesy of Fitchburg Public Library.)

Alice B. Cushman (1904–1994)

Affectionately known as "ABC" and "Auntie Cush," Cushman is a native of Bernardston, Massachusetts. She was hired as Fitchburg Public Library's first full-time children's librarian in September 1937 and served in that capacity until her retirement in 1965. For most of those years, she lived at 33 School Street, where she enjoyed being part of the Greek neighborhood. She received her library training at the Westfield Athenaeum Library, the Simmons Library School in Boston, the Columbia Library School in New York, and the Carnegie Library School in Pittsburgh. During her tenure as librarian in Fitchburg, Cushman notably developed the children's book collection, established storytelling programs and a special reading room for young adult literature, and worked tirelessly with teachers and administrators of local schools to encourage reading. She was also the professional consultant for the new youth library, which opened in 1950. The first library intended only for young people, the Fitchburg Youth Library made national news due to the fact that the children of Fitchburg saved their pennies to help finance the project. While in the Hillcrest Nursing Home at the end of her life, Cushman remained in touch with many of the children, now parents and grandparents, she had served. Though small in stature, she had a way of making it known that she was in charge. Hoping to find just the right book, many might still recall her favorite four words heard upon entering the library: "Are your hands clean?" You had to show her, and if you failed her test, she sent you to the washroom. Cushman died on February 13, 1994, at the age of 90. (Courtesy of Fitchburg Public Library.)

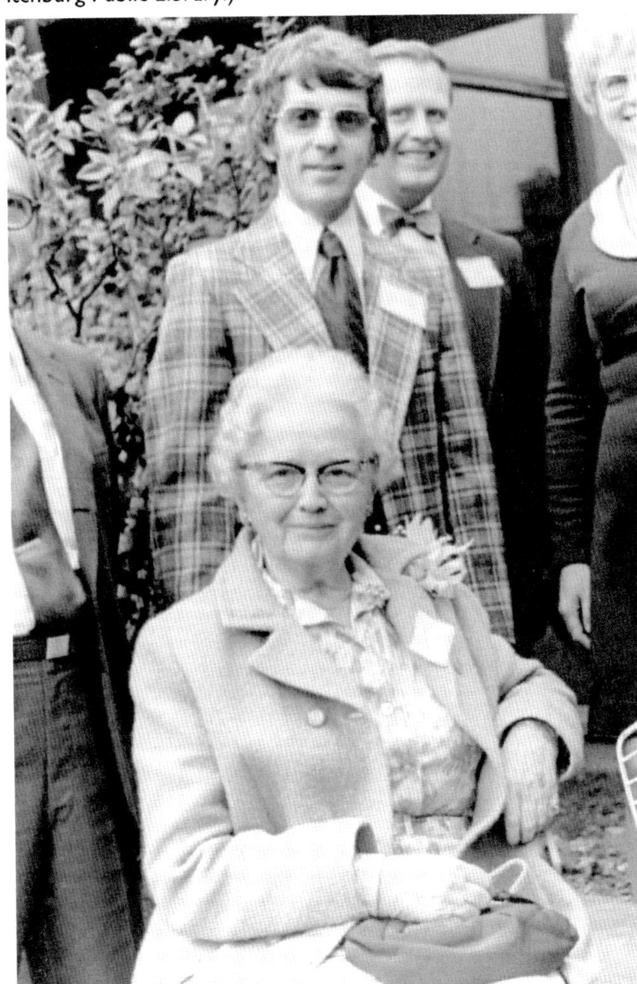

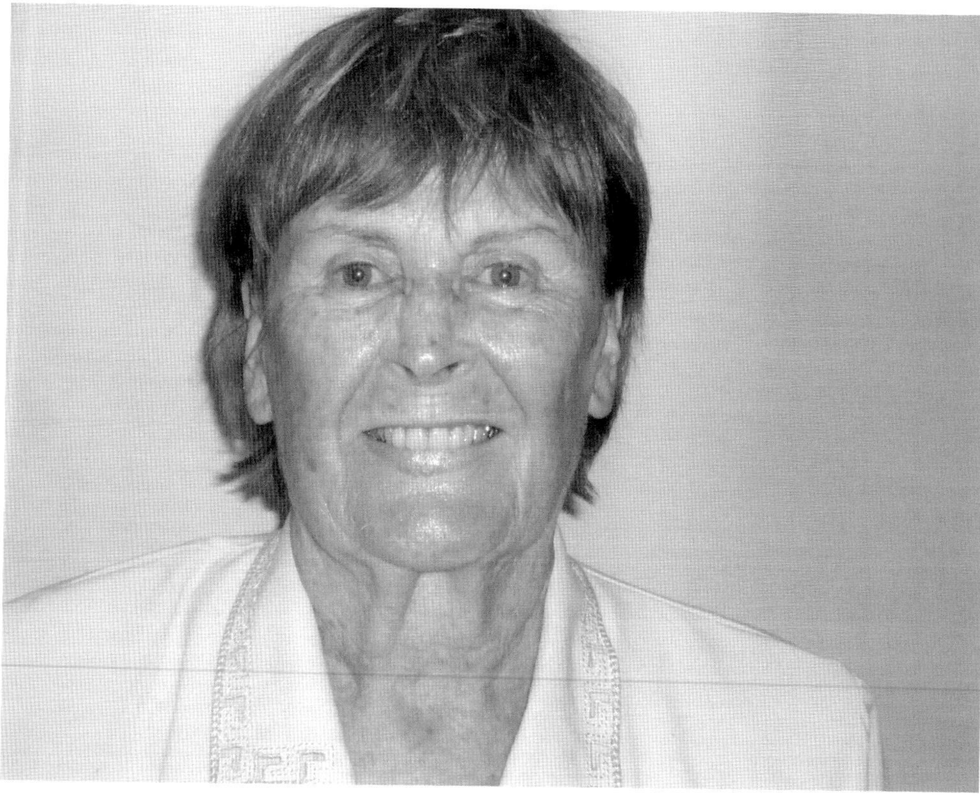

Annie K. Byrne DeMartino (1938–present)
DeMartino emigrated from Ireland in 1965 as a governess. After marrying Fitchburg native Phillip DeMartino, she began studying for a degree in human services. DeMartino worked for the Herbert Lipton Center, Battered Women's Resources (BWR), and the Massachusetts Department of Health and Human Services, where she continued after graduation. She has been an advocate for the homeless and is a founder of Our Father's Table. Then governor Michael Dukakis presented her with the national award for fighting homelessness in 1988, and she was selected as ABC News "Person of the Week" in 1987 and 1989. Wanting to obtain help for the homeless, DeMartino ran for Ward 6 councilor in 1989. She had no campaign, just a handmade sticker on her green coat, but she won by a large margin. From 1995 to 2010, DeMartino served as Fitchburg councilor-at-large. (Courtesy of Simone Blake.)

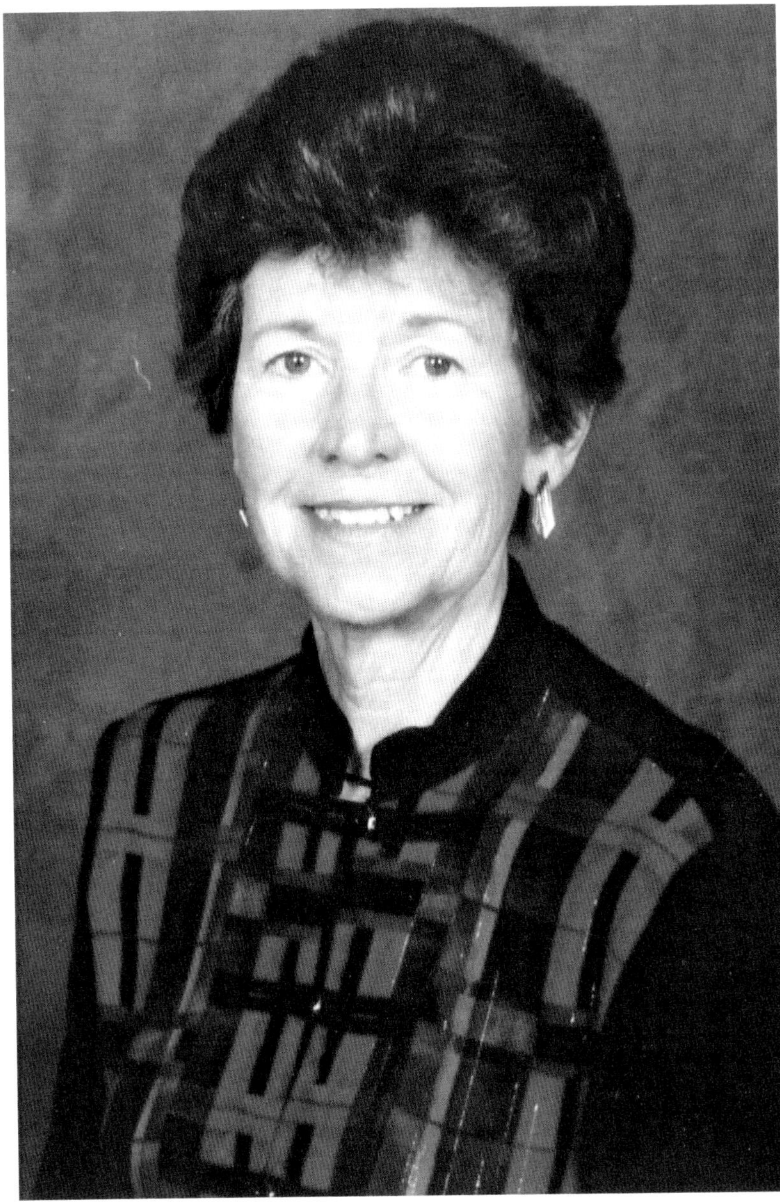

Eleanor Gilmartin (1929–present)
A licensed social worker, Gilmartin received her graduate degree from Fitchburg State College. She began her career in elder services in 1972, when she was appointed director of Fitchburg's Council on Aging. She was responsible for Meals On Wheels, as well as a senior meals program at B.F. Brown School. She also opened a drop-in center on Elm Street. In 1974, Gilmartin founded the Montachusett Home Care Corporation (MHCC) and served as executive director until her retirement in 1996. At MHCC, she developed case-managed services for elders designed to allow them to remain at home. She also established auxiliary programs, including Crisis Intervention, Friendly Visitors, Adult Family Care, and Congregate Housing. At its inception, MHCC served three communities from an office in Fitchburg. At the time of Gilmartin's retirement, more than 1,000 elders in 21 communities were receiving MHCC assistance. (Courtesy of Eleanor Gilmartin.)

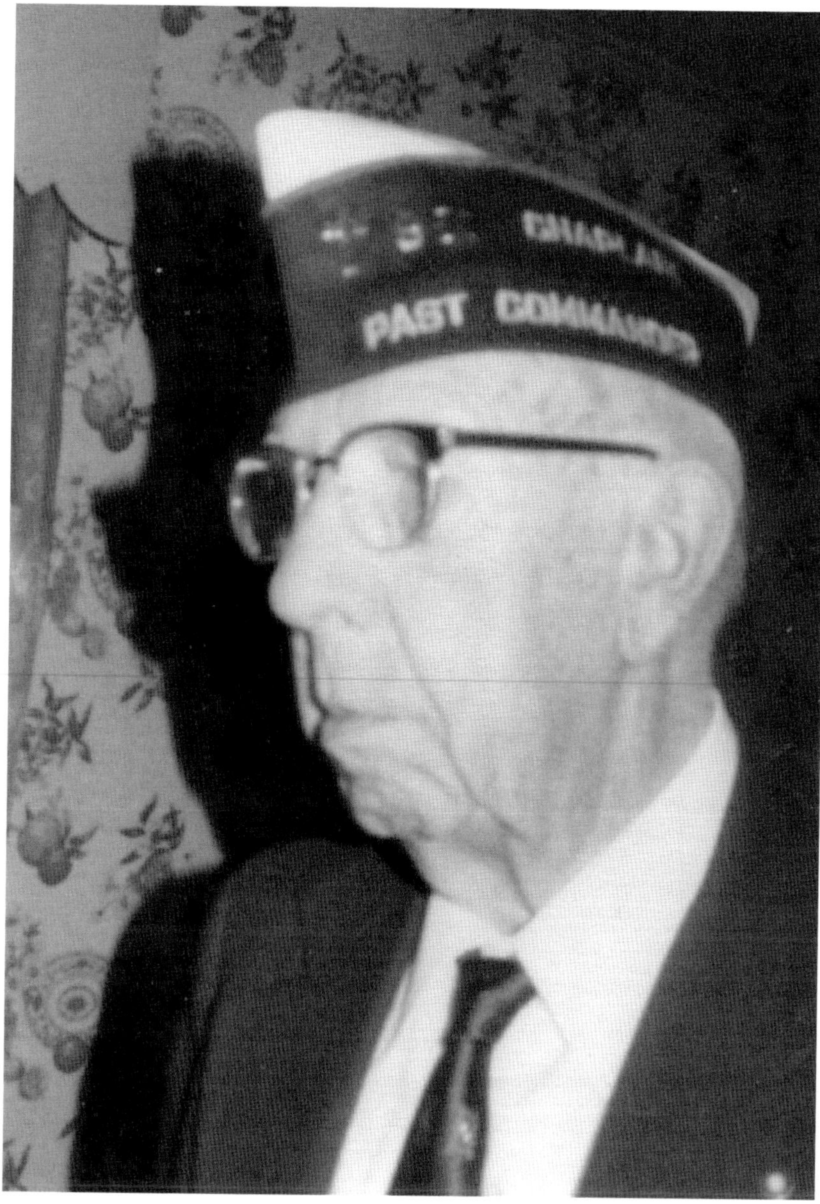

Elliott Wellington (1890–1986)
When asked how he was doing, Wellington would reply, "Sick abed and dying," or "Do you really have the time to listen to how I am?" Elliott was a World War I veteran who served in France. Employed by the Fitchburg *Sentinel & Enterprise* before and after he returned from the war, he was proud to say he ran the handpress, now part of the historical society collection. He established the Sentinel Credit Union for fellow employees, which remained active for 46 years. Wellington grew up in Fitchburg, where he would ride with his dad on a horse-drawn wagon to deliver lumber. On one such occasion, he recalled falling from the wagon and having to visit the so-called "painless dentist," Dr. Palmer, to have his jaw wired. Wellington always claimed that Dr. Joseph Palmer was *not* painless. (Courtesy of Simone Blake.)

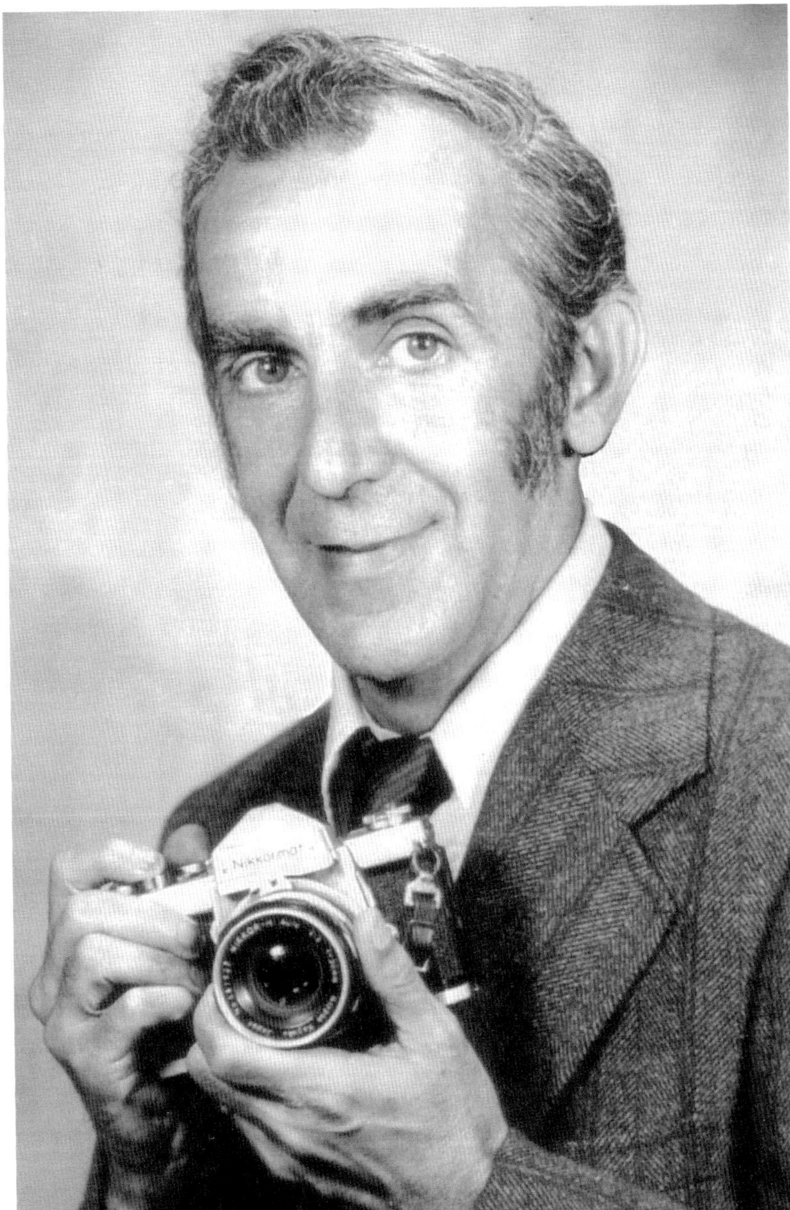

Robert W. Jollimore (1928–2003)
For more than 20 years, "Photo by Bob Jollimore, Staff Photographer" followed the photograph captions of local newspapers. During those years, Jollimore could be found at nearly every event in the Fitchburg-Leominster area. Born in Springfield, Bob was adopted and brought to Fitchburg by his parents, Elizabeth and Hastings Jollimore. Fulfilling his love for photography, he left the confines of factory work to become a freelance photographer. After working for the Worcester *Telegram & Gazette* for a short time, he began his career at the Fitchburg *Sentinel & Enterprise* around 1957. He was a respected photographer who never refused or missed an assignment. His passion for his profession was evident in every newspaper. His son Richard, a Fitchburg firefighter, has displayed a similar passion with his photographs, some of which are now owned by the historical society. (Courtesy of Rick Jollimore.)

Patricia "Pat" Goguen (1929–present)
Goguen left Laconia, New Hampshire, in 1953 to work at the Fitchburg *Sentinel & Enterprise* as the editor of the Family Page, later known as the Women's Page. She walked to work and made many friends along the way; some even say they could set their watches by her. In 1969, she began the popular "Patter by Pat" column, which she wrote with warmth and humor. Goguen was also responsible for theater reviews, both at the Whalom and Stratton Playhouses. She interviewed many stars, including Mickey Rooney, Gloria Vanderbilt, Gypsy Rose Lee, and Shelley Winters. Long after retiring in December 1991, Goguen still believes interviewing is an art and continues to do so, whether in line at the supermarket or in the doctor's waiting room, and then invites the people she meets for coffee in her backyard under her Norwegian maple. (Courtesy of Pat Goguen.)

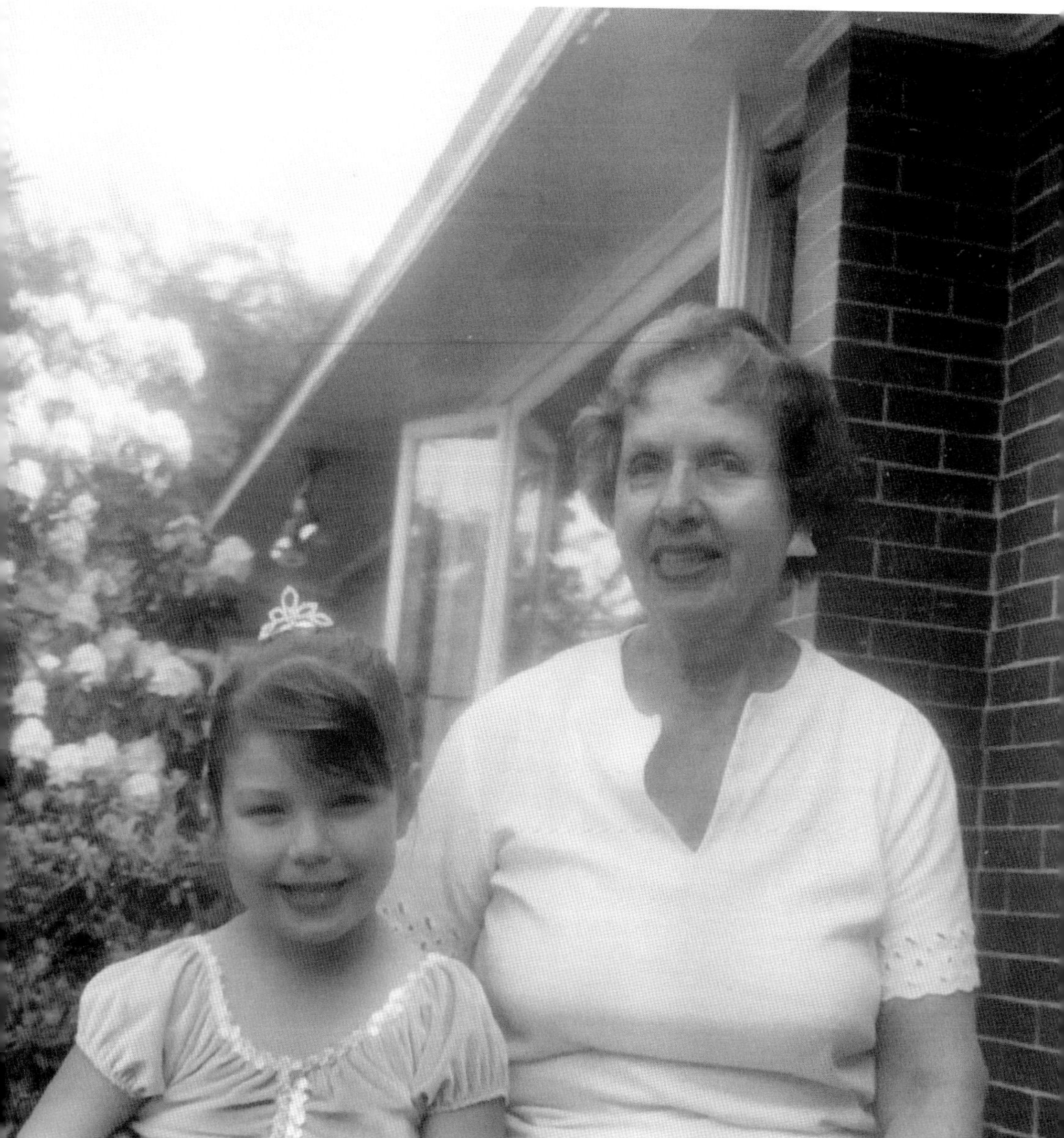

William T. "Bill" Casey (1925–present) and Julia Tomasini Casey (1922–present)

William, a Boston native who admittedly enjoys anything as long as it requires no heavy lifting, came to Fitchburg in 1967. After serving for three years in the Navy, he received graduate degrees from Boston College and Simmons Collage, the latter in library science. He had first planned to become a teacher, but a chance meeting with a friend at the Boston Public Library (BPL) led him to what he calls his "accidental library career." In 1967, Bill was hired as the first full-time director of the library at Fitchburg State College. Prior to that, he worked at the BPL, and in 1964, he had the dubious honor of being hired as the first male director of a branch library, at Connolly. The college library was then located in the Sanders Building, and in 1975, Bill oversaw the construction of the library space in the Hammond Building, in which the excellent core book collection he developed is now housed. After his retirement in 1990, the public service area of the current Amelia V. Gallucci-Cirio Library was dedicated to him to commemorate his many years of service to the Fitchburg State community. He continues to be an active volunteer with the Montachusett Opportunity Council (MOC), the board of which he was appointed to by Pres. Vincent J. Mara in 1985 to represent the institution.

A discussion about Bill would not be complete without mentioning the other bookend of the pair, Julia Tomasini Casey, also a Boston native, whom he took as his bride in 1951. Even though they grew up in the same section of Boston, Bill met Julia through her brother Raymond, who served with him in the Navy. "It was meant to be," they both say. After raising their seven children, Julia worked for the Department of Health and Human Services for 18 years, retiring in 1988. She also began what would be a 19-year college career, finally earning her bachelor's degree in 1990, the year Bill retired. "I took one course at a time. It was all about enrichment," she said. She ignited her love for gardening as an urban gardener while growing up. In 1993, she joined the Laurelwood Garden Club, another of her enriching experiences. (Courtesy of Simone Blake.)

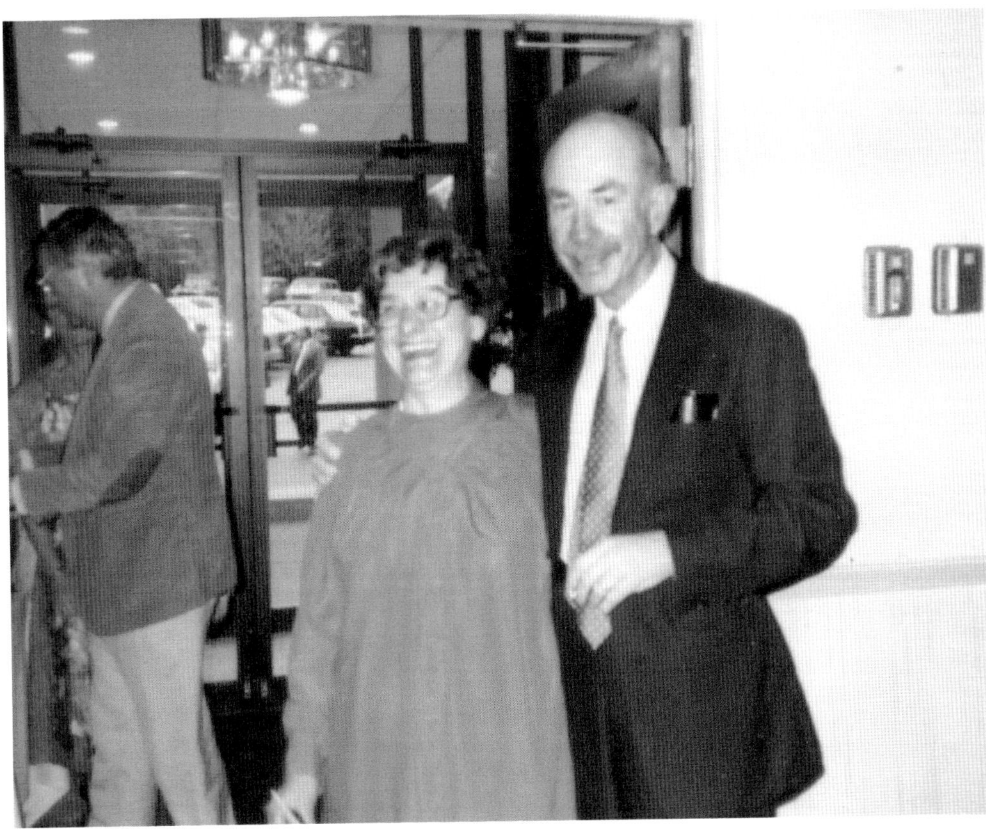

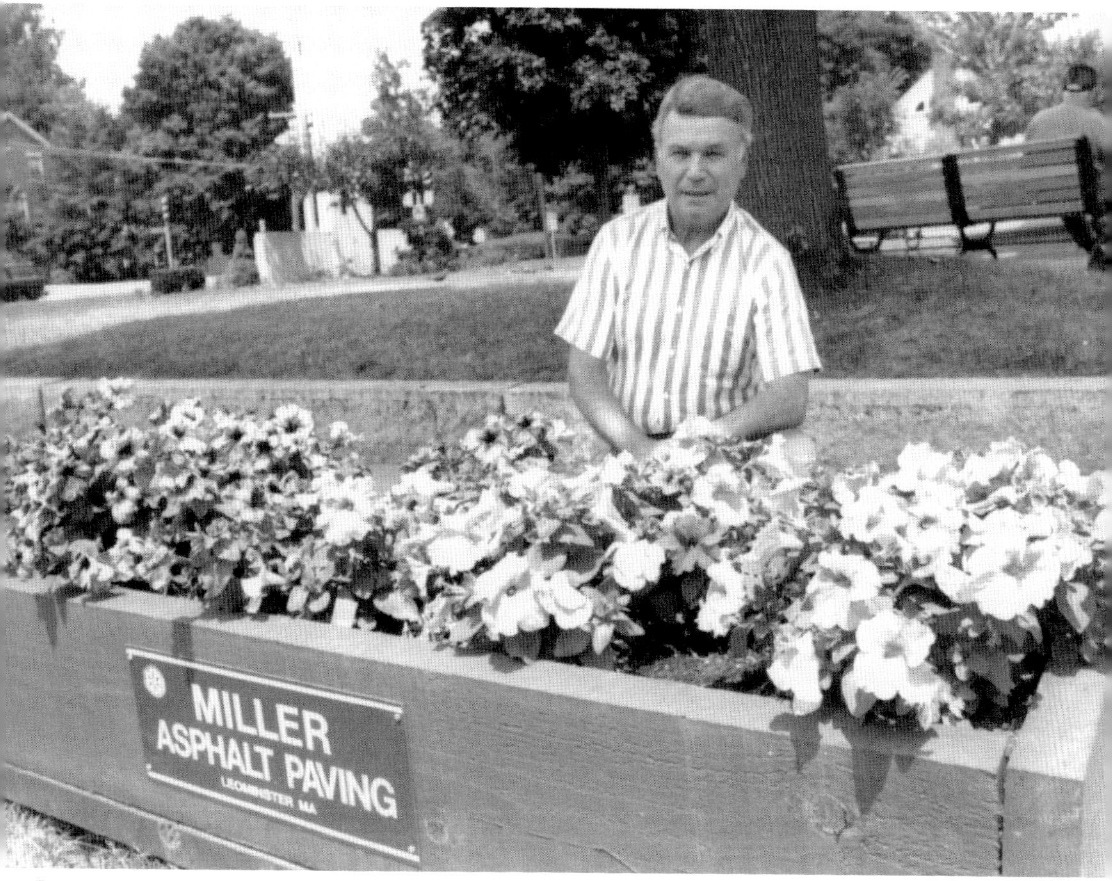

Rocco "Rocky" Piccicuto (1922–1988)
Piccicuto was born in Fitchburg and graduated from St. Bernard's High School in 1940. During World War II, he served in the US Navy Seabees. For 50 years, he owned Rocky's Barbershop at 280 Main Street in Depot Square. Piccicuto was a founder of both the Fitchburg Men's Club and the Rotary Club East, a board member for the Thayer Conservatory and the Fitchburg Civic Center, and a supporter of the Special Olympics. In the mid-1970s, he had an idea for beautifying the city with flowers, which he presented to the Rotary Club East. Members built wooden flower boxes filled with petunias that were sponsored by local businesses and displayed along city sidewalks. Piccicuto passed away in 1988, but the Rotary Club East still supports the flower boxes with local business and individual sponsors.

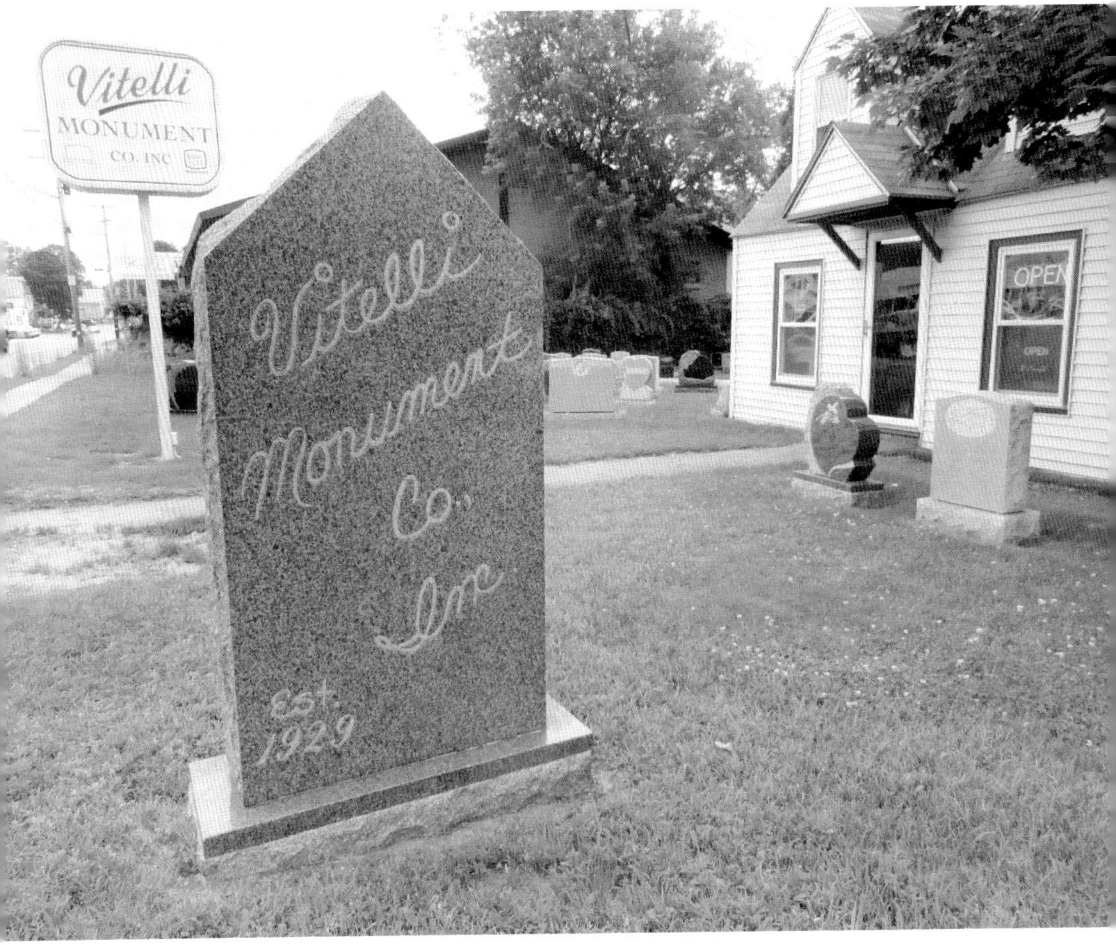

The Vitelli Family

Since 1929, members of the Vitelli family have served Fitchburg residents in a special way—by carving monuments to honor those who have died. Around 1898, Alfredo Vitelli came to Fitchburg from Italy and worked at the Rollstone Quarry. He started the Vitelli Monument Company in his garage. Alfredo's son Mitchell took over the business in 1938. He also owned three diners, including the Moran Square Diner, where his three sons—Louis, Alfred "Butch," and Anthony—all worked. Mitchell's son Anthony took over the monument business when Mitchell died. Anthony passed away in 1989, and Tina, his daughter, owned the business until 1996. Anthony's son Mitchell is now the owner, helped by his son Nicholas. The Vitelli Monument Company has carved thousands of individual monuments and several public monuments, including the Longsjo, policemen, and firefighters memorials.

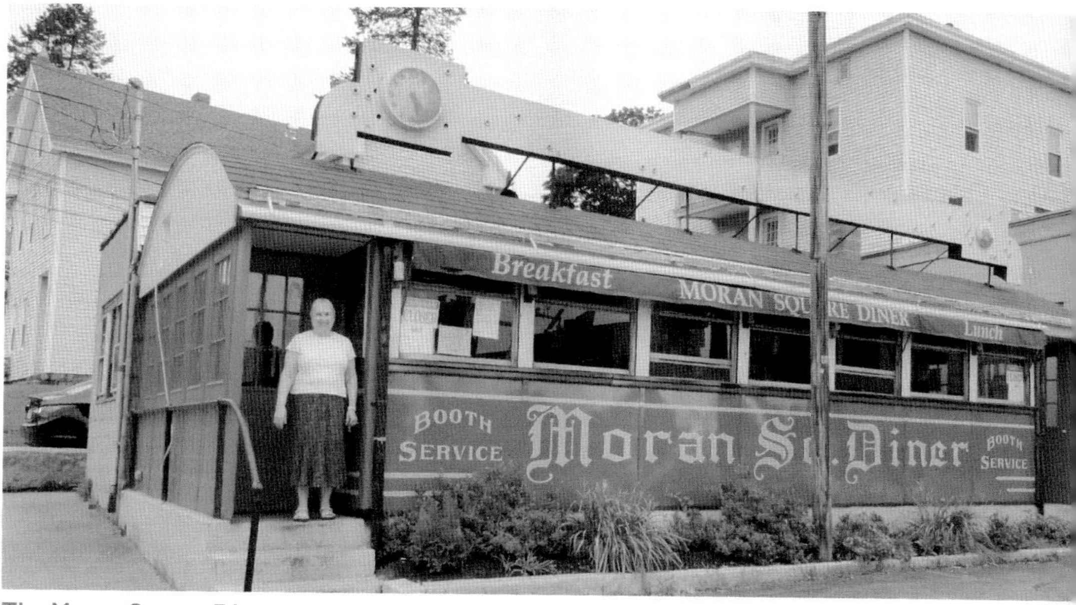

The Moran Square Diner
The Moran Square Diner—a 1940s, red-and-yellow Worcester dining car—caters to all ages. Since 1994, the owners have been Chris and Mary Giannetti. Chris has a hotel and restaurant management degree and is the cook, while Mary, a dietician, helps create the menus. With its swivel stools and wooden booths, the Moran Square Diner is a downtown treasure that, according to *Roadside* magazine, "deserves preservation in a museum."

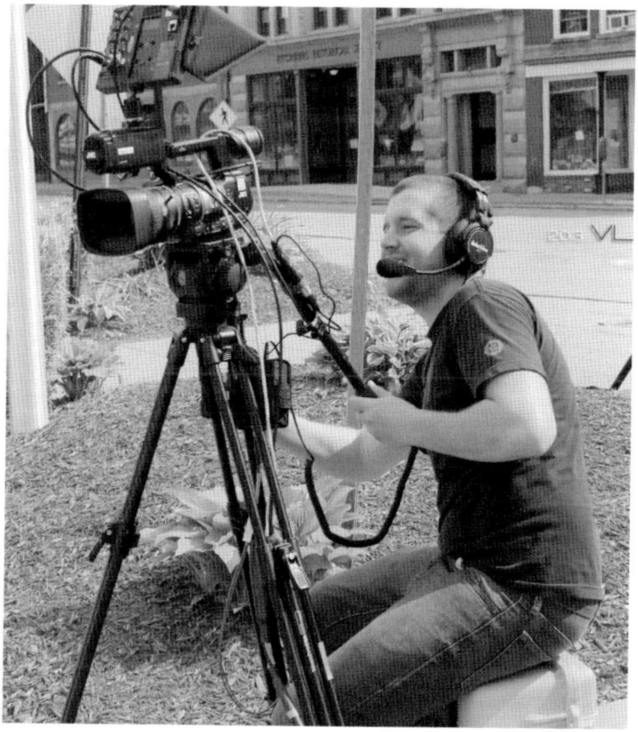

Fitchburg Access Television
Dave Svens has served FATV in several positions, beginning in 1992. In 2011, he became the executive director. Dave credits an excellent professional staff and hundreds of volunteers for making FATV successful for 25 years. Most watched by individuals who cannot attend local events are the city council and school committee meetings, the high school football games, and the programs on Fitchburg history. (Courtesy of FATV.)

INDEX